Eastern Wisdom: Five Paths to Enlightenment

The Creed of Buddha
The Sayings of Lao Tzu
Hindu Mysticism
The Great Learning
The Yengishiki

Eastern Wisdom: Five Paths to Enlightenment

The Creed of Buddha
by Edmond Holmes

Preface

AS I do not know a word of Pâli or any other Eastern language, I owe a debt of gratitude to those distinguished scholars whose translations of the Buddhist scriptures and expositions of the teaching of Buddhism have made it possible for me to attempt to interpret the creed of Buddha. If I have found their treatises less helpful and less illuminative than their translations, the reason is, no doubt, that the qualities which make a man a successful scholar differ widely from those which might enable him to enter, with subtle sympathy and imaginative insight, into the thoughts of a great Teacher. That the task of expounding Buddhism to the Western world has devolved upon a small group of linguistic experts is due partly to the obvious fact that these experts had early access to, and for a time a practical monopoly of, the available materials; partly to that singular lack of interest in the spiritual life and thought of ancient India which is characteristic of Western culture, and which predisposes even the more thoughtful and enlightened minds to accept with indolent acquiescence the ideas of others about Indian religion and philosophy, instead of trying to evolve ideas for themselves. There was a time when ignorance of the Pâli language was a final disqualification for the task of studying the philosophy of Buddha. But it is so no longer. For the disinterested labours of the scholar have provided the "lay" student with a mass of materials of which he may be able to make a profitable use; and one who feels impelled, as I have done, to fathom the deeper meaning of Buddha's wonderful scheme of life, and to guess the secret of his mysterious silence, has now as good a right as any Orientalist to attempt the solution of that fascinating problem.

That the problem has not yet been even approximately solved is my sincere conviction. I have read many treatises on Buddhism; but I have yet to find the writer who, when expounding the philosophy (as distinguished from the ethical system) of Buddha, teaches "as one having authority and not as the Scribes." The indisputable fact that Buddha himself kept silence with regard to the ultimate realities and ultimate issues of life, shows that the task of interpreting his creed is one for "criticism" (in the widest and deepest sense of the word) rather than for "scholarship,"—for judgment, the judgment that enables a man to make use of the learning of others, rather than for learning as such. One of my objects in writing this book has been to vindicate the right of the "layman" to explore a region which the linguistic expert has hitherto been allowed to regard as his private preserve. Should any other "layman" feel disposed to follow my example, he may start on his enterprise with the full assurance that the field before him is as open as it is wide.

One or two words of warning I may perhaps be allowed to offer him. He will do well to suggest to himself at the outset that the Western way of looking at things may not be the only way which is compatible with sanity, that the Western standard of reality may not be the final standard, that the world which is encircled by the horizon of Western thought may not be the whole Universe. The student of Buddhism who is bound, hand and foot, by the quasi-philosophical prejudices of the Western mind, will be unable to survey his subject from any Eastern standpoint, or to approach it along the line of Eastern thought. This fundamental disability will be fatal to his enterprise. There is a special reason why the student of Buddhism should be able (on occasion) to look at things from Eastern standpoints, and to enter with sympathy into Eastern modes and habits of thought. The teaching of Buddha can in no wise be dissociated from the master current of ancient Indian thought. The dominant philosophy of ancient India was a spiritual idealism of a singularly pure and exalted type, which found its truest expression in those Vedic treatises known as the Upanishads. The great teacher is always a reformer as well as an innovator; and his work is, in part at least, an attempt to return to a high level which had been won and then lost. Whether Buddha did or did not lead men back (by a path of his own) from the comparatively low levels of ceremonialism and asceticism to the sublimely high level of thought and aspiration which had been reached in the Upanishads is, perhaps, an open question. But that he had been deeply influenced by the ideas of the ancient seers can scarcely be doubted; and the serious and sympathetic study of their teaching should therefore be the first stage in the attempt to lift the veil of his silence and interpret his unformulated creed. The student who has gone through this preliminary process of initiation will find that he has begun to fit himself for other tasks than that of communing with the soul of Buddha: and he will also find that those other tasks will in due season claim his devotion. When he has solved the problem of the indebtedness of Buddha to the philosophy of the Upanishads, he will be confronted by another problem which for us of the West is of even greater importance, the problem of the indebtedness of Western thought—of Pythagoras, of Xenophanes and Parmenides, of Plato, of Plotinus, of Christ himself and those who caught the spirit of his teaching—to the same sacred source. That problem, too, will have to be grappled with, if the West is ever to discover the secret of its own hidden strength, and if Christendom is ever to understand Christianity.

Table of Contents

EAST AND WEST

THE religions of the civilized world may be divided into two great groups, those of which the paramount deity is the Jewish Jehovah, and those of which the paramount deity is the Indian Brahma. Jehovah reigns, under the title of God the Father, over Europe and the continents which Europe has colonized; and, under the title of Allah, over western Asia and northern Africa. Brahma reigns in the far East, India being under his direct rule, while Indo-China, China, and Japan belong to his "sphere of influence." Even in India he receives but little formal recognition. But he is content that this should be so. He is content that men should worship other gods until the time comes for them to give their hearts to him.

Between these two worlds, which I will call—loosely and inaccurately—the Western and the Eastern, there is a great gulf fixed, a gulf which few minds can pass over from either side. This gulf has been hollowed out by the erosive action of speculative thought. Western thought, which has always been dominated by the crude philosophy of the "average man," instinctively takes for granted the reality of outward things. Eastern thought, which, so far as it has been alive and active, has been mainly esoteric, instinctively takes for granted the reality of the "soul," or inward life. Such at least is the general trend of thought, on its various levels, in each of these dissevered worlds.

As is a man's conception of reality, so is the God whom he worships. Jehovah, the God of the Western world, is an essentially outward deity. Debarred by its instinctive disbelief in the soul from seeking for God in the world within, constrained by the same cause to identify "Nature" with the world without, the Western mind has conceived of a natural order of things which is real because God has made it so, and of a supernatural order of things which is the dwelling-place of God. But because the Western mind, in its quest of reality, must needs look outward, this supernatural order of things is conceived of as a glorified and etherealized replica of the natural order; and God, though veiled from sight by a cloud of splendour and mystery, is made in the image of man. Thus in the Western cosmology there are two worlds, the natural and the supernatural; and two bases of reality, lifeless matter and supernatural will.

In the East, where the soul is the supreme and fundamental reality, the identification of God with the world-soul, or soul of universal Nature, is the outcome of a movement of thought which is at once natural and logical. This divine soul is the only real existence: by comparison with it all outward things are shadows, and all inward things, so far as they hold aloof from the all-embracing consciousness,are dreams. Thus in the Eastern cosmology there is one world, and one centre of reality, the world of our experience seen as it really is, seen by the soul, which, passing inward, in its quest of absolute reality, from veil to veil, and gathering within itself all things that seem to bar its way, arrives at last at the very fountain-head of its being, at its own true self.

There are evils incidental to the worship of each of these sovereign deities. The despotism of the supernatural God tends to reduce to a minimum the spiritual freedom of his subjects. To tell men in precise detail what they are to believe and what they are to do, is to prohibit (under tremendous penalties) all spiritual initiative, and to pander to one of the most demoralizing of all human weaknesses,—the spiritual indolence of the "average man." And as in the higher stages of soul-growth freedom is not merely one of the first conditions of life, but is scarcely to be distinguished from life itself, the autocratic restriction of the spontaneous energies of the soul by codes and creeds, by scriptures and churches, must needs bear deadly fruit. In the present condition of the Mahometan world we see what devastation can be wrought by centuries of blind devotion to the irresponsible Lord of Fate. In Christendom the character of Jehovah has been profoundly modified (though the change which has been effected is as yet potential rather than actual) by the influence of the Founder of Christianity, whose ideas, whatever may have been the history of their development in his mind, belong in their essence to the creed of the Far East. The gospel of spiritual freedom which Christ consistently preached was long ignored by Christianity—so potent was the sway of Jehovah—and has not yet been consciously accepted; but the leaven of Christ's teaching is now producing a visible ferment, and the struggle of the European mind for freedom bears witness to the efficacy of its action. Yet even in the development of that life-giving and soul-redeeming struggle one can trace the baneful influence of the commonplace and unimaginative philosophy which underlies the worship of Jehovah. The deification of the Supernatural too often ends, as it always begins, in the despiritualization of Nature; and the rejection by progressive thought of a supernatural deity prepares the way for the conscious acceptance of a materialistic "theory of things."

There is another way in which the shadow of the Supernatural tends to blight human life. If freedom is to be strangled, love, which is the most expansive and emancipative of all forces, must first be Wounded and disarmed. Dogmatism, intolerance, and uncharitableness are by-products of the worship of Jehovah. The people or the church which believes itself to have received a supernatural revelation, naturally claims to have exclusive possession of "the truth," and therefore regards all who are beyond the pale of its faith as either outcasts from God's presence or rebels against his will. The attitude of the Jew towards the Gentile, of the Christian towards the "Heathen," of the Mahometan towards the "Infidel," is an attitude of spiritual intolerance in which the "believer" reproduces towards his fellow men the supposed attitude of the "jealous God" whom he worships towards all but a faithful remnant of mankind. In this way supernaturalism tends to introduce hatred—the most anti-spiritual of all passions—into the most sacred of all spheres. The history of the Western world, since it accepted Jehovah as its Lord and Master, has been in the main the history of religious persecutions and religious wars; and men, in perfect good faith, have proved their zeal for God by devoting the bodies of their fellow men to the flames, and their souls to the torments of Hell.

The evils to which the worship of Brahma is exposed are of an entirely different order. Of the creed of him who gives his whole heart to the all-embracing Life I will not attempt to speak. Silence is the true language of cosmic adoration; and it is in sympathetic silence that one should contemplate so pure and profound a creed. When the Western mind accuses the Eastern of pantheism, it instinctively assumes that the Eastern standpoint is the same as its own. In point of fact the "higher pantheism" of the East is an entirely different thing from the materialistic pantheism into which Western thought, in its seasons of revolt from the worship of a supernatural God, is liable to relapse. The only fault that can be found with the former is that very few persons can breathe freely on its exalted heights. To give his heart to One who is not merely supremely real but alone real, and who is therefore in very truth the All of Being, "exceeds man's might." For all but a chosen few the figure of Brahma must needs recede into the dim background. As it recedes, lesser Gods—some beautiful, some terrible, some loathsome, some grotesque—emerge from the darkness and claim man's homage. The further it recedes, the lowlier are the Gods that man worships. In China and Japan, where faith in the individual soul is strong but the "intuition of totality" is weak, Brahma (or his equivalent) becomes the mere shadow of a shade, and the souls that are worshipped are those of departed men. Thus the creed of the East tends to degenerate either into polytheism, which becomes at last the dead worship of dead Gods, or into ancestor-worship, which is indeed within its limits a living faith and does much for the stability of social life, but which, even in its most exalted moods, can present no higher ideal than that of patriotism to the aspiring souls of its votaries.

From the uncharitableness of supernaturalism the creed of the East is, in theory at least, entirely free. All men, without exception, are near and dear to the Universal Soul, for all are sparks from its central fire. More than that, life as such, be it high or low, is sacred because of the fountain from which it issues. Not religious toleration only, but all-embracing charity is of the very essence of the faith that directs itself towards the All. One needs but a superficial acquaintance with the sacred writings of the East to convince oneself that, unlike his Western rival, Brahma is not, in any sense of the word, a "jealous" God. Jehovah's jealousy of other Gods and vindictiveness towards those who worship them suggest that he is conscious of his own limitations and is not secure of his position. Brahma knows that the lesser Gods whom men worship are his Viceroys,—embodiments in their several ways of the ever-changing dream of him, who is All in All, which possesses the growing soul of Humanity; and, far from resenting the worship that is paid to them, he accepts it as meant for himself:—

Nay, and of hearts which follow other Gods
In simpler faith, their prayers arise to me,
O Kunti's Son! though they pray wrongfully;
For I am the Receiver and the Lord
Of every sacrifice.

Religions have indeed been persecuted in the East, but always for social or political reasons. Of Buddhism, the dominant creed of the East, one may say more than this; one may say that it has never persecuted, that, in practice as well as principle, it is an entirely tolerant creed. "Throughout the long history of Buddhism," says Dr Rhys Davids, ". . . the Buddhists have been uniformly tolerant; and have appealed, not to the sword, but to intellectual and moral suasion. We have not a single instance, throughout the whole period, of even one of those religious persecutions which loom so largely in the history of the Christian church. Peacefully the Reformation began; and in peace, so far as its own action is concerned, the Buddhist church has continued till to-day." The idea of torturing a fellow-man to death because his theology happens to differ from one's own, is wholly alien from the Eastern tone and temper of thought, as alien as is the assumption which makes religious persecution possible,—the atheistical assumption that Divine Truth can be imprisoned in a form of words.

Each of these dominant types of religion has, as might be expected, its own psychology, its own eschatology, and its own moral and social life. The West regards the soul as dependent on the body, coming into being with the latter, growing with its growth, and either dying at its death or surviving it by the grace of the Supernatural God. The immediate destiny of the departed soul is a matter with regard to which Western theology is, speaking generally, in a state of complete bewilderment. That survival is not regarded as a natural process is proved by the fact that, both in Christendom and in Islam, the immortality to which the believer is taught to look forward is supernatural and quasi-material. On some future day the outward and visible world (which Western thought identifies with "Nature") will pass away, and a supernatural order of things, also outward and visible, will take its place. The bodies of the dead will then be raised from the grave, and their souls, which meanwhile have been leading a dubious twilight kind of existence, will be restored to them, and will dwell in them for ever, either in the light of God's visible presence or in the lurid darkness of Hell. So the two great religions which sprang from the parent stem of Judaism have authoritatively taught, and so for many centuries the whole of Christendom and the whole of Islam were content to believe. Supernaturalism is now being slowly undermined; but wherever belief in the Supernatural is dying, belief in survival is dying with it. Modern scepticism, which is based, like the faith that it repudiates, on an instinctive belief in the reality of the outward world and an instinctive disbelief in the reality of the inward life, sees in death the extinction of the soul (which indeed has never been anything but a name) as well as the dissolution of the body.

Morality is a function of many variables, of which psychology and eschatology are perhaps the most important. The Soul, which is at once One and Many, is the real bond of union among men; and all communal sentiments, such as attachment to country, clan, or family, are ultimately rooted in the sense of oneness in and through the Universal Self. The Western disbelief in the reality of the soul has hastened the dissolution of communal bonds and interests, and has helped to bring in, perhaps prematurely, the régime of individualism,—a necessary stage in the development of the soul, but one in which selfishness is not merely permitted but directly fostered. The Western belief in the reality of the outward world, and therefore in the intrinsic worth of outward goods, has made the struggle for wealth, both by nations and individuals, one of the most prominent features of Western civilization. Against this materialistic individualism, this régime of "competitive selfishness," the moral precepts of the founders of Christianity and (in a lesser degree) of Islamism have waged an honourable warfare. But in this struggle they have found the eschatological teaching of the churches a hindrance rather than a help. The idea of a natural connection between this life and the after life, or lives, has been almost wholly lost sight of in the West. A mechanical interpretation has been placed upon each of the rival doctrines of salvation, "faith" having been degraded to the level of belief, and "works" to the level of ceremonial observance. The false dualism (so characteristic of Western thought) which divides the future world into Heaven and Hell, has borne its inevitable fruit. However tamely the Western mind may have seemed to acquiesce in the formal conceptions of infinite bliss and infinite misery, it has never failed (at any rate in more recent years) to rise in secret revolt against the assumption that in a single brief earth-life either extreme can fairly be earned. The shadow of Hell has at times fallen heavily on human life; but each man in turn has managed to persuade himself that so tremendous and unjust a penalty was not for him. The doctrine of eternal punishment, when steadily faced, is so intolerable as to become at last incredible; and as there are no intermediate states between Heaven and Hell (Purgatory being merely the ante-room of the halls of Heaven), the instinctive recoil of the soul from the latter throws open to all men the portals of the former. The average man of to-day too readily flatters himself that somehow or other he and his friends will all be "saved." But a Heaven which can be so cheaply earned is scarcely worth striving for. The practical abolition of Hell carries with it the practical abolition of Heaven, for in proportion as the former ceases to deter the latter ceases to attract. Even among those who call themselves believers there is an ever-growing tendency to live wholly in the present, and to turn away from the contemplation of death and its consequences.

Yet the very materialism of the West has been, in a sense, its salvation. The soul of man has grown in the Western world, not because religion has directly fostered its growth, but because circumstances which the very irreligiousness of popular thought—its very indifference to what is inward and spiritual—has helped to create, have actually compelled it to grow. The intense interest which the Western mind takes in the outward world, has caused it to devote itself with whole-hearted energy to the study of physical science. Scientific research prepares the way for practical discoveries and inventions; and these are ever tending to modify—some of them have in recent years revolutionized—the material conditions of human life. In its efforts to adapt itself to the never-ending changes in its environment which Western inventiveness tends to produce, the soul is not only kept alive and awake, but must needs make considerable growth in certain directions. That the growth which it makes is inharmonious and one-sided; that the spiritual side of it has not kept pace, in its development, with the intellectual; that its spiritual faculties have been to some extent atrophied by the diversion of its vital energies into the channel of mental growth, is unhappily true. But the fact remains that the sap of life is running strongly in the soul of the Western world; and from this one may perhaps infer that it will make vigorous growth in the right direction, when the higher impulses and the higher guidance for which it is waiting are given to it.

Even that strong and ever-growing individualism which, for the time being, seems to have raised selfishness and ambition to the rank of virtues, has a moral value which cannot well be over-estimated. It is in the soil of social individualism that the seeds of freedom and of the love of freedom must be sown; and though in its earlier stages the struggle for freedom may take the form of selfish rebellion against wise and lawful restraint, it is certain that, with the gradual growth of the soul, man's conception of freedom will be expanded and purified, till at last the prize of which he dreams will reveal itself to him as the first condition, nay, as the very counterpart, of spiritual life. In this way—so ready is Nature to turn her loss to gain—the social individualism which is one of the by-products of Western philosophy, tends to become the champion of spiritual freedom against the tyrannical encroachments of supernaturalism,—itself one of the more direct and obvious products of the selfsame tendency of thought.

The psychology of the East is as simple as it is profound. The soul, or inward life, alone is real. Eternity is a vital aspect of reality. Birthlessness and deathlessness are the temporal aspects of eternity. The present existence of the soul is not more certain than its pre-existence and its future existence; and these three—the past, the present, and the future lives—are stages in an entirely natural process. The present life is always brief and fleeting; but the past begins, as the future ends, in eternity, in the timeless life of God himself. Issuing from the Universal Soul, and passing through axons of what I may call pre-natal existence, the soul at last becomes individualized, and enters on a career of conscious activity. Far from being dependent on the body, it accretes to itself, on whatever plane it may energize, the outward form that it needs and deserves; and, in each of its many deaths, it is the body that dies, deprived of the vitalizing presence that animated it,—not the soul.

> Never the spirit was born; the spirit shall cease to be never;
> Never was time it was not; End and Beginning are dreams!
> Birthless and deathless and changeless remaineth the spirit for ever;
> Death hath not touched it at all, dead though the house of it seems!

The destiny of the soul is determined by its origin. Issuing from the Universal Soul, it must eventually be reabsorbed into its divine source. Beginning its individualized career as a spiritual germ, it passes through innumerable lives on its way to the goal of spiritual maturity. The development of the germ-soul takes the form of the gradual expansion of its consciousness and the gradual universalization of its life. As it nears its goal, the chains of individuality relax their hold upon it; and at last,—with the final extinction of egoism, with the final triumph of selflessness, with the expansion of consciousness till it has become all-embracing,—the sense of separateness entirely ceases, and the soul finds its true self, or, in other words, becomes fully and clearly conscious of its oneness with the living Whole.

This pure and exalted creed, besides placing before man the highest and truest of all ideals—that of utter selflessness—has the merit of bringing the whole of human life under the dominion of natural law. Indeed, it applies to the life of the soul that great natural law, the discovery of which in the sphere of physical life has been one of the foremost achievements of modern thought,—the law of evolution. One consequence of this is that the notions of arbitrariness, favouritism, and caprice, which cling, de facto if not de jure, to the conception of a supernatural God, and which introduce a gambling element—a readiness to take risks, a tendency to put off things to the eleventh hour—into the practical morality of the West, have no place in the ethical philosophy of the East. The Catholic belief in the efficacy of the last rites of the Church, the Protestant belief that a deathbed repentance may open the door of Salvation to one who has led an impious life, bear witness, each in its own way, to the presence in the religious atmosphere of the West of a fantastic conception of God which is absolutely irreconcilable with the primary assumption of Eastern thought. It is of Brahma rather than of Jehovah that the words of the Lawgiver hold good: "God is not a man that he shall lie, neither the son of man that he shall repent." The successive lives of the soul, to which Eastern thought looks backward and forward, are linked together by a chain of natural causation. What a man sows that shall he reap, not in this earth-life only but also in the lives that are yet to be. The primary relation between the individual and the Universal Self is an essentially natural relation; and through this vast conception the whole spiritual world is brought under the dominion of natural law.

So pure, and so exalted is the inner faith of the East, that the excess of these qualities is perhaps its only defect. The ideas that it embodies immensely transcend the normal range of human desire and human thought, with the result that it has ever been and will long continue to be an esoteric creed. Yet the life of the masses in the East owes much to its occult influence. Besides investing the ethics of half the human race with an atmosphere of natural law, the Brahmanic ideal of duty, though beyond the apprehension of ordinary mortals, makes two contributions of inestimable value to the popular morality,—the sentiment of devotion to impersonal causes, and the kindred sense of detachment from material aims and interests. We have seen that, as the figure of Brahma recedes into the dim background, lesser Gods come forth and claim man's homage. So too, as the Brahmanic ideal (devotion to, culminating in reunion with, the Universal Self) fades into the background, lesser ideals, such as patriotism, tribal loyalty, filial piety, and the like, come forth and claim man's devotion. In Japan, whose people during the past 50 years have transferred to their country the devotion which they formerly gave to the family and the clan, patriotism—as wide-spread as it is intense—has transformed an obscure, remote, and apparently helpless country into one of the foremost nations of the world. In China, where patriotism has but an embryonic existence, filial piety will move a man to sell himself into slavery or to devote himself to certain death. Men who value life lightly will set but little store on those perishable accessories of life which the Western world esteems so highly. Among the personal desires which the sentiment of devotion to impersonal causes tends to suppress, the first and most obvious is the desire for material possessions,—the thirst for wealth. One might wander far and wide through Europe and America without finding such calm indifference to the charms of property, on the part of a man of business, as the Burmese contractor displayed who spent five-sixths of his modest income in charity, and was ready to retire from business because he had enough to live on quietly (his personal wants being very few) for the rest of his life. "His action," says the writer who tells of him, "is no exception, but the rule."

But the very disinterestedness of the Oriental mind may well become the cause of its undoing. Just as the West has the qualities of its defects, so the East has the defects of its qualities. The communism and idealism of the East have been unfavourable to the growth of physical science (the nidus of which has been in the main utilitarian), and to the development by man of the material resources of the earth. As science and industrialism are among the chief causes of change in the external conditions of human life, and as the endeavour to adapt itself to a changing environment is one of the chief causes of the development of the human spirit, we seem to be driven to the paradoxical conclusion that the periodic immobility of the East, which arrests the growth of the soul, both by denying it the opportunities for growth and making it revere custom for its own dead sake, is due in no small measure to the very strength of the Eastern faith in the soul. So too, though the suppression of individuality is the last and highest achievement of the soul in its struggle for spiritual freedom, the war which Eastern thought has ever waged against individualism tends to keep the mass of men in leading strings, and to deny them that initial boon of social freedom without which the struggle for spiritual freedom—a struggle in which the soul is schooled by its very blunders, and taught to conquer by its very failures cannot well be begun.

Separated from each other for thousands of miles by impassable mountain-chains and pathless deserts, the two worlds—the Eastern and Western—have had so little intercourse with each other, that each in turn has been free to develop, without let or hindrance, its own type of civilization, its own philosophy, its own ideal of life. Of late years, intercourse between the two worlds has been fostered by various causes, and there is reason to believe that it will become closer and more continuous as time goes on. With the removal of the barriers that held the two worlds apart, their respective ideals will begin to influence each other; and one may venture to hope, or at least to dream, that in the far-off future a new ideal, higher and truer than either of these "mighty opposites," will be evolved by their reciprocal action, and will become the common possession of the whole human race. Meanwhile, it is essential that an attempt should be made by the more advanced spirits in each world to understand the thoughts, the dreams, the aims, the aspirations of the other. Recognition of the profundity of the abyss that parts the two types of mind, is the first step in the direction that I have indicated. Recognition of the possible one-sidedness and inadequacy of one's own spiritual prejudices, is the second. The thinker of either world who cannot divest himself, even provisionally and hypothetically, of his own habits of thought will never be initiated into the mysteries of the other world. The abyss between East and West is not to be crossed by any bridge of controversial argument; for, owing to the two philosophies having, as philosophies, no common ground of agreement, the piers that should support the bridge could never get down to the bedrock of proof. It is only by outsoaring the abyss on the wings of imaginative sympathy that one may hope to span its depths.

The Wisdom of the East

THERE were mighty warriors before the days of Agamemnon, and mighty thinkers before the days of Socrates and Plato. Greatest of all the forgotten thinkers of antiquity, greatest, as it seems to me, of all who have ever consecrated their mental powers to the service of Humanity, was the sage whose vision of reality found expression in the parables and aphorisms of the Upanishads. So lofty was the plane on which his spirit moved that, however high the fountain of idealistic speculation may ascend in its periodic outbursts of activity, it can never do more than seek the level of his thought.

Philosophy is, in its essence, the quest of reality. In the attempt to determine what is real, one has to choose, in the first instance, between the percipient self and the things that it perceives. This choice may seem to be purely metaphysical, but sooner or later it becomes a moral choice and one which is decisive of the chooser's destiny. For him who can face the problem steadily there is, in the last resort, but one possible solution of it. If we may assume that each term of the given antithesis has some measure of reality, we need be in no doubt as to which is the more real. The problem solves itself, for the simple reason that the decision as to whether the self or the outward world is (relatively) real rests with the self, not with the outward world. It is I who have to make the choice between myself and the world that surrounds me; and I have to make it to my own satisfaction. Is it possible for me to remain impartial? Am I not inevitably prejudiced in favour of myself? If I invest the outward world with reality of any degree or kind, if I persuade myself that it is more real than I am, if, by some metaphysical tour de force, I go so far as to regard it as the substance of which I am merely the shadow, the fact remains that it is I who am guaranteeing its reality; and, that being so, the question inevitably suggests itself: If the guarantor is metaphysically insolvent, what is the value of his guarantee? The man who can allow himself to say: "I can see the outward world; therefore it is real. But I cannot see my self; therefore I am non-existent": is obviously the victim of a singular confusion of thought. It is sometimes said that the idealist starts with himself, and never gets to the outward world. There are certain dialectical developments of idealism of which this criticism may perhaps hold good; but, as a general criticism of idealism, it is, I think, entirely untrue. The idealist starts, where every thinker must start, with provisional acceptance of the outward world as well as of the percipient self; and, in I common with all his fellow men, he invests the former with some measure or degree of reality; but, in the act of guaranteeing its reality, he guarantees (as he has discernment enough to realize) a fuller measure and a higher degree of reality to himself. Nor is the value of the latter guarantee impaired by the patent fact that it is illogical to go surety for oneself. To prove the reality of what alone enables one to prove reality is, for obvious reasons, impossible. But the Universe (as I know it) would melt into a dream-world if I could not place my self at the centre of it; and my inability to prove, or even begin to prove, that my self is real, matters little so long as Nature herself constrains me—with or without the consent of my consciousness—to postulate its reality.

In the choice between the percipient self and the objects of its perception, the thinkers of India threw the whole weight of their thought on the side of the former. The philosophy of the Far East, which has ever been dominated by the "ancient wisdom" of India, bases itself on acceptance of the self or soul, just as the philosophy of the West bases itself on acceptance of the outward world. This is a point on which I have already dwelt, and need not further enlarge. What it now concerns us to notice is that there are vast philosophical conceptions implicit in the germinal assumption of Eastern thought, and that the thinker who speaks to us in

"The grand, sonorous, long-linked lines"

of the Upanishads, proved his greatness by the profound insight and the speculative daring with which he developed those conceptions into a world-embracing system of thought.

Let us, with the aid of the Upanishads, attempt to do his thinking for him. If in the microcosm, the world which directly and obviously centres in the individual, the self or conscious subject is real and the objects of its knowledge are by comparison unreal, must it not be the same—one instinctively argues—in the macrocosm, or totality of things? Is there not at the heart of the Universe a conscious life, and is not this all-conscious life—this Universal Self, as we may call it the supreme reality by reference to which all existent things, when their claims to reality are tested, take their several "stations and degrees"? To argue from one's own experience (whether rightly or wrongly interpreted) to the world at large is permissible, for the simple but sufficient reason that it is inevitable. The man who inclines to materialism when he makes his choice between his own self and the world that environs him, will be a materialist in his general conception of the Universe. The transition from personal to impersonal idealism is equally natural and necessary. The truth is that the distinction between the microcosm and the macrocosm is a tentative and provisional one, which readily melts away under the solvent influence of speculative thought. The microcosm, as we try to define its boundaries, gradually expands into the macrocosm; and the relation between the two is seen to be one, not of analogy merely, but of ultimate identity. The reality of the Universal Self is as certain as the reality of the individual self; and in the act of accepting the latter we accept the former, with all that it implies.

For Indian thought, then, which started with acceptance of the individual self, Brahma—the Universal Soul or Self—was and is alone real. The first thing that we can say about him is that he is unknown and unknowable. In the world which centres in me, it is I, the knower, who am unknown and unknowable. It is the same in the Cosmos. We must either keep silence when we meditate on Brahma, or speak of him (as the Upanishads habitually do) in the language of paradox and negation. Speech cannot reveal him, for he makes speech possible. Thought cannot reveal him, for he makes thought possible. Sight cannot reveal him, for he makes sight possible. Hearing cannot reveal him, for he makes hearing possible. He is afar and yet near. He is innermost and outermost. Though swifter than the mind, he moveth not. All things are in him, and he is in everything. Allow opposites are harmonized in him,—being and non-being, wisdom and unwisdom, right and wrong. He is beyond sight, beyond speech, beyond mind, beyond the known, beyond the unknown. "If thou thinkest 'I know him well,' but little sure of Brahma dost thou know."

"He is unknown to whoso think they know,
But known to whoso know they know him not."

But though he is in very truth the Unknown and Unknowable, he is not "the Unknowable" of
modern European thought. In the "synthetic" philosophy the Unknowable is a background of unreality which brings out into strong belief the reality of the phenomenal world. Or, again, it is a convenient hypothesis which bears, like the scapegoat of old, the sins and follies of idealism, and takes them away into the wilderness of non-existence, and so sets the thinker free to develop, without let or hindrance, a materialistic system of thought. But the Unknowable of Indian philosophy is the most real of all realities. Indeed it is the sum total of reality, the beginning and end of all that really is.

"This is that ultimate and uttermost
Which shall not be beheld, being in a
The unbeholden essence!"

Brahma, then, far from being the pale reflection of our own complacent ignorance, is the innermost reality, in the sense that all existent things have their life and their power in him. This conception finds fitting expression in the parable of Brahma and the Gods. The story goes that Brahma once won a victory for the Gods,—Wind, Fire, and the rest. They thought, "Ours is this victory, our very own the triumph." Knowing their thought, Brahma stood before them. They knew him not, and wondered who he was. They said to Fire, "Find out, all-knowing one, who that wondrous Being is." Fire did their bidding, and, as he drew near to the stranger, was greeted with the words, "Who art thou?" "Why, I am Fire," he answered, "all-knowing Fire am I." "What power is in thine I-ness, then?" said the stranger. "Why, I can burn up everything on earth," said Fire. Then the stranger set a straw before him, and bade him burn it. He smote it with all his might, but could not even scorch it. So he returned and said, "I could not find out who that wondrous Being is." Then Air was sent on the same quest, and he too was asked, "Who art thou?" "Why, I am Air," he answered, "breather in mother space am I." "What power is in thine I-ness, then?" said the stranger. "Why, I can blow away all things on earth," said Air. Then the stranger set a straw before him, and bade him blow it away. He smote it with all his might, but could not stir it. So he too returned and said, "I could not find out who that wondrous Being is." Then "the Lord" (Indra) was sent; but the stranger, as he drew near to him, vanished from his sight, and where he had been standing there stood a beautiful woman arrayed in gold. Of her the Lord asked who the stranger was. "Brahma," she said. "In Brahma's conquest do ye triumph."

The moral of this story is plain. Individuality is the negation of reality. Apart from the One the individual is nothing. Even the high Gods triumph in Brahma's might. Left to themselves, they have no power, no life. Their selfhood, when severed from the Universal selfhood, is a pure delusion. Fire cannot of himself burn a straw. Air cannot of himself blow a straw away. The Universal Self is the true self of each of the high Gods. It follows, a fortiori, that it is the true self of each individual man. We have seen that the microcosm, as we try to define its boundaries, gradually expands into the macrocosm, and that the relation between the two worlds is one, not of analogy merely, but of ultimate identity. There is a corollary to this general conception of things, which Indian thought did not fail to draw. As the microcosm expands into the macrocosm, so does what is real in the former—the individual self—expand into what is real in the latter,—the Universal Self. The relation between the two selves, like the relation between the two worlds, is one, not of analogy merely, but of ultimate identity. As I try to determine what my self really is, I find that it begins to melt into the Universal Self; and at last the idea begins to dawn upon me that the Universal Self, the All-Consciousness, is the real self of each individual man, and that until I have found the Universal Self, made myself one with it, made it in some sort my own, I am not really free to say, "I am I."

This grand conception is the keystone of the whole arch of Indian thought. Let us consider its bearing on human life. We must first remind ourselves that the philosophy of ancient India brings the whole Universe under the dominion of natural law. The Divine Self does not dwell above or apart from the world of Nature, but at the very heart of it, being indeed the vital essence of Nature,—the revelation to him whose inward eyes are open, of what Nature really is. It follows that the natural order of things is the expression, or at any rate an expression, of the Divine Self; that the central forces of Nature are a manifestation of the Divine Will; and that through the whole system of natural law the One, who "remains," proves his presence in and through the Many, which "change and pass." The physical science of the West believes itself to have evolved the conception of natural law, and claims to have exclusive rights in it. But in this, as in other matters, we must distinguish between the conscious and the unconscious apprehension of a philosophic truth. The sense of law and order in Nature is not only common to all human beings, from the savant in his laboratory to the "burnt child" that "dreads the fire," but is also present, however dimly or inchoately, in every organism, however lowly, which adapts itself with any measure of success to the world in which it lives. But, whereas in the West the conception of natural law has in the main been applied to the outward and visible world, in the East, where the outward and visible world owes such reality as it possesses to its own inward and spiritual life, the conception of law has not merely been applied to the inward and spiritual life, but has been more intimately associated with it than with any other aspect of Nature. In the Universe, as the popular thought of the West conceives of it, there are two worlds,—the natural, which is under the dominion of law, and the supernatural, which is under the sway of an arbitrary and irresponsible despot, who can also suspend or modify at will the laws of the natural world. But Eastern thought, in conceiving of the inward life as the real self of Nature, conceived of it also as the ultimate and eternal source of all natural law. Indeed, it is in and through the inward life that Nature—the totality of things—is transformed from a chaos into a Cosmos, from an aggregate of atoms into an organic Whole.

Now the Universal Soul is not only the real self of the whole Universe, but is also, more particularly, the real self of each individual soul. This fundamental fact determines the destiny of Humanity, and the duty (or individualized destiny) of each particular man. Applying to the life of the human soul the highest of all natural laws—that of organic growth—the thinkers of the East evolved a sublime idealism which may be said to have centred in the following "sovereign dogma." As the destiny of every animal and plant is to find its true self, or, in other words, advance towards the perfection of which its nature is capable,—so the destiny of man, as a "living soul," is to find his true self, by growing into oneness with the Divine or Universal Soul, which is in very truth the ideal perfection of all soul-life.

Having set man this tremendous task, they gave him ample time in which to accomplish it. There is no respect in which the Eastern mind differs so widely from the Western as in the range of their respective visions. The temporal horizon of Western thought had never, until the discoveries of physical science transformed its conceptions, been more than a few hundreds or, at most, thou-sands of years from the mental eye of the spectator. A generation ago, it was possible for learned men to believe, in all seriousness, that the Universe was created 4004 years before the birth of Christ. Nor did this grotesque belief begin to fall into discredit until Science had convinced men that the changes which are registered in the strata of the earth's surface had taken millions of years to accomplish. The idea that cons are needed for the spiritual development of each individual man is one which is still foreign to the Western mind. That a single earth-life, or fraction of a life on earth (for it is never too late for the sinner to repent and be "saved"), can fit the soul for "eternal life," can fit it, in other words, either for immediate admission into the pure light of God's unclouded presence, or for entrance into that Purgatorial world which is the ante-room of Heaven,—this, with the correlative belief that one brief earth-life can earn for a man the tremendous penalty of eternal damnation, is one of the accepted doctrines of all the Christian churches. The very glibness with which the pious Christian talks of dwelling in Heaven "for ever," is the outcome of his spiritual myopia. Eternity, as he calls it, is but a high-sounding name for the wall of darkness which bounds his vision as he looks down the vista of soul-life.

But the Eastern mind has always moved with ease through vast cycles of time; and as its philosophy brings all things—spiritual as well as physical—under the dominion of natural law, and therefore forbids it, in any sphere of thought, to pass from finite causes to infinite effects, it has always instinctively assumed that the process of growth which is to transform the individual into the Universal Self is, speaking generally, of practically immeasurable duration. In other words, it has always believed that the soul will pass through innumerable lives on its way to its divine goal. That many of these lives must be passed on earth has always been taken for granted. The obvious fact that in one earth-life man can learn but little of what earth has to teach him, and the further fact that most men die with the desire for the goods and pleasures of earth still strong in their hearts, lead one to expect (once the idea of a plurality of lives has been accepted) that the soul, in the course of its wanderings, will return to earth again and again,—will return, partly in order to widen and enrich its experience, partly in response to attractive forces which it has not yet learned to control. It was in this way that the doctrine of re-incarnation—of a re-incarnating self or Ego—became one of the cardinal articles of the faith of the East.

Let us follow this doctrine into some of its momentous consequences. The prospect of attaining, in the fullness of time, to the infinite bliss of conscious union with the Divine Life must needs disparage the attractions of earth. Those who believe that they will never again return to earth may well cling fondly to this temporal life,—so fondly that they will even project it in imagination into the Heaven to which they look forward. But for the Eastern mind each temporal life was (and is) a stage in a long and toilsome journey,—a journey which seemed to grow ever longer and more toilsome, in proportion as the grandeur of the destiny that awaited the journeying soul was more and more vividly realized. Hence it was that a kind of high-souled impatience, a "divine home-sickness" (to use Heine's beautiful words), took possession of the nobler spirits in the Eastern world; and the desire to shorten the journey, to escape as early as possible from the "whirlpool of rebirth," grew up and made its presence felt. The Western mind, which is constitutionally incapable of seeing more than a few years into the future, finds much to satisfy it in the pleasures and pursuits of earth. But the far-sighted Eastern mind, looking beyond the immediate horizon of man's aims and interests, sees that disillusionment and disappointment are the inevitable sequels to success; sees that there is nothing of earth worth possessing, except what is intrinsically unattainable in any earth-life,—nothing, except those prizes which will not be won until the soul, after many wanderings, has entered into possession of its kingdom,—nothing, in fine, except Beauty and Love.

But how was the journey to the inward and spiritual Heaven to be shortened? It was by the actual growth of the soul, with the concomitant expansion of its consciousness, that the goal was to be reached. When the individual consciousness had become all-embracing, the union of the soul with God would obviously be complete. What if the process of soul-expansion could be abridged? What if the soul could be made to realize—in this or in any future life—to realize fully, finally, and with unfaltering certitude, that all outward things are unsubstantial as shadows, that all the pleasures and interests of earth are evanescent as breaking bubbles, that its own individuality is an illusion,—that nothing, in fine, is real, either in the inward or in the outward world, except the Universal Self, the all-embracing One? If the hollowness and unreality of earth and its treasures could once be realized, would not the attractive force of earth—that subtle power by which it draws the soul back to itself again and again—have ceased to act? Would not the cycle of births and deaths have come to an end? Would not the "peace that passeth all understanding" have been won?

The Upanishads are dominated by this idea. The beautiful story of Nachiketas and Death has one burden,—that "he who sees seeming difference" (he who thinks that differences are real, and cannot see the One for the Many) "goes from death to death," whereas he who knows the One, the "all-comprehending One" who is "far beyond distinction's power," escapes from death and inherits eternal life. It is desire for the things of earth that draws man back to earth; and desire for the things of earth is generated by belief in their reality. Know that they are unreal, and you will cease to desire them. Cease to desire them, and they will no longer draw you back to earth. "When all desires that linger in his heart are driven forth, the mortal immortal becomes, here Brahman he verily wins. When every knot of earth is here unloosed, then mortal immortal becomes." He who would escape from death must turn his eye away from outward things, and "behold the inner self." "After outward longings fools pursue, they tumble into death's wide-spreading net; whereas, the wise, sure deathlessness conceiving, want nothing here below among uncertain things." The vision of the One discredits the reality of the Many, and in doing so frees the soul from bondage to desire, and therefore to death and re-birth. "Sole sovereign, inner self of all creation, who makes the one form manifold—the wise who gaze on him within their self, theirs and not others is the bliss that aye endures." To say that knowledge of reality subdues desires for outward .things, is to say, in simpler and homelier language, that reason teaches man self-control. "The man who is subject to reason and mindful, constantly pure, he unto that goal truly reacheth from which he is not born again. Aye, the man who hath reason for driver, holding tight unto impulse's reins, he reacheth the end of the journey, that home of the Godhead supreme." But the man "who is the prey of unreason, unmindful, ever impure, to that goal such a man never reacheth, he goeth to births and to deaths."

It is clear, from these and kindred passages, that the thinkers of the East attached immense importance to the effort and initiative of the individual soul. It is also clear that the highest achievement of the soul (as they conceived it) was to know the real from the unreal, and to translate that knowledge into feeling and action. Knowledge of reality was at once the goal of the soul's wanderings, and the path that led to the goal; and, that being so, the goal had but to become fully realized in order to make a sudden and final end of the path that led to itself.

The stress that the Sages of the Upanishads laid on knowledge, and the emancipative power that they ascribed to it, may seem strange to our Western minds. Our own ideas about knowledge have so long been dominated by the provisional assumptions of Physical Science, that there is now only one kind of knowledge—that which has scientific certitude for its counterpart—to which we are willing to apply the name. But, in truth, the range of knowledge is as wide as that of Nature, and the word has as many shades of meaning as there are degrees in that "diameter of being" which leads from the pole of abstract and impersonal theory to the anti-pole of actual oneness with reality. To know the supreme truth—that the Universal Self is the only reality, and is therefore the real self of each of us—delivers a man from the circle of life and death, and enables him to enter the great Peace. Were the thinkers of India justified in making salvation dependent on knowledge? Our answer to this question will depend on what we mean by knowledge. Such a truth as that in which the faith of India was rooted, may be apprehended in many ways. Let us consider four of these:

In the first place the truth may be apprehended notionally, as the conclusion to a chain of metaphysical argument.

In the second place it may be apprehended emotionally, as a living personal conviction, akin to the pious Christian's faith.

In the third place it may be apprehended intuitively, as the result of a sudden illumination of consciousness, which, while it lasts, gives a man perfect certitude, making him as sure of what he discerns as he is of his own existence.

In the fourth place it may be apprehended really. A man may become conscious—clearly, fully, and finally—of his own absolute oneness with the Universal Self. This is obviously the highest imaginable type of knowledge; and it is obviously the ultimate outcome of the whole process of soul-growth. It is not until the soul has become divine that it can realize its oneness with God.

Of these four types of knowledge, the sages of the East, in their quest of absolute truth, wavered between the first and the third. The second did not appeal to them, partly because the emotional apprehension of truth is generated and fed by personal influences and is therefore foreign to the impersonal mind of the East, and partly because the ultimate identity of the individual with the Universal Self is a truth too large and fundamental to be apprehended with anything of the nature of personal emotion. The fourth type of knowledge was, in a sense, the goal of their desire; but they believed that there were short cuts to it; and it was their very endeavour to find those short cuts that led some into the path of metaphysical speculation, and others into the path of mental discipline and inward illumination. The idea of at once following and abridging the path of soul-growth—the only path to the goal of real knowledge, and the one path which is open to all men—did not suggest itself to them. Yet one of the many advantages of that path is that by following it we necessarily abridge it; and it was inevitable that, sooner or later, some master-mind should discover and reveal to mankind this too obvious truth.

Meanwhile, those whose mental bias predisposed them to approach the sovereign dogma of Eastern philosophy from a dialectical standpoint, set to work to establish its truth by quasi-logical methods,—to demonstrate its soundness as a theory, to show that it was the last link in a flawless chain of metaphysical argument. But as, in the region of speculative thought, theory and counter-theory are always equal and opposite, each in turn evoking and being evoked by the other, the attempt to grasp the truth of things in a purely "notional" form plunged those who made it into a whirlpool of metaphysical strife. A truth which, if true at all, is the very counterpart of supreme reality, and which therefore needs, for its apprehension, an atmosphere of perfect mental serenity, became a war-cry in one of those dialectical controversies

"Where friend and foe are shadows in the mist"

and inflamed the angry passions of those whom it should have filled with inward peace. Apart from this, it is obvious that the "notional" apprehension of spiritual truth does not necessarily stimulate the soul to bring forth the fruits of good living; and that in any case it is far beyond the reach of ordinary men.

Other thinkers who had no turn for metaphysical speculation, or to whom the atmosphere of controversy was distasteful, tried to arrive at the truth of things by another and a more direct path. In various ways—by mental discipline, by ascetic practices, by concentrated meditation—they tried to realize that rare but very real experience, a sudden illumination of consciousness, an experience which, while it lasts, solves all riddles and mysteries by making the inner meaning of life as clear as the light of noon. Such a mode of seeking truth may seem to our Western minds to savour of madness. But there is always method in the madness of the East. It is possible that some of us, even in the West, have at one time or another experienced, if only for a fleeting moment, a feeling akin to that of which I speak; a feeling of absolute certitude with regard to the ultimate realities of existence; a sense of having been initiated into a mighty mystery, in which all the lesser mysteries that distress and bewilder us are obviously, and of inner necessity, summed up and solved; a sudden and overmastering conviction that the world has, after all, a real and sufficient meaning, and that life is, in its essence, a movement towards a glorious goal. Generated, as it ordinarily is, by the shock of an overwhelming sorrow or of an overwhelming joy,—a shock which for the moment benumbs all the mental faculties of the ordinary self, and wakes to consciousness a higher and more inward self,—the feeling too often passes away before one has had time to realize its presence. But, evanescent though it be, the memory of it is ineffaceable; and those who have once experienced it can understand the attraction which that esoteric pathway to reality had for the Indian sage. Nor are we to assume off-hand that the labours of those who tried to find and follow the pathway were wasted. It is possible and even probable that, in the search for inward illumination, important "psychical" discoveries were made; that some at least among the seekers were enabled to realize, each for himself, the presence in man of clairvoyant senses and occult powers; and that by exercising these they gained, in exceptional cases, clear insight into the very heart of their cherished truth. There is something in the philosophy of the East, even on its more popular and practical side, which suggests that those who expounded it spoke, not merely out of the abundance of their hearts and the conviction of their minds, but also out of a personal experience, which, though supernormal, was by no means supernatural, and which was at once convincingly actual and transcendently real. But the pathway to the inward light is hard to find and easy to lose; and the methods by which recluses in Indian forests tried to acquire intuitive knowledge of the truth of truths, are not to be followed by ordinary men.

How, then, was that life-giving knowledge to be communicated to the rank and file of mankind? The solution which this problem received was in keeping with the esoteric tendency of Indian thought. The grand ideas in which the Soul of the East had found refuge could not be communicated as ideas to the average man, who was, ex hypothesi, as incapable of high thinking as of self-culture and mental self-control. Personal faith such as that which the devout Christian reposes in Christ, and in God the Father for Christ's sake, was not expected from him; for it was a vast conception that was presented to him, not a personality or a life. The truth of things must be taught to him, for he could neither evolve it nor discern it for himself; and though the notion of his growing, in the fulness of time, into oneness with that living truth of things which is the counterpart of supreme reality, was implicit in the creed of his teachers, the immediate bearing of the notion had not yet been realized. The truth of things must be taught to him; but it was not to be taught to him as abstract truth. What then? One course only remained. The truth must be taught to him symbolically. It must be embodied for him in a ceremonial system, and he must express his belief in it by the due discharge of a series of prescribed rites. This is what happened in India; and the seed which was thus sown bore its inevitable fruit. The inner meaning of the symbol was gradually forgotten, until at last the symbol was mistaken for the reality to which it bore witness. Then the forces in the East which periodically make for immobility asserted themselves without let or hindrance. The tyranny of ceremonialism—a tyranny which is inherent in the assumption that the truth of things is to be taught ab extra—extinguished spiritual feeling, and suspended, if it did not wholly destroy, the inner life of the people. "Deeper than ever plummet sounded," the Soul of India "lay (as it is lying now) inactive." The process of its evolution was arrested; and the last and safest pathway to reality—the pathway of soul-growth, of the actual expansion and vivification of consciousness—was closed to mankind.

What remedy was there for this state of things? There was a remedy; but it was too obvious to be easily found, and centuries had to pass before it could suggest itself to Eastern thought. The symbolical, equally with the formal, teaching of spiritual truth, ends at last in the substitution of machinery for life. The path of salvation lies else-where. If you want the rank and file of mankind to realize the truth of a given conception of life, get them to act—to order their own lives—on the assumption that it is true.

The Path of Life

LET us suppose that a great prophet appeared on earth, one who was in equal degrees a lover of his kind and a dreamer of spiritual dreams. Let us suppose that this prophet had drunk at the pure fountain of Indian thought, that he had accepted and assimilated the ideas which found expression in the Upanishads, the idea of the reality of the soul, of the development of the individual soul through a chain of earth-lives, of the consummation of this process of development in the union of the individual with the Universal Soul and its consequent admission into a life of unimaginable peace and bliss. Let us further suppose that, when his heart and mind had become saturated with these ideas, he became possessed with the desire to communicate them to his fellow-men. Let us imagine him looking down, from the standpoint of his exalted faith, on the toiling, suffering masses of mankind. Let us picture to ourselves the sorrow that must have pierced his heart when he saw how profoundly ignorant were the masses of the great truth which he had made his own; how entirely they were absorbed in the pursuit of what was material, trivial, perishable, unreal; how they were living, without knowing it, in a world of shadows and illusions; how even religion, which must once have had an inward meaning, had become for them a round of ceremonies and a network of formula; how dense, in fine, and how deadly were the mists that overhung their lives, and how seldom could those mists be parted by any breath of spiritual freedom, or pierced by any ray of spiritual hope and joy. Let us suppose that he then looked forward into the future, and saw his fellow men returning to earth again and again, and leading lives as hollow, as purposeless, and as joyless as the lives which they were leading then; the process of their soul-growth being so slow, owing to their fundamental ignorance of reality, that for a long sequence of earth-lives no appreciable progress could be made. Would not the sympathetic sorrow which the vision of the present had awaked in him, be intensified by his vision of the future; and would not the longing to help his fellow men, to enlighten them, to lead them into the path of light and life, become at last an absorbing passion which left no room in his heart for any other desire?

But how could he give men the knowledge that they needed? It was ignorance of reality that had darkened and debased their lives. It was knowledge which they were waiting for, knowledge of what was real and what was true. How could he give them this most rare and most precious of all gifts? How could he transform their sense of reality, and quicken and purify their perception of truth? Philosophical knowledge of the truth of things is, for obvious reasons, beyond the reach of the masses. The average man has no turn for metaphysical speculation, and the worse service that one can render him is to tempt him to indulge in it; for in the atmosphere of verbal controversy reality becomes an abstraction, truth becomes a formula, while love, which is the real unsealer of all spiritual secrets, inevitably withers and dies. The intuitive apprehension of the truth of things is equally, and for equally obvious reasons, beyond the reach of the masses. The "psychical" faculties, which generate that rare but vividly real type of knowledge, though potentially present in all men, are developed in an exceedingly small minority; and the premature attempt to develop them would end in hysteria being mistaken for inspiration, and hallucination for divine truth. The emotional apprehension of the truth of things may seem to be within the reach of ordinary men. In reality it also is reserved for a chosen few; for it is only in the genuinely poetic nature that it can maintain its equable heat and pristine purity. In lower natures it burns itself away in the pitchy flames of undisciplined sentiment, and dies out at last into formalism, dogmatism, and other "bodies of death." Moreover, the teacher who appeals to the spiritual emotion of his disciples, and who thereby enters into emotional relations with them, and through them with their disciples and .spiritual descendants, runs one serious risk. The chances are that, sooner or later, those who come under his influence, without having known him in the flesh, and who are therefore free to construct imaginary pictures of his life and person, will transfer to his personality the devotion which he wished them to give to his ideas, and will end by regarding his inevitable limitations, or rather the limitations of their own imagination— for by this time the teacher will have become a legendary hero—as the very boundaries of reality.

There remains what I have elsewhere called the real apprehension of ultimate truth. This, and this alone, is within the reach of all men. The actual expansion of the soul, in response to the forces in Nature that are making for its development, will give men, little by little, the knowledge that they need; for, as the soul expands, as it increases in wisdom and stature, its consciousness will enlarge its horizon, its vision will become clearer and deeper, and its sense of proportion will be transformed. When the knowledge of reality has been finally won, the attractive forces of earth, which will then be felt to be wholly illusory, will have ceased to act, and the end of the soul's pilgrimage will be at hand. The best service, then, that a man can render to his fellow men is to persuade them to enter the path of soul-growth. Or rather—for they entered it long ago—to follow it, no longer blindly and instinctively, but deliberately and of their own free will; and, by thus consciously co-operating with the expansive forces of Nature, to shorten the path of soul-growth, and to hasten the advent of its glorious goal.

That our prophet, looking at things from the standpoint of his own higher knowledge, should desire to render this service to his fellow men, may be taken for granted. But how should he persuade men that escape from the cycle of earth-lives was intrinsically desirable, that the path of soul-growth was the path of real life, that the goal to which it would lead them was worthy of their highest aspiration and their most strenuous endeavour? If their ignorance of reality was as dense as it seemed to be, to what faculty should he appeal and on what ground of admitted truth should he take his stand? The relation between knowledge and action, in the sphere of moral life, presents a problem which is insoluble, except on one hypothesis. Our difficulty is that for right action we need right knowledge; that for right knowledge we need inward enlightenment; that for inward enlightenment we need the transforming influence of a life of right action. There is but one way of escape from this seemingly vicious circle. Apply the law of development to the inward life of the soul; and it will become clear that the sense of reality, like every other sense and power, exists in embryo in each individual man. It is to this embryonic sense of reality that our prophet would make his appeal. In doing so, he would provide both for the development of that sense, and for the concurrent development in the soul of his disciple of the germ of his own teaching. For the sense of reality, like every other sense and power, grows by being exercised; and if it is to be exercised, it must be appealed to and called upon to exert itself. It follows that, in appealing to a man's sense of reality, one helps it to grow; and it follows that, in helping the sense to grow, one trains it to understand and respond to the appeal that is made to it.

We may conjecture, then, that the teacher who wished to lead men to the knowledge of reality would begin by assuming that the sense of reality was latent in every heart. He would say to them, "Does this earth-life really satisfy you? Cannot you see for yourselves that in the last resort it is hollow and unreal? Do the prizes for which you strive content you when you have won them? Do they not crumble into dust as you grasp them? Everything that earth can give you—health, wealth, pleasure, power, success, fame—proves to be either transient or illusory. Health lasts a few years, and is then undermined by disease and decay. Wealth has neither meaning nor value except so far as it enables you to buy pleasure, power, success, and fame. Pleasure palls upon you, and at last ceases to please. Or, if it does continue to please, age and disease forbid you to enjoy it. Power brings with it a weight of care and responsibility. Success has its counterpart in failure, for

'Things won are done: joy's soul lies in the doing.'
Fame is
'Enjoyed no sooner but despised straight.'

Look down the vista of the years. If you continue to desire the things of earth, you will return to earth, drawn by the influences that now attract you, again and again. Does this prospect content you? Has your experience of earth been so happy that you wish to renew it again and again? Is it not true that the earth-life brings real happiness to those only who have found inward peace? And is it not true that inward peace, though it can transfigure earth and make it spiritual and beautiful, is won by detachment from earth, not by devotion to it? This inward peace, in enjoying which you drink the only draught of real happiness that the earth-life can offer you, is a faint foretaste of what is in store for the soul when all its wanderings are over. Beyond all earth-lives a goal awaits you—a goal which crowns and completes the process of the soul's evolution—the goal of deep, perfect, inexhaustible bliss. This reward will be yours when you have broken the last of the ties by which earth attracts you, and in doing so have escaped, once and for ever, from the 'whirlpool of rebirth.'"

If there was anything in the heart of man which could respond to this appeal, the seed of the prophet's teaching would have been safely sown. His philosophy would have taught him that his appeal would not be made in vain. The germ of divine wisdom is implicit in the germ of soul-life; and the teacher who took for granted that men could see for themselves the inner truth of things, would find that the insight with which he credited them would evolve itself, little by little, in response to his appeal. But, be it carefully observed, he would make his appeal to the people as simple and direct as possible. He would not attempt to base it on metaphysical or theological grounds. He would not employ arguments which appeal to the intellectual faculties only, for he would know that the people have no capacity for abstract speculation, and he would infer from this that the more cogent a metaphysical or a theological argument might seem to be, when addressed to popular thought, the more certain it would be to delude and mislead. The reticence which he would thus impose upon himself might carry him very far, but he would respect all its obligations. He would make no attempt to lead the undeveloped minds of his hearers into the presence of what was ultimate, either in themselves or in the world at large. He would say nothing to them about the "Ego," nothing about God. He would put no truth before them which was not in some measure self-evident. To say that life, as we know it, is full of pain, sorrow, and disappointment; that its pleasures are transitory and delusive; that its prizes are intrinsically worthless; that the inward peace which moral goodness generates is the only real happiness; and that to escape into a world of inward peace is, therefore, the highest imaginable bliss; to advance such arguments as these is to appeal to an inward sense which exists potentially in all men. But to go beyond the limits of those simple yet profound conceptions, would be to lead men into a region of doubt, bewilderment, and wordy strife.

Having won from men some measure of assent to the self-evident truths which he had set before them, the teacher would proceed to draw for them the practical inferences from his premises. He would tell them that there was a path, by following which they would become gradually detached from earth and its shadows and delusions, and brought within sight of their spiritual goal; and he would then teach them how to enter that path and walk in it. The path of deliverance is the path of soul-growth. As the soul grows, and its perceptive faculties widen and deepen, the unreality of the earth-life will become gradually apparent; and when this has been fully realized, the last chain that binds the soul to earth will snap of its own accord, and deliverance will be won. The one thing needful, then, the one thing which every man ought to do and which any man can do, is so to live as to make his soul grow. How is this to be done? We need not go far for an answer to this question. In the first place, all the influences which directly thwart the growth of the soul must be subdued and disarmed. The lusts and passions of the animal self; the desires and ambitions, the moods and impulses, that are generated by petty egoism; the tendencies, whatever they may be, that make for the contraction of the life of the soul, for the restriction of its vital energies to the plane of the lower self,—all these must, for obvious reasons, be kept under due control. To allow the soul to identify itself with any of the lower selves which egoism seeks to magnify, would be fatal to its spiritual progress. Also, since it is of the essence of the new scheme of life to entrust to each man in turn the duty of ordering his own goings, it is clear that if any carnal or semi-carnal desire or passion were allowed to seize the helm of the will, the voyaging soul would make early shipwreck.

This is the negative side of soul-growth. The positive side is of even greater importance. If the soul is to grow, it must go out of itself into some sphere of being which seems for the moment to lie beyond its own. Now there are many avenues of escape from the ordinary self; and each of these helps, in its own way, to foster the growth of the soul. But there is one and one only which is open to all men,—the avenue of sympathy, of living or beginning to live in the lives of other persons and other things. In teaching men to live in the lives of others, our moralist would be content to lead them on from strength to strength, and would make no attempt to initiate them, while they were still in pupilage, into the esoteric mystery of an all-embracing, all-consuming love. He would take for granted that the germ of sympathy was in every heart, and that the germ would evolve itself, under the stress of the natural forces that make for the expansion of the soul, when once the adverse influences that hindered its outgrowth had been removed or, at least, reduced to inaction. What hinders the outgrowth of sympathy is not the lust of cruelty (for that is a rare and artificial by-product of human development), but the reckless egoism which prompts the strong, in the general struggle for existence, to trample down the weak. The impulse—half fear, half anger—which makes a man strike in self-defence; the "instinct to live" which makes him ready to sacrifice life in other beings in order that he may preserve it in himself; the desire for material comfort and well-being, which makes him reckless of the comfort and well-being of others, these tendencies are not in themselves incompatible with sympathy, though they may, if uncontrolled, develop into darker and deadlier passions, and generate an egoism more callous and more self-seeking than that from which they spring. But the scheme of life which we are considering has provided for all the animal and semi-animal passions being placed under due control; and he who had laid this teaching to heart would be ready to receive the further lesson, that he ought to refrain from wanton unkindness, first to his fellow-men, and then to all other living things. In other words, though he would be left free to take whatever steps might prove to be necessary for the protection and preservation of his life, he would be taught that no wound was to be wantonly inflicted, no life to be recklessly destroyed; and that, speaking generally, each man in turn was to make his pilgrimage on earth as free as might be possible from harm and offence to others. Under the influence of this teaching, gentleness, kindness, and tolerance would gradually impregnate the atmosphere of man's daily life; and in that atmosphere the germ of sympathy would make strong and steady growth.

To trace the stages in the growth of that soul-expanding germ would be beside my present purpose. That the destiny of sympathy is to trans-form itself into the passion of spiritual love, can scarcely be doubted. It is of the essence of the individual life to seek to outgrow itself, to seek to mingle itself with other lives on its way to that Universal life which is its own true self; and when once the individual life has begun to lose itself in the lives of others, a process has been initiated, of which absorption into the Universal life—itself the highest imaginable development of love—is the natural and necessary consummation. But one who was addressing himself to the rank and file of mankind, and was therefore taking thought for the earlier stages of soul-growth, would be careful to disabuse the minds of his disciples of the idea that there was any short cut to spiritual perfection. The critic who looks at things from the standpoint of the "enthusiasm of humanity," may possibly condemn the gospel of sympathy as a cold and pallid substitute for the gospel of love; but the moralist who had taken upon himself to lead the average man into the path of life, would not allow this criticism to deflect him from his purpose. Knowing that in the earlier stages of soul-growth self-control was the one thing needful, and that until the self-seeking desires had been mastered the outgrowth of the soul-expanding desires was not to be looked for; and knowing further that sympathy, which has much in common with self-control, and follows naturally from it, would gradually prepare the way for the outgrowth of spiritual love and the desires that are akin to it, or rather would itself, in the natural course of things, develop into these;—knowing this, the idealistic moralist would be content that men should aim in the first instance at the skyline which was visible to them, and that the heights which this hid from view should unfold themselves, little by little, as the soul surmounted the foothills of its life. Herein he would show his practical wisdom and make good his claim to be a teacher of mankind. The premature development of the "enthusiasm of humanity" and other spiritual passions might well have fatal consequences; for experience has amply proved that the lower desires and impulses are all too ready to masquerade as the higher,—lust, for example, as love, race-hatred as patriotism, religious intolerance as spiritual devotion, egoism as self-respect, censoriousness and uncharitableness as moral zeal. The truth is that in ordinary men the passion of love necessarily directs itself towards what is individual and quasi-concrete, whereas sympathy, just because it is a colder and paler sentiment, has an immeasurably wider and more abstract range. There are indeed exceptional natures which can sublimate personal into impersonal love; but, speaking generally, if the impersonal passion of universal love is to be our goal, the safer path to it,—at any rate in the earlier stages of man's development,—will be that of the impersonal sentiment of sympathy rather than the personal passion of love.

The master principle, that deliverance from the illusions of earth is to be won by self-control and sympathy, would be embodied in a simple "Law." It is in this form, and no other, that the new philosophy of life would have to be presented to the rank and file of mankind. It may be possible for ordinary men to see for themselves that escape from the "whirlpool of rebirth" into the calm haven of inward peace and spiritual bliss, is a desirable end; but the teacher who should try to explain to them that this end was to be compassed by the practice of self-control and the cultivation of sympathy, would find that his words had missed their mark. The average man has no turn for abstract thinking; and to ask him to trace the logical connection between this or that moral principle and the paramount end of life, is to set him a task beyond his power. What is needed for his edification is to give him a few simple moral rules, and to tell him that these, if faithfully followed, will lead him to the goal that he desires to reach.

But the rules that are given him must be simple and few. In other words, they must be the axiomata media of morality, the broad rules of life which mediate between the master principles of moral action and those meticulous details into which the mind that values rules for their own sake is so ready to descend. The force and authority of each rule must be self-evident. The teacher must be able to say to his disciples: "Cannot you see for yourselves that this course of action is better than that,—that continence (let us say) is better than incontinence, sobriety than intemperance, kindness than cruelty, gentleness than violence?" In making this appeal to his disciples he would at once exercise and cultivate their spiritual intelligence and their power of moral choice. When we say that the force and authority of the axiomata media of morality are self-evident, we imply that they stand very near to the moral principles which are behind them, so near that, in yielding to their attractive force, the soul is brought into subconscious contact with the truth and beauty of the teacher's philosophy of life. We imply, in other words, that the simple rules of a sane morality are in themselves a source of inward illumination, and that the soul which disregards them sins, in some sort, "against light and knowledge" and misuses its power of choice.

To this proposition there are corollaries which are of profound importance. The growth of the soul, and its consequent absorption into itself of forces and influences which seem to be external to its life, are necessarily accompanied by the diminution of outward pressure and the consequent growth of freedom; and it stands to reason that, when the individual has become one with the Universal Self, so that all forces and all influences are gathered at last within the compass of its conscious life, absolute freedom will have been won. It follows that freedom is the very counterpart of spiritual life. Now freedom is of two kinds,—freedom to know and freedom to do; and these two are in the last resort one. The teacher who would lead men into the path of life must assume at the outset that man is free, potentially if not actually,—free both to discern good from evil and to make his choice between the two; and he must so shape his teaching that this dual faculty shall be constantly exercised, and to that extent encouraged to grow. It is because the teacher who limits himself, when framing his Law, to a few axiomata media and refuses to go further into detail, makes ample provision, first for the recognition and then for the culture of spiritual freedom,—it is for this, if for no other reason, that he must take rank as the wisest of Lawgivers.

The superiority of a simple to an elaborate Code of Law, in respect of the services that they respectively render to the cause of spiritual freedom, may be looked at from another point of view. The connection between the broader rules of conduct and the goal by which obedience to those rules is at last to be rewarded, though possibly not directly traceable by the man of average insight and intelligence, is always felt by him to be natural and real. In an elaborate Code of Law, on the other hand, nine-tenths of the rules that men are directed to obey are so unreasonable and so unattractive that the man who obeys them can neither discern their moral significance, nor see that there is any natural connection between his obedience and his promised goal. The consequence is that he gets to regard both the law and its reward as wholly alien from his own inward life. He is to obey such and such rules of conduct because he is told to obey them, and for no other reason; and if, and so far as, he is obedient to them, he is to reap such and such rewards, not because there is any natural connection between his conduct and its recompense, but because the irresponsible despot who framed the Code of Law chose, for reasons of his own, to attach certain prizes to obedience, and certain penalties to rebellion. When such a conception of life and duty has fully established itself, spiritual freedom has been mortally wounded, and the soul has entered the valley of the shadow of death. Against this danger the teacher who regarded soul-growth as both the way and the end of "salvation," would be ever on his guard. Not only would he make his moral rules as few, as simple, and as broad as possible, but he would also impress upon his disciples that by obeying those rules, by following the path, which they marked out for them, they would, in the natural course of things, arrive in due season at the promised goal of inward peace and bliss;—a goal which is so vitally connected with the way of living that leads up to it, that those who seek it enjoy it in some measure before they reach it, its foreglow—"the peace which passeth all understanding"—falling in ever deepening splendour on each successive stage in the path of life. He would therefore warn his disciples against whatever scheme of conduct might tend to substitute a mechanical for a spiritual, a supernatural for a natural, conception of life and duty. Thus he would teach them that "sacrifices and burnt offerings" could profit them nothing; that ceremonial observances had no intrinsic meaning or value; that obedience to rules, for the mere sake of obedience, far from strengthening their souls, would entangle them at last in the clinging meshes of the infinitesimal. He would teach them, further, that actions produce their natural and necessary consequences, and that the most vital of these is the reaction of what is done on the soul of the doer. Is the soul really growing? Are the earth-ties being strengthened or weakened? These are the questions which men must learn to ask themselves, and to answer. It is by the strictly natural process of growth, and in no other way, that the soul is to be "saved alive"; and the idealistic teacher would urge his disciples to repudiate the authority of his own law, if it set any other path or any other ideal than that of soul-growth before them.

Above all—and this is perhaps "the conclusion of the whole matter"—the teacher who preached the gospel of soul-growth would impress upon his disciples that each of them must work out his salvation for himself; that he must take the conduct of his life into his own hands; that he must enlist his will-power on the side of those natural forces which are ever making for the expansion of his life; that his will-power was in fact the last and the highest of those natural forces; that its outgrowth had come, gradually and naturally, with the outgrowth of his soul; that whatever tended to arrest its growth tended also, and in an equal degree, to arrest the growth of his soul; that in this, as in other matters, the end of life must control the way, and the way foreshadow the end; that in this, as in other matters, a man must achieve his ideal by applying it to the solution of his practical problems, and giving expression to it in the daily round of his life.

The Teaching of Buddha

IN the Sixth Century before the birth of Christ, India, which had long been seething and fermenting with spiritual thought, gave to the world a great teacher. The son of an Indian chieftain, Gaudama Buddha 1 strove for many years to find that inward illumination on "great matters," which was the cherished dream of every serious thinker in that remarkable era. After having followed, to no purpose, the paths of metaphysical speculation, of mental discipline, and of ascetic rigour, he reaped on one memorable night the fruit of his prolonged spiritual effort, the truth of things being of a sudden so clearly revealed to him that thenceforth he never swerved for a moment from devotion to his creed and to the mission that it imposed upon him.

What was the creed of Buddha? What did he teach mankind, and what were the dominant ideas on which he based his teaching? It is, I think, at once easier and more difficult to interpret the creed of Buddha than that of Christ. Unquestionably easier, within certain clearly defined limits. Perhaps more difficult, when once those limits have been passed.

That the moral teaching of Buddha was of such and such a character, that the carefully elaborated scheme of life which has always been attributed to him was really his, can scarcely be doubted. On this point it will suffice if I cite the authority of two well-known Buddhist scholars. "When it is recollected," says Dr Rhys Davids, "that Gaudama Buddha did not leave behind him a number of deeply simple sayings, from which his followers subsequently built up a system or systems of their own, but had himself thoroughly elaborated his doctrine, partly as to details, after, but in its fundamental points even before, his mission began; that during his long career as teacher, he had ample time to repeat the principles and the details of the system over and over again to his disciples, and to test their knowledge of it; and finally that his leading disciples were, like himself, accustomed to the subtlest metaphysical distinctions, and trained to that wonderful command of memory which Indian ascetics then possessed; when these facts are recalled to mind, it will be seen that much more reliance may reasonably be placed upon the doctrinal parts of the Buddhist Scriptures than upon correspondingly late records of other religions." Dr Oldenberg speaks to the same general effect: "On the whole we shall be authorized to refer to Buddha himself the most essential trains of thought which we find recorded in the Sacred Texts, and in many cases it is probably not too much to believe that the very words in which the ascetic of the Sakya house couched his gospel of deliverance, have come down to us as they fell from his lips. We find that throughout the vast complex of ancient Buddhist literature which has been collected, certain mottoes and formulas, the expression of Buddhist convictions upon some of the weightiest problems of religious thought, are expressed over and over again in a standard form adopted once for all. Why may not these be words which have received their currency from the founder of Buddhism, which had been spoken by him hundreds and thousands of times throughout his long life devoted to teaching?" Whatever else Buddha may have been, he was a serious and systematic teacher who was deeply impressed with the belief that it was his mission to lead men into the path of salvation,—a broad path, as he conceived it, but clearly defined; and as his missionary life lasted for forty-five years, and was one of incessant preaching and teaching; we may well believe that he mapped out the path with extreme care and accuracy, and that the chart of life which he thus elaborated was preserved in all its detail by the retentive memory of his listeners and their disciples, and has come down intact to the present day. We way also assume with confidence that tradition has faithfully preserved that part of his teaching in which he gave reasons for the faith that was in him. It is certain that he urged men to enter and walk in the path in order that, by extinguishing all desire for earthly things, they might win deliverance from the earth-life, with its attendant suffering, and attain to that blessed state of being which he called Nirvâna. It is further certain that he believed in re-incarnation, and took for granted that those who listened to him held the same belief; and that therefore he meant by deliverance from earth deliverance from the "whirlpool of rebirth," deliverance from the cycle of earth-lives which the unenlightened soul is bound to pass through.

This much is practically certain. But when we ask ourselves what Buddha meant by re-incarnation—a question which must be asked, and which obviously gives rise to other questions wider and deeper than itself—we come to the verge of what is obscure and dubious; and the very next step takes us into a region of pure conjecture in which at present there is neither path nor guide.

For this sudden and complete change there are two chief reasons. The first is that, even when a great teacher says much about the ultimate realities of existence (or what he regards as such), it is extremely difficult to make out what he really believes. In the realm of metaphysical speculation, whether we are thinking for ourselves or trying to interpret the ideas of others—the two enterprises are really one—we feel (if we have any qualification for either task) that our thoughts are utterly inadequate to the solution of our problems, and that our words, besides being of Protean instability, are utterly inadequate to the expression of our thoughts. Who but the novice at speculative thinking would venture to make any statement with confidence when he had to use such words as Soul, Ego, Person, Consciousness, Being, Reality, Universe, God;—words that have different meanings for different minds; words that take new shades of meaning from each new standpoint which the thinker finds it needful to adopt, and even from each new context which the course of his thinking suggests to him; words that stand on guard at the portal of every metaphysical inquiry, and refuse to allow us to pass until we have read the riddle of their meaning and so answered their unanswerable challenge?

The second reason for our uncertainty as to the metaphysical grounds on which Buddha based his ethical teaching, is that he himself was so far from dogmatizing about what is ultimate as to preserve a deep and consistent silence with regard to it. The meaning and the significance of this silence will presently be considered. Meanwhile I can but say, with Dr Oldenberg, that in the

Buddhist philosophy (as it is presented to us in the Sacred Scriptures) "we have a fragment of a circle, to, complete which and to find the centre of which, is forbidden, for it would involve an inquiry after things which do not contribute to deliverance and happiness."

Let us now set forth what is clear and certain in Buddha's teaching, and then advance from this in the direction of what is dubious and obscure. It is fitting that we should begin, as Buddha himself began, with the Four Sacred Truths. In the Sermon to Five Ascetics at Benares, which tradition gives as the opening act of the ministry of Buddha, the Four-fold Truth is set forth in the following words:

"There are two extremes, O monks, from which he who leads a religious life must abstain. What are those two extremes? One is a life of pleasure, devoted to desire and enjoyment; that is base, ignoble, unspiritual, unworthy, unreal. The other is a life of mortification; it is gloomy, unworthy, unreal. The Perfect One, O monks, is removed from both these extremes and has discovered the way which lies between them, the middle way which enlightens the mind, which leads to rest, to knowledge, to enlightenment, to Nirvâna. And what, O monks, is this middle way, which the Perfect One has discovered, which enlightens the eye and enlightens the spirit, which leads to rest, to knowledge, to enlightenment, to Nirvâna? It is this sacred eightfold path, as it is called: Right Faith, Right Resolve, Right Speech, Right Action, Right Living, Right Effort, Right Thought, Right Self-Concentration. This, O monks, is the middle way, which the Perfect One has discovered, which enlightens the eye and enlightens the spirit, which leads to rest, to knowledge, to enlightenment, to Nirvâna.

"This, O monks, is the sacred truth of suffering; birth is suffering, old age is suffering, death is suffering, to be united with the unloved is suffering, to be separated from the loved is suffering, not to obtain what one desires is suffering, in short the fivefold clinging to the earthly is suffering.
"This, O monks, is the sacred truth of the origin of suffering; it is the thirst for being, which leads from birth to birth, together with lust and desire, which finds gratification here and there: the thirst for pleasures, the thirst for being, the thirst for power.
"This, O monks, is the sacred truth of the extinction of suffering; the extinction of this thirst by complete annihilation of desire, letting it go, expelling it, separating oneself from it, giving it no room.
"This, O monks, is the sacred truth of the path which leads to the extinction of suffering; it is this sacred, eightfold path, to wit, Right Faith, Right Resolve, Right Speech, Right Action, Right Living, Right Effort, Right Thought, Right Self-Concentration."

This is the Four-fold Truth, on which Buddha's whole scheme of life is hinged. Let us try to set it forth in other and fewer words:

(1) Life on earth is full of suffering.
(2) Suffering is generated by desire.

(3) The extinction of desire involves the extinction of suffering.

(4) The extinction of desire (and therefore of suffering) is the outcome of a righteous life.

There is one link in Buddha's teaching which seems to be missing. Why does desire generate suffering? The answer to this question is given in a discourse which Buddha is said to have held with the five ascetics shortly after he had expounded to them the Four Sacred Truths.

"'The Exalted One,' so the tradition narrates, "spake to the five monks thus:

'The material form, O monks, is not the self. If material form were the self, O monks, this material form could not be subject to sickness, and a man should be able to say regarding his material form: My body shall be so and so; my body shall not be so and so. But inasmuch, O monks, as material form is not the self, therefore is material form subject to sickness, and a man cannot say as regards his material form: My body shall be so and so.

"'The sensations, O monks, are not the self'"—and then follows in detail regarding the sensations the very same exposition which has been given regarding the body. Then comes the same detailed explanation regarding the remaining three component elements, the perceptions, the conformations, the consciousness, which, in combination with the material form and the sensations, constitute man's sentient state of being. Then Buddha goes on to say:

"How think ye then, O monks, is material form permanent or impermanent?"

"Impermanent, Sire."

"But is that which is impermanent, sorrow or joy?"

"Sorrow, Sire."

"But if a man duly considers that which is impermanent, full of sorrow, subject to change, can he say: that is mine, that is I, that is myself?"

"Sire, he cannot."

Then follows the same exposition in similar terms regarding sensations, perceptions, conformations, and consciousness: after which the discourse proceeds:

"Therefore, O monks, whatever in the way of material form, sensations, perceptions, etc., respectively, has ever been, will be, or is, either in our case, or in the outer world, or strong or weak, or low or high, or far or near, it is not self: this must he in truth perceive, who possesses real knowledge. Whosoever regards things in this light, O monks, being a wise and noble hearer of the word, turns himself from sensation and perception, from conformation and consciousness. When he turns therefrom, he becomes free from desire; by the cessation of desire he obtains deliverance; in the delivered there arises a consciousness of his deliverance; rebirth is extinct, holiness is completed, duty is accomplished; there is no more a return to this world, he knows."

We now understand what the desire is that generates suffering, and why it generates it. It is the desire for what does not belong to "self"—the real self —that generates suffering; and the reason why such desire generates suffering is that what does not belong to the real self is impermanent, changeable, perishable, and that impermanence in the object of desire must needs cause disappointment, regret, disillusionment, and other forms of suffering to him who desires. The tendency to identify self with what is material and temporal, and therefore to desire for oneself material and temporal goods and pleasures, is the chief cause of human suffering; for, when such goods and pleasures are desired, success in the pursuit of them is perhaps more hurtful and scarcely less painful than failure. And not only does this tendency, with its derivative desire, cause suffering in the present earth-life, but it also causes suffering to be reproduced for the self in future earth-lives; for it is desire for the goods and pleasures of earth which, acting as a strong magnetic force, draws the self back to earth again and again. Desire in itself is not evil. On this point Buddha's teaching must not be misunderstood. His disciples are expressly told—this is the very sum and substance of his teaching—to desire and strive for enlightenment, deliverance, Nirvâna. Desire for the pleasures, or rather for the joys, that minister to the real self, is wholly good. It is desire for the pleasures that minister to the lower self; it is the desire to affirm the lower self, to live in it, to cling to it, to rest in it; it is the desire to identify oneself with the individual self and the impermanent world which centres in it, instead of with the Universal Self and the eternal world of which it is at once the centre and the circumference;—it is this desire, taking a thousand forms, which is evil, and which proves itself to be evil by causing ceaseless suffering to mankind. If the self is to be delivered from suffering, desire for what is impermanent, changeable, and unreal must be extinguished; and the gradual extinction of unworthy desire must therefore be the central purpose of one's life.

But how is desire, with the suffering that it generates, to be extinguished? The answer to this question is the Fourth of the Sacred Truths: "This, O monks, is the sacred truth of the path which leads to the extinction of suffering: it is the sacred eightfold path, to wit, Right Faith, Right Resolve, Right Speech, Right Action, Right Effort, Right Thought, Right Self-Concentration."

There is no part of Buddha's teaching in which his wisdom shines out more clearly than in this. At first one might feel disposed to think that Right Action was everything. Buddha does not think so. Right Speech, Right Action, and Right Living may perhaps be grouped together under the general head of Right Conduct; but there are other elements of Righteousness which Buddha seems to regard as not less important than these, to wit, Right Faith, Right Resolve, Right Effort, Right Thought, Right Self-Concentration. In other words, Buddha lays as much stress on the inward as on the outward side of morality; and he would have us realize that conduct, when divorced from faith and thought and purpose, is worth nothing. Under the Jewish Law—at any rate in the later developments of legalism—correct action was regarded as the one thing needful. The consequences of this assumption were disastrous in the extreme. A mechanical and quasi-material conception of life and duty was introduced into the very heart of religion and morality; and spiritual freedom was crushed out by an ever-growing burden of narrow, rigid, and despotic rules. Buddha, like other moral teachers, found it necessary to give men rules for the conduct of life; but not only did he make his rules as few, as simple, and as comprehensive as possible, but by associating faith, thought, and purpose with speech and action, by impressing on his disciples that the inward side of conduct counts for at least as much as the outward, he provided against that miserable pullulation of trivial rules, which is sure to arise whenever correct action is regarded as an end in itself; and in doing so he shielded spiritual freedom from the most oppressive and most deadly form of constraint.

Nevertheless, when we have once realized that the inward side of action—the inward approaches to it and the inward consequences of it—is to the full as real and as significant as the outward, we may safely affirm, what Buddha would not have denied, that Right Conduct is the aspect of Righteousness which concerns us most. What we do, besides being the outward and visible sign of our inward and spiritual state, reacts, naturally and necessarily, on what we are, and so moulds our character and controls our destiny—for "character is destiny"—both in this and in future earth-lives. That being so, and conduct being the aspect of a man's general bearing for which directions are at once most needed and most easy to give, it is not to be wondered at that Buddha should have thought it necessary to formulate moral rules for the guidance of his followers,—men who were presumably ignorant and unenlightened (for his message was addressed to all men) and therefore in need of some measure of ethical direction.

In framing his moral code, Buddha, according to his wont, departed widely from precedent, and showed that, as regards his outlook on life, he was far in advance of his age. The ethical legislators of antiquity addressed themselves to a comparatively narrow audience,—a city, a tribe, or a people; they went fully into detail, their rules being many and minute; and they went far beyond the limits of ethics proper, nine-tenths of their rules being civil or ceremonial rather than ethical (in the stricter, and yet broader and more spiritual sense of the word). Buddha, on the contrary, addressed himself to the widest of all audiences,—to the whole human race: he carefully abstained from going into detail, his rules being few, simple, and comprehensive; and he kept entirely within the limits of ethics proper, limits which he may almost be said—so original and so formative was his teaching—to have been the first to define.

Here is his Code of Moral Law.

The believer is required

1. To kill no living thing.
2. Not to lay hands on another's property.
3. Not to touch another's wife.
4. Not to speak what is untrue.
5. Not to drink intoxicating drinks.

A simple code this, but as profound as it is simple. To begin with, its extreme simplicity means that its authority is in the main self-evident; in other words, that it makes a direct appeal to a man's latent moral sense, and, in appealing to it, trains it and helps it to grow. In the next place, the fact that the rules are all prohibitions means that the believer is, first and foremost, to exercise self-control. The reason why he is to exercise self-control is that deliverance from suffering is to be won by the suppression of unworthy desires, and that without the exercise of self-control desire cannot be suppressed. The five rules indicate five arterial directions in which his self-control is to be exercised. Thus the first rule calls upon him to control the passion of anger; the second, the desire for material possessions; the third, the lusts of the flesh; the fourth, cowardice and malevolence (the chief causes of untruthfulness); the fifth, the craving for unwholesome excitement. It is to be noted that the desires and passions which the believer is called upon to suppress, are those which are most hurtful to his own inner life, most productive of suffering to himself, and most productive of suffering to his fellow men. By learning self-control with regard to these, he not only brings happiness to himself and to others, but he also strengthens himself for the more general work of suppressing unworthy desires of every sort and kind. But the five rules are something more than mere prohibitions. Self-control necessarily prepares the way for the development of the more positive and active virtues. When the baser tendencies of man's nature are kept under such strict control that at least they lose their baseness and cease to obstruct the outgrowth of the nobler tendencies, the latter must needs begin to germinate. Thus the control of anger will prepare the way for the outgrowth of gentleness and compassion; the control of covetousness, for the outgrowth of charitableness and generosity; the control of lust, for the outgrowth of purity and unselfish love; and so forth. "How does a monk become a partaker of uprightness?" asks Buddha. The answer is, "A monk abstains from killing living creatures; he refrains from causing the death of living creatures; he lays down the stick; he lays down weapons. He is compassionate and tender-hearted; he seeks with friendly spirit the welfare of all living things. This is part of his uprightness." Let a man abstain from unkindness to his fellow men and other "living creatures,"—and the germs of kindness, gentleness, and compassion which are lying dormant in his nature will begin to make spontaneous growth. And so with the other rules.

Yet Buddha was wise to limit his formulated law to negative commandments. If a positive commandment is to move men to well-doing, it must be in some sort a counsel of perfection; and there are few men who can receive a counsel of perfection in the spirit in which it is, or ought to be, given to them. Some natures are over-wrought by it, and lose their spiritual balance. Others interpret it literally, and so make nonsense of its transcendent sense. Others again (the majority) listen to it, but pay no heed to it. For ordinary men it is best that the active, positive side of virtue should be approached—gradually and naturally—from the side of self-control. Also, it must be remembered that the formulation of a positive moral law tends, especially in an age of ceremonialism, to arrest the development of conscience,—the very faculty which, in the Buddhist scheme of life, there is most need for men to cultivate. When a man does kind and compassionate deeds (let us say), not because his better nature, acting through his moral sense, prompts him to do them, but because he is authoritatively commanded to do them, there is a danger lest the man's moral sense, finding that there was little or no work for it to do, either as a prompter or as a guide, should gradually cease to energize, and the man should at last become entirely dependent for moral guidance on formulated rules and their professional exponents. Obedience to a negative commandment—provided that the commandment is sufficiently broad and simple for the spirit of it to appeal to one—can do no harm to him who obeys, and may do much good, for the discipline of self-control is one of the best of moral tonics. But when the self-control has done its work, when the soul, braced and disciplined, is ready to walk in the path of active virtue, it is in the highest degree desirable that it should be allowed to walk by itself (or with no more guidance than is implicit in the prohibitions which it has obeyed), and that nothing should be done to impair its insight or weaken its will.

There were weighty reasons, then, why Buddha's ethical teaching should have been mainly negative. There is, however, one positive virtue which is inculcated in all the Buddhist Scriptures—the virtue in which, in its embryonic stage, all other virtues are present in embryo—the virtue in which, in its ideal stage, all other virtues are crowned and consummated—love. Not the impersonal passion of universal love—that would come at the end of the Path, not at the beginning—but the impersonal sentiment of sympathy, with all that it involves,—kindness, gentleness, unselfishness, compassion. That this should have found a prominent place in the Buddhist scheme of life was inevitable, for, when egoism has been subdued, the self is constrained, by the expansive stress of its own inward nature, to find channels for the overflow of its abounding life; and the safest and most accessible channel of overflow is that of sympathy, first with other men and then with every living thing. But the process which is thus initiated—a process of self-realization through self-expansion—will not cease until sympathy has transformed itself into the passion of spiritual love, and the individual life has at once lost and found itself in the Universal Life, which is and has always been its own true self.

When a teacher tries to bring salvation within the reach of all men, he is confronted by the difficulty that men are in various stages of spiritual development, and that rules of life which are sufficient for the many may prove to be too elementary for the few. Not that the few are to ignore those rules or neglect to observe them. That they observe them fully and faithfully, and would never dream of breaking them, is taken for granted. But the simpler rules of life need to be supplemented, in these exceptional cases, by others which are at once more elevating and more exacting. When the foothills of life have been surmounted, the more difficult and dangerous mountain heights will come in view, and directions for climbing these will be needed and will have to be given.

In the Eight-fold Path there are Four Stages, each of which is marked by the breaking of some of the "Fetters"—ten in all—which bind man to earth and to self.

In the First Stage, the stage of "Conversion" or "entering upon the stream," three fetters are broken:

(1) The delusion of self; the delusive belief that the individual self is real and self-existent. This fetter is rightly placed at the head of the list; for the clinging to individuality, the desire to affirm the apparent or actual self instead of looking forward to its expansion into the real or universal self, has its ethical counterpart in egoism, and egoism is the beginning and end of sin.

(2) Doubt: doubt as to the wisdom of the teacher and the efficacy of the prescribed Path.

(3) Belief in the efficacy of good works and ceremonies. The disciple must free himself, first from the general delusion that correct outward action will ensure a man's salvation, and then from the particular delusion that religious rites and ceremonies have intrinsic value.

Having broken these fetters, the disciple enters the Second Stage, "the path of those who will return only once to earth." In this, and in the Third Stage, "the path of those who will never return to earth," two more fetters are broken:

(4) The fetter of sensuality or fleshly lust. The belief that fleshly lusts war against the soul is not peculiar to Buddhism. The difficulty for most religions, and indeed for most men, is to hit the man between rigorous asceticism and moral laxity. Buddha, who regarded the "life of mortification" as "unreal" and "unworthy," carefully abstained from overstraining human nature in that particular direction. It was only in the case of the "monk," or "religious devotee," that complete renunciation of the pleasures of the flesh was enjoined. But in the third stage, "the path, of those who will return to earth no more," every one is in a sense a religious devotee; and there can be little doubt, I think, that in that stage the final extinction of lust was contemplated. If so, that achievement would be the consummation of a long course—perhaps pursued through many lives—of continence and self-control.

(5) The fetter of ill-will. The disciple has to subdue all the feelings of anger, resentment, envy, jealousy, hatred, and the like, which spring from his sense of separateness from the rest of mankind, or rather from the rest of living things, and from his subsequent reluctance to identify himself with the Universal Life. In other to get rid of those feelings, a spiritual exercise was prescribed by the early Buddhists, which is eminently characteristic of the general spirit of Buddhism.

"He [the disciple] lets his mind pervade one quarter of the world with thoughts of love, and so the second, and so the third, and so the fourth. And thus the whole wide world, above, below, around and everywhere, does he continue to pervade with heart of love, far-reaching, grown great, and beyond measure. Just as a mighty trumpeter makes himself heard and without difficulty towards all the four directions, even so of all things that have shape or form, there is not one that he passes or leaves aside, but regards them all with mind set free and deep-felt love." The exercise is then repeated, substituting each time for love, first pity, then sympathy, then equanimity. By this means the strength of the fifth fetter is gradually weakened, and at last destroyed.

The whole of the Second and Third Stages is occupied with the struggle against the many enemies of the higher life who fight under the banners of sensuality and ill-will. When all of these have been finally conquered, the disciple enters the Fourth Stage, "the path of the Holy Ones, or Arahats." There he breaks, one by one, the five remaining fetters, to wit:

(6) The desire for life—for separate life—in the worlds of form.

(7) The desire for life—for separate life—in the formless worlds.

(8) Pride.

(9) Self-Righteousness.

Ought not the eighth and ninth fetters to have been broken long ago? Perhaps they ought; but Buddha knew that even in the last stage of the upward Path the shadow of egoism may fall on one's thought. The man who can say to himself: "It is I who have walked in the Path. It is I who have scaled these heights. It is I who have suppressed egoism. It is I who have won deliverance: "is still the victim of delusions. There are still fetters for him to break.

(10) Ignorance. The last fetter, like the first, is ignorance. As the Path begins with enlightenment, so it ends with it. It begins with potential enlightenment.

It ends with actual enlightenment. It begins with partial enlightenment. It ends with perfect enlightenment. It is for the sake of knowledge—real, final, absolute knowledge—that the Path has been followed. To know that the Universal Self is one's own real self,—to know this truth, not as a theory, not as a conclusion, not as a poetic idea, not as a sudden revelation, but as the central fact of one's own inmost life,—to know this truth (in the most intimate sense of the word know) by living it, by being it,—is the final end of all spiritual effort. The expansion of the Self, which is the outcome of spiritual effort, carries with it the expansion of consciousness; and when consciousness has become all-embracing, the fetter of ignorance has been finally broken, and the delusion of self is dead.

When the last fetter has been broken, the disciple—the "Arahat" or "Holy One" as he is now called—has reached his goal; in other words, he has attained to a state of perfect 1 knowledge, perfect love, perfect peace, perfect bliss.

There is something esoteric, one feels inclined to say, in this Path of the Four Stages. One finds some difficulty in identifying it with the Eightfold Path of the Fourth Sacred Truth. From Buddha's day down to our own, there has never been an age in which the number of men who could really break even the first of the Ten Fetters was not exceedingly small. What of the rest of mankind? Was no provision made for them in Buddha's scheme of life? Was that scheme meant for recluses and "adepts"—or would-be "adepts"—only? Were ordinary men to be left to their own devices until the time came for them to be "converted" (by what miracle we cannot well conjecture), and to realize what is so hard for even the best of us to realize,—the unreality of the individual life?

Surely not. "Conversion" has been happily defined as the "effective realization of admitted truth." The process that leads up to "conversion" is carried on, for the most part, in silence and obscurity. There is always a long period of ante-natal growth before the new idea, the new way of looking at things, can come to the birth. The authorities on Buddhism whom I have consulted do not make it clear whether the First Fetter was to be broken at the entrance to the First Stage of the Path, or whether it was the first delusion to be got rid of after the soul had entered that stage. In the latter case the difficulty of identifying the Path of the Four Stages with the Eight-fold Path vanishes; for it is quite conceivable that the soul should linger long in the First Stage, should even pass, during its sojourn in it, through a sequence of earth-lives, before it could realize that its sense of separateness was illusory. In the former case we must adopt another hypothesis. We must assume that, before the first of the Four Stages can be entered, there must be for most men a long preliminary stage of preparation, during which they follow, perhaps through a sequence of lives, the rules of Right Conduct—the simple rules of kindness, honesty, continence, truthfulness, temperance—until at last the reaction of Right Conduct on character, and the consequent expansion of the Self and enlargement of the field of its consciousness, makes it possible for them to enter the Path proper,—the Path which will lead them in the fullness of time to the goal of conscious union with the Living Whole. In either case we may take for granted that, before the First Fetter can be broken and flung aside, the soul must set itself to acquire the strength which will enable it to perform that initiatory act of renunciation, and that it is only by a course of "Right Conduct"—by the consistent exercise of self-control, and culture of sympathy—that it can acquire the strength which it needs.

In any case we are free to regard the Fourfold Truth as a message to the rank and file of mankind. Men might accept that message, and even begin, in their feeble, faltering way, to walk by it, before they were fit to advance into the more esoteric stages of the Path of Life. But those stages must be passed through—on this Buddha would have insisted with all the weight of his authority—before the goal can be reached. Miracles, in the supernatural sense of the word, are not to be looked for in the moral, any more than in the physical world. It is conceivable that my neighbour, whose spiritual development is far in advance of mine, may complete the Path in 50 years, whereas my sojourn in it may last for 50,000; but by him as by me, and by me as by him, every stage must be passed through and every fetter must be broken, if the promised prize is to be won. It is sometimes said that for ordinary men the path of spiritual ascent is spiral, whereas for men of exceptional spiritual development it is direct. This may be so; or it may be that for all men the path is spiral up to a certain point, and beyond that point direct. But be it spiral or direct or both, it is certain that it must free us from every delusion that separates us from the Real Self, if it is to lead us to our goal.

Whatever view we may take of Buddha's teaching, we must admit that in its essence it belongs to no one nation and no one age. Moses legislated for the Jews, Lycurgus for the Spartans, Zoroaster for the Persians, Confucius for the Chinese, Buddha for all men who have ears to hear. Man, as Buddha conceived of him, is not a citizen but a "living soul." The life which the scheme prescribed, though compatible with good citizenship and even conducive to it, is quite independent of it. It is also quite independent of caste, of social gradation, of distinctions such as that between priest and layman, between the learned and the ignorant, between gentle and simple, between rich and poor. Dr Oldenberg's contention that Buddha had no message for the poor and lowly, is scarcely tenable. The inward and spiritual life can be lived by the poorest of day-labourers not less than by the richest of millionaires. If anything, it is easier for the poor than for the rich to enter "the Kingdom of Heaven," for there are fewer earth-ties for the former to break. When Dr Oldenberg quotes the saying "to the wise belongeth the law, not to the foolish," and argues from it that "for children and those who are like children the arms of Buddha are not opened," he is playing on the word "wise." The wisdom which Buddha magnified was not the wisdom of the intellectual, the learned, the cultured, but the wisdom of those who have taught themselves, by walking in the Path of Life, to distinguish between shadows and realities. The simplicity Of Buddha's ethical code brings it within the reach of the simplest natures. It is surely open to those "who are like children" to be kind to their fellow-men, to abstain from envy and covetousness, to control the lusts of the flesh, to be truthful in word and deed. If there are heights to be climbed beyond those which the "child-like" can dream of, the soul will not be asked to attempt these until, by the practice of the life of simple goodness, it has grown strong enough for the more arduous task. The greatness of Buddha as a teacher is proved by the fact that his scheme of life, so simple and yet so complex, so obviously and yet so profoundly true, so modest in its aims and yet so daringly ambitious, so moderate and yet so extravagant in the demands that it makes on our spiritual resources,—provides for the needs of all men, in all stages of development, of all moulds of character, of all types of mind.

There is one feature of Buddha's teaching which demands our special attention because it seems to pervade, like an atmosphere, the whole of his scheme of life. We know from experience that our actions produce far-reaching consequences which we can follow out, both laterally and lineally, to a considerable distance. We know, for example, that our actions affect the material conditions of our own and of other lives; that they produce social consequences which have a wide circle of disturbance; that they affect, for good or for evil, our own characters, and—to a lesser extent—the characters of those with whom we are much in contact. We know also, if we take the trouble to consider the matter, that these consequences are the natural and necessary effects of causes which our action sets in motion; and, if we follow out this line of thought, we shall probably come to the conclusion that the whole moral world, under both its aspects—the outward and the inward—is, like the physical world, under the dominion of natural law. It was to this aspect of morality that Buddha attached supreme importance. According to the law of Karma, which he was not the first to formulate but which he unreservedly accepted, the consequences of a man's action—foremost among which is its effect on his character—follow him, not merely through life (in the vulgar sense of the word) but also from life to life, until they have exhausted their influence.

"The Books say well, my Brother! each man's life
The outcome of his former living is."

What we have done has made us what we are. What we are doing is moulding our character and determining the direction of its development. When a man dies, he takes his character away with him. When he returns to earth, he brings his character back with him,—a character which determines the very nature of his material surroundings, for the re-incarnating soul seeks (according to the doctrine of Karma), or has assigned to it, the particular environment which is at once most in keeping with its nature and most suitable for its development.

"That which ye sow, ye reap. See yonder fields!
　The sesamum was sesamum, the corn
Was corn. The Silence and the Darkness knew!
　So is a man's fate born.
"He cometh, reaper of the things he sowed, . . . "

The idea that pervades the whole of Buddha's teaching is that whatever we sow we must reap; in particular, that nothing can come between our conduct and its inward consequences; that every thought, every word, every deed is either making or marring us; in fine, that our spiritual destiny, which after all is our real destiny, is in our own hands.

With characteristic wisdom Buddha made no attempt to reconcile human freedom with the supremacy of natural law. He probably saw that the opposition of freedom to law is a false antithesis,—one of the fatal by-products of the dualism of ordinary thought. One who looked at things from the standpoint of the philosophy of the Upanishads would know that the free-will riddle, which has tied Western thought into so many desperate tangles, is a mere "Idol of the Cave." He would know that the Real or Highest Self—being, ex hypothesi, universal and eternal, and therefore exempt from all external constraint—is absolutely free. He would know that the Real Self is present in potency in each individual life, and that every "living soul" is, therefore, potentially free. He would know, further, that the development of the soul, in the direction of its own true self, is always marked by the outgrowth of freedom; and he would infer from this that freedom varies, in the degree of its development, from soul to soul, and that, speaking generally, it is lost or won by conduct. But though no man is absolutely free, and though in most men freedom has but a rudimentary existence, he would realize that the best way to foster its growth is to postulate its existence and appeal to it, as the wise teacher always appeals (though here too he is probably appealing to what has but a rudimentary existence) to a man's better self. In fine, far from teaching that freedom is incompatible with law, he would realize that the law of the growth of freedom—the seemingly paradoxical law that freedom, without which moral action is impossible, is itself generated by moral action—is one of the master laws of human life. Whether Buddha did or did not accept the ideas of the Upanishads, is a question which will presently be considered. Meanwhile, it is enough to know that, with his own practical ends in view, he not only postulated freedom in man, but—by bringing the inward life under the dominion of natural law, and so excluding from it all extraneous influences—he laid a tremendous burden on the human will; for he told men that it rested with them, and with them only, to determine what course the process of their development should take, and how long their pilgrimage on earth (from life to life) should last.

Now the first and last of Nature's laws is that of growth; and the teacher who brings the inner life of man under the dominion of natural law brings it also, by implication, under the dominion of the law of growth. Wherever there is life there is growth; in other words, there is a gradual passage from embryonic existence to maturity, from the seed-state, in which all the potentialities of future perfection are wrapped up, to perfection itself,—the perfection of the particular species or type. This law applies to the self, not less than to the animal or the plant. Indeed, it applies first and foremost to the self, and applies to the living things that surround us because, and just so far as, they too are manifestations of the one self-evolving life. There is, however, a vital difference between the growth of the soul and the growth of any animal or plant. "The lilies of the field . . . toil not, neither do they spin: and yet . . . Solomon in all his glory was not arrayed like one of these." But if the soul is to be arrayed in glory it must both toil and spin. "Which of you," asks Christ, "by taking thought can add one cubit unto his stature?" Buddha's teaching bases itself on the assumption that by taking thought we can add to our spiritual stature, that the soul can make itself grow. Buddha would, I think, if we could question him, pass on from can to must. He would say that, when a certain stage in our development has been reached, the soul can make no further growth except what it wills to make, that it is only by the action of the will—itself one of Nature's master "streams of tendency"—that the expansive forces of Nature which are at work in the soul can be co-ordinated and made effective. He would say that the power of the soul to make itself grow is the very fruit of the whole previous process of its growth; that its presence is the proof that the process has (thus far) been successfully accomplished; that if it be wanting, the preliminary process of growth has not been carried far enough; that if, having been won, it has become atrophied through disuse, the growth of the soul has been arrested and the counter-process of degeneration has begun.

That we may the better realize the meaning and ulterior bearing of this conception, let us contrast it with the conception which has long dominated the ethical philosophy of the West. Owing to the myopia of the Western mind, the doctrine that the soul can work out its eternal destiny in a single earth-life has been able to win general acceptance. This doctrine is obviously incompatible with the idea that the destiny of the soul is to be achieved by the actual vital process of growth; for it stands to reason that, in the natural order of things, neither utter depravity nor absolute perfection can be achieved in the brief space of a single life. How then is "salvation" to be won? Israel, from whom the Western mind inherited its popular philosophy, persuaded himself that salvation was to be won by obedience to a formal Law. This Law was the work of the supernatural God, by whom it was miraculously delivered to man. There was no reason why all or even many of its commandments should be moral, in the stricter sense of the word. The supernatural God, whose ways are presumably inscrutable, might, for reasons of his own, order man to do things which were apparently trivial or unreasonable. If he did, man must obey. Apart from this, there was a special reason why many of the commandments of the Jewish Law should be non-moral. The frailty of man is such that he is always liable to disobey God. Disobedience is hateful to God, and draws down his wrath upon the sinner. In order to appease God and avert his wrath, man must offer up something which he himself especially values,—a bullock, a he-goat, or whatever the victim may be. Thus the idea of propitiation through sacrifice is bound up with the idea of salvation through obedience to a divinely formulated Law. Sacrificial observances, being an important part of man's life, must be duly and formally regulated. In other words, ceremonial directions must always form an essential part of a Law which has come to man from a supernatural source. Now it is obvious that in matters of ceremonial punctilio there can be no inward standard of right and wrong. Correctness of outward action is all that is asked for; but absolute correctness is indispensable, and the general idea that action must be outwardly correct if it is to please God easily spreads from the ceremonial to the more strictly moral side of the Law. In the attempt to define correctness with perfect accuracy, rules and sub-rules spring up in rank profusion, until at last the burden of legalism threatens to extinguish spiritual life.

This is what happened to Israel in the days of his national decadence. Christianity inherited his ideas, but rejected the intolerable burden of his Law. It inherited the idea of salvation being won by obedience; but it started, under the stress of Christ's vivifying influence, by assuming that the Law which God wished men to obey was mainly, if not wholly, moral. To obey a moral law is, however, even more difficult than to obey a ceremonial law; and in the one case, as in the other, the penalty of disobedience, when the Law comes from God, is eternal death. How then was the wrath of God to be averted from disobedient man? "By the Sacrifice of Christ, the Mediator between God and Man," is the answer which Christian theology gave and still gives to this question. In the Catholic Church the sacrifice of Christ is perpetually repeated by the priest. In the Protestant Churches the Sacrifice is supposed to have been performed once and for all; and faith in the efficacy of the Cross opens the door of salvation to the believer. The reappearance—the inevitable reappearance—of the sacrificial idea in the religions of the West tended, for obvious reasons, to discredit morality and to substitute machinery for life. A man might conceivably have climbed to the highest pinnacle of virtue (in the human sense of the word), he might even have climbed to the highest level of holiness (in the inward and spiritual sense of the word), and yet be doomed to eternal perdition, either because he had no faith in the efficacy of the Sacraments of the Church or because he rejected the doctrine of the imputed righteousness of Christ. Contrariwise, a man might have sinned deeply, basely, and consistently, and yet, having made a late repentance, be forgiven—and therefore "saved"—for Christ's sake. Where such anomalies were possible, there could be no causal connection between conduct and its results. The doctrine of forgiveness of sin has ever tended to demoralize human life, by undermining the idea that virtue is rewarded by virtue, and vice punished by vice. A Heaven in the future is reserved by official Christianity for those who fulfil certain clearly prescribed conditions; a Hell in the future, for those who neglect to fulfil them. But neither in Heaven nor in Hell does a man reap the actual crop that he has sown. If he did, the false dualism of Heaven and Hell would disappear, and there would be millions of after-states instead of only two. Even when Hell has been fairly earned it may conceivably be evaded, for it is always open to the sinner to fall back on the uncovenanted mercies of God.

From first to last, this theory of things—a theory from which the ideas of natural law and natural growth are conspicuously absent—is wholly foreign to Buddha's scheme of life. Miraculous intervention, whatever form it may take, is beyond the horizon of his thought. The sacrificial system, ceremonialism, sacerdotalism, legalism,—all these he entirely rejects. Correct outward action counts for nothing in his eyes. The inward motive to and the inward consequences of action are all that he regards. Mediators count for nothing. Redeemers count for nothing. Priests count for nothing. Casuists and such like spiritual directors count for nothing. The most that one man can do for other men is to tell them of the Path of Life—the broad Path of self-development through self-surrender—and give them general directions for finding and following it. The true Saviour of men is he who does this. But each man in turn must walk in the Path, by using his own sight, his own strength, his own judgment, his own will.

"Therefore, O Ânanda! be ye lamps unto yourselves. Be ye a refuge to yourselves. Betake yourselves to no external refuge. . . . Look not for refuge to anyone except yourselves." External rewards are not to be looked for. External penalties are not to be feared.

It knows not wrath nor pardon; utter true

Its measures mete, its faultless balance weighs;
Times are as nought, to-morrow it will judge,
Or after many days.

Virtue rewards itself by strengthening the will, by subduing unworthy desire, by generating knowledge of reality, by giving inward peace. Sin punishes itself by weakening the will, by inflaming unworthy desire, by generating delusions, by breeding fever and unrest. For sin to be "forgiven" is as impossible as for virtue to forego its reward. To walk in the Path is its own reward; for the Path is lit by the ever-deepening foreglow of its goal. To depart from the Path is its own punishment; for the erring steps must, at whatever cost, be retraced. Must be retraced,—for all the forces of Nature are making for the growth of the soul, as surely as in springtime all the forces of Nature are making for the outgrowth of flower and leaf. It is Nature 3 herself that, acting through his sense of right and wrong, constrains him who has left the Path to seek to regain it. But the Path is not to be regained, except by a steep and arduous ascent; and the longer the return to it is delayed, the more steep and arduous will the ascent prove to be.

This is, I think, the most inward conception of life, and the most intrinsic standard of moral worth, that has ever been presented to human thought. When Christ says: "Take heed that ye do not your alms before men, to be seen of them: otherwise ye have no reward of your Father which is in Heaven"; when he bids us pray and fast in secret so that we may be rewarded, not by the applause of men, but by "the Father, which seeth in secret"; when the author of the "Imitation"—in some ways the most Christ-like of all Christians—reminds us that "what each man is in Thine eyes, that he is and no more,"—we are taken as far in the direction of pure inwardness and intrinsic reality as it is possible for men to go who worship and have long worshipped a "personal God." That "the Father in Heaven" whom Christ adored coincides, in the last resort, with Brahma—the all-knowing, all-thinking Self, the all-embracing, all-sustaining Life—is more than probable. But though the inspired teacher, whose thoughts are all poems, may be able to purify and spiritualize the conception of a personal God, the average man is quite sure to debase and externalize it. If we could but listen to the prayers that at any moment were being addressed "in secret to the Father which seeth in secret," we should realize how widely popular thought had departed from a really inward conception of life, and from a really intrinsic standard of moral worth. What is unique in Buddha's scheme of life is that every influence which might conceivably come between conduct and its consequences is rigidly excluded. God himself—if we are to continue to think and speak about God—"knows not wrath nor pardon." But can we continue to think and speak about so impersonal a God? Buddha must, I think, have asked himself this vital question. A great spiritual life-work is always the outcome of a great renunciation; and it is possible that what Buddha renounced was something dearer than wealth or power, dearer even than wife or child. The austere inwardness of his teaching had its counterpart, as we shall presently see, in a deep silence about what is ultimate and innermost, a silence which he must have imposed upon himself at the beginning of his long ministry, and which he never broke.

A Misreading of Buddha

SET forth in as few words as possible, Buddha's message to man is an appeal to him to find his true self, with all that this can give him—joy, peace, knowledge, love—by suppressing egoism, with all the desires and delusions on which it feeds, and breaking, one by one, the fetters of the surface life and the lower self.

Those who have followed me thus far will, I think, admit that Buddha's scheme of life coincides, at all its vital points, with the scheme that I worked out by drawing practical deductions from the master ideas of that deeply spiritual philosophy which found its highest expression in the Upanishads. One who accepted the central idea of that philosophy—the idea that the Universal Soul is the real self of each one of us—and realized its spiritual consequences, and who at the same time saw clearly that none of the current modes of apprehending it—the metaphysical, the intuitional, the poetical, the symbolical—was available for ordinary, unenlightened, undeveloped men, would probably come to the conclusion that, if the world at large was to be brought under the influence of that great spiritual idea, a practical interpretation of it must be presented to and followed by the rank and file of mankind.

Such a teacher would begin by appealing to the very sense which it was his most cherished desire to cultivate,—the sense of reality, which is present in embryo in every breast. He would tell men that life is full of suffering, and that the chief cause of suffering is the impermanence—and therefore the unreality—of the objects of man's desire; and he would expect them to assent to these propositions.

This is what Buddha did.

He would explain to them that the desire for unreal things not only caused suffering in this or that earth-life, but also caused the suffering to be reproduced in other earth-lives,—desire for the shadows and illusions of earth being the subjective side of the attractive force by which earth draws the unemancipated soul back to itself again and again; and he would ask them to infer from this that deliverance from suffering (now and in the future) was to be won by the subjugation, and at last by the extinction of desire,—not of desire as such, but of the base, carnal, worldly, self-seeking desires, which, by keeping the soul in ignorance of its true nature and destiny, cause it to eddy round and round in the "whirlpool of rebirth."

This is what Buddha did.

He would tell them—though not in so many words—that, if their baser desires were to be subdued, they must practise self-control and cultivate sympathy; and, with that end in view, he would give them a few simple rules for the conduct of life,—rules which would provide for the development of self-control and sympathy along the arterial lines of morality, and the authority of which would therefore be in a measure self-evident.

This is what Buddha did.

For those who had mastered their baser desires and passions, and who, by a parallel process, had cultivated the latent virtues of gentleness, kindness, and compassion, and, speaking generally, begun to live in the lives of others, he would make further provision; he would help them in various ways to conquer their hydra-headed enemy, the lower self; he would teach them to distinguish between the shadows and the realities of life, to rid themselves of every self-seeking desire and every self-affirming delusion, to quench lust and anger, to extend in every direction the radiating light of sympathy and good will.

This is what Buddha did.

He would tell them that, when the last taint of egoism and the last shadow of ignorance had disappeared, the happiness to which they had always had an indefeasible title, but a title which each man in turn had to make good for himself, would at last be theirs; that the Path which they had followed for so long would lead them at last to the fullness of knowledge, the fullness of peace, the fullness of love,—and therefore to unimaginable bliss.

This is what Buddha did.

But he would impress on them that they lived in a world in which causes always produce their natural and necessary effects; that the consequences of their conduct would therefore follow them wherever they went; that external rewards were not to be hoped for; that external punishments were not to be dreaded; that virtue was its own reward and vice its own punishment, in the sense that whatever is done or left undone inevitably reacts upon the character, and, through the character, affects for weal or for woe the destiny of the soul; that interference from without was in the nature of things impossible; that the whole sacrificial system was based on a delusion; that ceremonial observances were of no avail:—he would teach them, in fine, that each man in turn must take his life into his own hands and work out his destiny for himself.

This is what Buddha did.

But, while he taught them all this, he would make no attempt to explain to them the deepest mysteries of existence; he would deliberately disconnect his scheme of life, so far as his own exposition of it was concerned, from theology and metaphysics; he would keep silence as to what is "ultimate and uttermost"; for he would know that the average mind has no capacity for deep thinking, and that, if he tried to disclose to his fellow-men his ultimate reasons for the course of life which he wished them to follow, they would make nonsense, first of his philosophical teaching and then of his whole scheme of life, giving themselves wrong reasons for everything that they did or left undone, and so (in the last resort) misinterpreting and misapplying every detail of his teaching.

This too is what Buddha did (or forebore to do). That he kept silence about "great matters" is as certain as that his ethical teaching was clear, coherent, and systematic.

The coincidences between the two schemes of life—that which Buddha taught and that which follows logically (in the deeper sense of the word) from the philosophy of the Upanishads—are so many and so vital that they cannot be ascribed to chance. Even if the age in which Buddha lived had been separated by a thousand years from the age which gave birth to the stories of Brahma and the Gods, and Nachikêtas and Death, we should feel justified, on internal evidence, in concluding that Buddha had somehow or other come under the influence of the ideas which those stories enshrined. But we need not trust to internal evidence only. We know that the spiritual atmosphere of India in Buddha's day was impregnated with the ideas of the Upanishads. We know that those ideas must have appealed with peculiar force to a thinker of Buddha's exalted nature, whether he ended by emancipating himself from their influence or not. We know that the teachers who had expounded those ideas had utterly failed to bring them into connection with the daily life of the ordinary man, and had thereby left a gap in the philosophical teaching of India, which was waiting to be filled by some master mind. The cumulative evidence afforded by these facts, added to the internal evidence which has already been set forth in detail, seems to point with irresistible force to one conclusion, namely that Buddha accepted the idealistic teaching of the Upanishads—accepted it at its highest level and in its purest form—and took upon himself as his life's mission to fill the obvious gap in it,—in other words, to make the spiritual ideas which had hitherto been the exclusive possession of a few select souls, available for the daily needs of mankind.

If this conclusion is correct, we shall see in Buddhism, not a revolt against the "Brahmanic" philosophy as such, but an ethical interpretation of the leading ideas of that philosophy,—a following out of those ideas, not into the word-built systems of (so-called) thought which the metaphysicians of the day were constructing with fatal facility, but into their practical consequences in the inner life of man.

But is the conclusion correct? I must admit at once that there is a preponderance of opinion against it. The Orientalist scholars into whose hands the work of expounding the ideas and doctrines of Buddha has perforce fallen, seem to be agreed in holding that in Buddhism the mind of India broke away from the Brahmanic line of thought. Some indeed go further than this. They tell us that Buddha's teaching was directly and openly subversive of the "sovereign dogmas" of Brahmanism. They admit indeed, with considerable reluctance, that he believed in re-incarnation, but they contend that he did not believe in any re-incarnating self or ego; and they accept on his behalf all the philosophical consequences of this sweeping denial, the last of these being that Nirvâna—the τέλος τελειότατον of Buddhist effort and aspiration—is the prelude to annihilation.

Foremost among the distinguished scholars who have satisfied themselves that Buddha was a negative dogmatist—a metaphysician, whose propositions were all fundamental negations—is Dr Rhys Davids, a writer on Buddhism whose works enjoy a well-deserved popularity, and whose influence in determining the attitude of contemporary opinion towards the Buddhist scheme of life is very great. In the following passages from his writings his own attitude is clearly defined. After expounding the hour Sacred Truths, he goes on to say, "The remarkable fact is that we have here set forth a view of religion entirely independent of the soul theories on which all the various philosophies and religions then current in India were based." Speaking of re-incarnation he says,

"There is no passage of a soul or I in any sense 1 from the one life to the other. Their [the Buddhists'] whole view of the matter is independent of the time-honoured soul-theories held in common by all the followers of every other creed." Speaking of the interest that the Brahmans took in Buddha's speculations, he says that "his [Buddha's] rejection of the soul-theory and of all that it involved was really incompatible with the whole theology of the Vedas." Elsewhere he says that no other school of religious thought is "quite so frankly and entirely independent as Buddhism of the two theories of God and the soul." Other significant passages in his writings are the following: "The victory to be gained by the destruction of ignorance is, in Gautama's view, a victory which can be gained and enjoyed in this life and in this life only."

"Man is never the same for two consecutive moments, and there is within him no abiding principle whatever." "Another proof of the prominence of the doctrine of the non-existence of the soul is the fact that the Brahmans who have misunderstood many less important or less clearly expressed tenets of Buddhism recognize this as one of its distinctive features." "Would it be possible in a more complete and categorical manner to deny that there is any soul—anything of any kind which continues to exist, in any manner, after death?" If there is no soul or ego, in any sense of the word, what is the meaning of Nirvâna? According to Dr Rhys Davids, it is a state of blissful repose which precedes annihilation, with which, however, it must not be confounded. "Death, utter death, with no new life to follow, is then the result of, but it is not Nirvâna."

These passages make it clear that Buddha, according to Dr Rhys Davids' estimate of him, was a daring speculative thinker who had thought out all the master problems of existence and solved them to his own satisfaction, his solution in every case, or rather in the one case which is decisive of the rest, being an unqualified negation. The uncompromising denial of the soul, which Dr Rhys Davids ascribes to Buddha, makes an end of all metaphysical speculation. If there is no soul, if the sense of self 1 is wholly delusive, we may know, without further inquiry, that there is no God (in any spiritual sense of the word), no inward life, no former life, no after life. But what of the outward things which the (so-called) self perceives and, in the act of perceiving, certifies as existent, and even provisionally certifies as real? According to Western thought these are real things; and the physical force which is behind them all, is the fundamental reality which it is the aim of speculation to discover. But, according to Buddha, outward things are all shadows and delusions; his primary aim, as a moral teacher, being to deliver men from belief in their reality,—a belief which is the source of all error, sorrow, and suffering. It is clear then that, if Dr Rhys Davids' interpretation of Buddha's metaphysical system is correct, he (Buddha) was not a materialist, like those modern thinkers with whom he may seem to have much in common, but a philosophical nihilist, who could find no centre of reality, no principle of permanence, in that whirl and flux of phenomena which for him constituted the Universe.

It is true that in more than one passage in his American lectures Dr Rhys Davids says that Buddha denied the existence of the soul in the Christian sense of the word: and one might infer from this that it was open to him to believe in the soul in some other sense of the word,—for example in the Brahmanic, which is diametrically opposite to the "Christian." 1 But whether Dr Rhys Davids has himself failed to distinguish between the Christian and the Brahmanic theories of the soul, or whether he regards the former as the only soul-theory which is in any degree compatible with mental sanity, I cannot pretend to say. What is certain is that he regards Buddha's rejection of the soul-theory as thorough-going and uncompromising. The words "There is no passage of a soul or I in any sense from the one life to the other. Their [the Buddhists'] whole view of the matter is independent of the time-honoured soul-theories held in common by all the followers of every other creed," are decisive on this point. Besides, it stands to reason that if "death, utter death," is the inevitable sequel to Nirvâna, there is no room in Buddha's philosophy for the soul, in any sense of the word.

My reason for setting forth in detail Dr Rhys Davids' interpretation of Buddha's philosophy is that it happens to be the one interpretation which has found its way into the outer world. Ask the man in the street what he knows of Buddha. He will tell you that Buddha was a pessimist and an atheist, who denied the soul, denied a supreme cause, denied that the world had any centre of reality, and taught his followers to look forward to annihilation as the final deliverance from the woes of earth. This, if not identical with Dr Rhys Davids' teaching, is at least an echo of it. Dr Paul Carus, who has taken upon himself to popularize Buddhism and to vindicate it from the disparaging criticism of its "Christian critics," is in the main in full agreement with Dr Rhys Davids, but is more ready than that distinguished scholar to accept the logical consequences of the dynamically atomistic philosophy which he ascribes to Buddha. Even the author of "The Soul of a People," a writer whose deep and delicate sympathy with, and insight into, the "soul" or inner life of a Buddhist people, besides investing his book with a charm which is all its own, entitles him to a respectful hearing whenever he speaks, in general terms, about Buddhism,—even he, when treating of the popular belief in re-incarnation, must needs shake his head over the credulity of the good, simple people, and remind them that belief in the survival of the "I" is "opposed to all Buddhism," the real teaching of Buddha—"that what survives death is not the 'I' but only the results of its action"—"being too deep for them to hold."

Such unanimity on the part of the popular exponents of Buddhism points to a large measure of unanimity on the part of its more learned interpreters and commentators. That Dr Rhys Davids has given voice to a general consensus of opinion on the part of the Western students of Buddhism, can scarcely be doubted. From Barthélemy Saint-Hilaire to H. C. Warren, the Orientalists of Europe and America are agreed, with one or two notable exceptions, in holding that Buddha denied the Ego and regarded Nirvâna as the prelude to annihilation; while the fact that the South Buddhist Church has given Dr Paul Carus a certificate of orthodoxy suggests that on these points the general trend of official opinion in the Buddhist world itself coincides, mutatis mutandis, with the general trend of learned opinion in the West.

What evidence can Dr Rhys Davids, and those who think with him, give in support of their thesis that Buddha was a negative dogmatist

"Who dropped his plummet down the broad

Deep Universe, and said 'No God' —
Finding no bottom."

There is this initial difficulty in the way of our accepting Dr Rhys Davids' interpretation of Buddha's metaphysical—as distinguished from his ethical—philosophy, that, on our author's own showing, Buddha was a true and consistent agnostic, who was so far from dogmatizing about what is ultimate that he regarded all metaphysical speculation as vain and foolish, and all metaphysical strife as morally wrong. "There were a certain number of questions to which it was his habit to refuse to reply. These were questions the discussion of which, in his opinion, was apt to lead the mind astray, and so far from being conducive to a growth in insight, would be a hindrance to the only thing which was supremely worth aiming at—the perfect life in Arahat-ship. Such questions as: What shall I be during the ages of the future? Do I after all exist, or am I not? are regarded as worse than unprofitable, and the Buddha not only refused to discuss them, but held that the tendency, the desire to discuss them was a weakness, and that the answers usually given were a delusion." With these words, which are to be found in Dr Rhys Davids' American lectures on Buddhism, we may compare Dr Oldenberg's statement that "the most serious obstacle in the way of our comprehending Buddhist dogmas is the silence with which everything is passed over which does not lead to the separation from the earthly, to the subjection of all desire, to the cessation of the transitory, to quietude, knowledge, illumination, to Nirvâna." Both writers are agreed in holding that the scheme of life which Buddhism set before its votaries was in all probability formulated by Buddha himself; but both writers are also agreed in holding that, though Buddha gave his followers what I may call the penultimate (or perhaps the ante-penultimate) reasons for entering "the Path," he not only carefully abstained from giving them the ultimate reasons, but positively forbade them to speculate as to what those reasons might be. What then becomes of Dr Rhys Davids' confident and often repeated statement that Buddha's philosophy centred in a fundamental denial? To deny the Ego is to gather all metaphysical problems into one pregnant question, and to answer that question with an everlasting "No." In other words, it is to say the last word that can be said in metaphysical speculation. Is it possible for the same thinker to be, at the same time and on the same plane of thought, a true agnostic and an aggressive dogmatist? If this is not possible, which rôle are we to assign to Buddha?

The teaching of Buddha, as Dr Rhys Davids presents it to us, may be divided into two parts,—an ethical scheme of life, and a metaphysical theory of things. Dr Rhys Davids will scarcely contend that the authenticity of the latter is as strongly vouched for by external evidence as that of the former. That there are passages in the Buddhist Scriptures in which Buddha is represented as having authoritatively denied the Ego, may perhaps be provisionally admitted. 1 But surely, in the light of Dr Rhys Davids' assertion that Buddha both abstained from and discountenanced metaphysical speculation, we are free to conjecture that, as statements of Buddha's own metaphysical teaching, these passages are entirely untrustworthy. It is surely conceivable that what is set forth in them is, not Buddha's own words or even his own opinions, but the writers' private interpretation of Buddha's deeper philosophy,—an interpretation which is based partly on what he said, partly on what he left unsaid (for his silence is both significant and suggestive), but chiefly on what the writers themselves happened to believe. It is conceivable that the writers felt, as Dr Rhys Davids evidently feels and as we must all feel, that behind Buddha's silence there was a living creed; and that, feeling this, they succumbed to a temptation which it is always hard to resist—the temptation to bring the ideas of a great writer into line with one's own—and ascribed to Buddha conclusions and arguments which he had never formulated, but which, in their opinion, he would certainly have endorsed. It is conceivable, to say the least, that many of the stories and discourses in the Buddhist Scriptures are as far from setting forth the inner creed of Buddha as the writings of Christian theologians in all ages are from setting forth the inner creed of Christ. At any rate, if I am to reconcile Dr Rhys Davids' authoritative statement that Buddha abstained on principle from metaphysical speculation with his equally authoritative exposition of Buddha's metaphysical system, I must assume that he has based the latter on internal rather than on external evidence; I must assume, in other words, that his interpretation of Buddha's philosophy is, in the main, the outcome of his study of Buddha's scheme of life, is in fact his own private attempt "to complete and to find the centre of the circle" of which Buddha has given us only a "broken arc."

If this is what Dr Rhys Davids has attempted to do, he has set us an example which I, for one, intend to follow. The specific passages to which he appeals in support of his general thesis will be considered in due course, and an attempt will be made to show that for the most part they admit of an interpretation which is the exact opposite of that which Dr Rhys Davids has put upon them. But as, on his own showing, the internal evidence is far more weighty than the external (which indeed he has expressly debarred himself from regarding as conclusive), and as on this point I am in full accord with him, I will now study the internal evidence in the light of his interpretation of it. He tells me that Buddha broke away, abruptly and completely, from the deeper spiritual ideas of his own age and country. That he should have done this, that any great Teacher should ever do this, is improbable in a very high degree. Christ was in open revolt against the legalism of his age and nation; but, far from rejecting the grandly poetical conception of God which Israel had evolved in the days of his spiritual greatness, and to which his sacred writings owe their charm and influence, he went back to that conception, went back to what was most spiritual and most poetical in it, reaffirmed this against the materialism and formalism of the Scribes and Pharisees, and then transformed it into a deeper and more spiritual vision of God than Israel, at his best, had ever fashioned. The relation of Christ to Judaism may well have been paralleled by the relation of Buddha to Brahmanism. That there was much in the Brahmanism of his day which Buddha rejected and even denounced, is certain; but it does not follow from this that he had broken away from the Brahmanic teaching at its highest level. On the contrary, the fact that the Brahmanism of his day had either forgotten that high teaching or deliberately betrayed it, makes it probable that in denouncing the former he was championing the cause of the latter. And the further fact that his own scheme of life, when surveyed from the standpoint of the Brahmanic philosophy, seems to be the practical application and expression of its spiritual ideas, raises to a high degree the probability of his having been in sympathy with those ideas, and raises to a still higher degree the improbability of his having formally renounced them.

Thus at the outset we are entitled to insist that the internal evidence which Dr Rhys Davids brings forward in support of his general position shall be convincingly strong. It happens, however, that, as an interpreter of the inner creed of an Eastern thinker, he, in common with other European exponents of Buddhism, labours under the disability of looking at "great matters" from standpoints which are exclusively Western. For example, that ultra-Stoical conception of life which makes it possible for him to say that "the true Buddhist saint does not mar the purity of his self-denial by lusting 1 after a positive happiness, which he, himself, shall enjoy hereafter," and which gives a strong bias to the general attitude which he and others have instinctively adopted towards Buddhism, is wholly foreign to Eastern modes of thought, and is in no way countenanced by Buddha's own ethical teaching. On this point there cannot be the shadow of a doubt. Buddha's own outlook on life, if, as all the commentators admit, it is faithfully mirrored in the "Four Sacred Truths," was not ultra-Stoical but essentially anti-Stoical. The two paramount ends which he set before his disciples, when he urged them to enter "the Path," were deliverance from suffering and the ultimate fruition of perfect bliss. In other words, his philosophy was hedonism of a pure and exalted type. It is true that he condemned the life of pleasure. But why? Not because those who led it were trying to be happy, but because they were trying to be happy in the wrong way,—because they had mistaken the shadow of happiness for the reality, because what they sowed as pleasure they were doomed to reap as pain. So far was he from condemning man's longing for happiness, that his whole scheme of life may be said to base itself on an appeal to, and resolve itself into a systematic attempt to cultivate, that instinctive desire, by teaching men to "fix their hearts" "where true joys are to be found."

More important even, and more characteristically Western, than the ultra-Stoicism which dominates Dr Rhys Davids' own ethical philosophy is the dualism which dominates his metaphysical theory of things. This tendency affects his interpretation of Buddha's ideas in more ways than one, but chiefly in this one way. He insists on things being divided into the existent and the non-existent, which are alternatives, whereas the higher thought of India seems to have divided them into the real and the unreal, which are not alternatives but polar opposites. Thus Dr Rhys Davids would say that the Ego exists or does not exist, whereas the Indian thinker would concern himself with the problem of the reality of the Ego, and would see that what is real (or unreal) from one point of view may be unreal (or real) from another. The difference between the two ways of looking at things goes very deep; goes in fact to the root of most of the problems that perplex the student of Buddhism. Existence and non-existence are alternatives; and, if we are to choose between alternatives, we must provide ourselves with a criterion by which we may know the true alternative from the false. But how shall man, who is presumably not omniscient, provide himself with a criterion which will enable him to define the boundaries of the Universe? For it is this, and nothing less, that he attempts to do when he takes upon himself to divide things into the existent and the non-existent. What is the criterion or test of existence? It is impossible to answer this question except by begging it. In other words, we must say what we mean by existence before we can attempt to distinguish between the existent and the non-existent. But in the very act of defining the word, we provide ourselves, whether we intend to do this or not, with a test of the thing. For example. We ask ourselves: Does a certain thing exist or not? Does a centaur exist or not? Does a mermaid exist or not? It is easy for us to answer these questions, so long as we agree among ourselves that the existent is that which is perceptible by man's bodily senses. In thus defining the word existent, we provide ourselves with a test of existence; and the test is valid just so long and so far as the definition is true. But the definition is, at best, only hypothetically and provisionally true. In the ordinary affairs of every-day life it is sufficiently true to answer our practical purposes. This is all that we can say about it. To take for granted that it is absolutely true, and that the corresponding test of existence is absolutely valid, is to beg every question which this hypothesis enables us to answer: for, the moment we accept the definition as true without qualification or reserve, we commit ourselves to a vast metaphysical assumption. Does the Ego exist or does it not? "No," answers the "uninitiated" thinker, "it does not satisfy my criterion of existence. It is not perceptible by my bodily senses." He fails to see that the question as to the existence of the Ego, which is, ex hypothesi, invisible and otherwise imperceptible, involves the further question as to the validity of his materialistic test of existence. To ask whether the Ego exists or not is to challenge, by implication, the validity of that particular test. Had the test been regarded as absolutely valid, the question as to the Ego would never have been raised. Yet it is only the thinker who has allowed the materialistic conception of existence to dominate his mind and limit his whole speculative outlook; in other words, who has allowed the practical demands of his ordinary everyday life to control the philosophical movement of his thoughts;—it is only the thinker of this crude and commonplace type, who can bring himself to ask whether the Ego exists or not. The teacher who rejects that particular test of existence knows that there is no (final) test, and he therefore abstains from asking a question which is of necessity begged in the act of being asked.

Not only must there be a recognized test of existence, if the controversy as to the existence of the Ego is to have any issue, but there must also be a tacit agreement among the disputants as to the meaning of the word Ego. In the absence of such agreement, the discussion can lead to nothing but loss of temper and confusion of thought. And as in the region of metaphysics such agreement is not to be looked for, since, if it existed, the very raison d'être of metaphysical inquiry would be gone, one can but conclude that to debate such a question as Does the Ego exist?—a question which takes one in an instant to the ultimate limits of human thought—is not merely a mischievous waste of mental energy, but also a proof of mental blindness on the part of those who allow themselves to indulge in so futile a controversy. Even such questions as Does a centaur exist? or Does a mermaid exist? become unanswerable the moment they become metaphysical. For, though neither a centaur nor a mermaid exists, in the sense of being perceptible by man's bodily senses, each of these fabled beings does exist as a creation of the human mind. Is existence, in that sense of the word, equivalent to non-existence? Perhaps it is: but the question goes to the root of human thought; and it is impossible to answer it offhand without begging all the deeper questions which it involves.

As metaphysical controversy was wholly repugnant to Buddha's type of mind, the antecedent improbability of his having indulged in the most futile of all metaphysical controversies and authoritatively solved the meaningless problem in which that controversy finally centres, is overwhelmingly strong. Moreover, there is, as it happens, positive evidence that, when he was invited to think and teach in the category of the existent and the non-existent, he deliberately refused to do so. The story of the dialogue between Buddha and Vacchagotta will presently be told, and its meaning will be considered. Meanwhile, it is enough for our present purpose to know that, when the wandering monk Vacchagotta challenged the "Exalted One" with the question "Is there the Ego?" and then with the question "Is there not the Ego?" he was in each case answered with silence.

The more carefully one studies the teaching of Buddha, the stronger does one's conviction become that the ultimate category in which he thought was that of the real and the unreal, not that of the existent and the non-existent. The difference between these two categories is that, whereas the existent and the non-existent are (as has been already pointed out) mutually exclusive alternatives, the real and the unreal are polar opposites, and as such always coexist—except of course at the ideal points of infinity and zero—varying together in inverse pro-portion, or, in other words, being so related to one another that the one falls as the other rises and rises as the other falls. If we are to choose between alternatives, we must be able to apply to each of them from without (so to speak) a recognized criterion or test. When our alternatives are ultimate conceptions, such as the existent and the non-existent, it stands to reason that to apply a test from without is impossible:—

"For God alone sits high enough above
To speculate so largely."

If we are to choose between polar opposites, we must be able to measure them by a standard. This standard is always internal to, and inherent in, the movement of the two opposites from pole to counter pole. It follows that, even when our opposites are ultimate conceptions, such as the real and the unreal, a standard of measurement is available, being inherent in the very movement of our thought. For example, to ask whether the inward and spiritual side of life is existent or non-existent, is to ask a meaningless and therefore an unanswerable question. To ask whether it is real or unreal is to ask a question to which life itself, both in its universal and in its individual movement, is the abiding, though never formulated, answer. That Buddha thought in the category of the real and the unreal is suggested by the whole tenor of his teaching. If there is any one thing which his sayings make quite clear, it is that he regarded outward things and the outward side of life as unreal. But he was not so foolish as to think of them as non-existent. Which is the real pole of existence? is the question which he must have asked himself; and his scheme of life is his answer to that question.

Let us now assume, for argument's sake, that the answer which he gave to life's master question was the opposite of that which the general tenor of his teaching would seem to suggest. Let us go further. Let us assume, with most of the Western exponents of Buddhism, that Buddha was a negative dogmatist, pure and simple,—that he regarded the Ego not merely as unreal but as non-existent. What follows with regard to his scheme of life? That scheme undoubtedly centres in the doctrine of re-incarnation, the very purpose of it being to deliver men from the "whirlpool of rebirth." If there is no re-incarnating Ego, what becomes of the doctrine of re-incarnation? And if this, the keystone of the arch of Buddhist thought, is withdrawn, what becomes of Buddha's scheme of life? Dr Rhys Davids, and those who think with him, have tried to face this difficulty. In his first exposition of Buddhism Dr Rhys Davids saw clearly that denial of the Ego turned the doctrine of re-incarnation into nonsense, and he accepted the consequences of this conclusion. He so expounded the Buddhist belief in re-incarnation as to make nonsense of it, and then boldly affirmed that the belief was in its essence nonsensical. Speaking of those who have trusted themselves to the seemingly stately bridge which Buddhism has tried to build over the river of the mysteries and sorrows of life, he said, "they have failed to see that the very keystone [of the bridge], the link between one life and another, is a mere word—this wonderful hypothesis, this airy nothing, this imaginary cause beyond the reach of reason—the individualized and individualizing force of Karma." But in his American lectures he departs from this logical and intelligible position, and tries to persuade himself that the doctrine of re-incarnation, even if there be no re-incarnating Ego, is sense. "There is a real identity between a man in his present life and in the future. But the identity is not in a conscious soul which shall fly out away from his body after he is dead. The real identity is that of cause and effect. A man thinks he began to be a few years—twenty, fifty, sixty years ago. There is some truth in that; but in a much larger, deeper, truer sense he has been (in the causes of which he is the result) for countless ages in the past; and those same causes (of which he is the temporary effect) will continue in other like temporary forms through countless ages yet to come. In that sense alone, according to Buddhism, each of us has after death a continuing life." This is an interesting statement of Dr Rhys Davids' own ideas about human immortality, but as a statement of what Buddha taught it is utterly misleading. It is doubtless true that all the forces of Nature, operating through millions of years, meet in me; and that what I do will produce consequences which will pass on, with an ever widening lateral movement, into the remotest future. But this is not what Buddhism teaches, in the doctrine of Karma, or has ever taught. "The peculiarity of Buddhism," says Dr Rhys Davids himself, "lies in this, that the result of what a man is or does is held not to be dissipated, as it were, into many streams, but concentrated together in the formation of one new sentient being." What Buddhism teaches is that I reap the crop which was sowed by some one man who lived before I did, and that in like manner some one man in the future will reap the crop which I am sowing now; and so on, both backwards and forwards. It teaches, in other words, that the current of moral cause and effect flows in the narrow channel of a succession of individual lives (or rather in a number of such channels), whereas modern science, to which Dr Rhys Davids seems to look for inspiration and guidance, teaches that there is always a dual movement,—from the collective life into the individual, and from the individual life into the collective.

The difference between these two conceptions of moral causation, and between the two derivative conceptions of human immortality, is as wide as it is deep. The question which we have to ask ourselves with regard to the Buddhist conception is a simple one: Is the identity between me and the inheritor of my Karma, or again between me and the man whose Karma I inherit, as real as the identity between the me of to-day and the me of twenty years hence (if I shall be living then), or again between the me of to-day and the me of my boyhood? If it is not as real, the doctrine of re-incarnation is pure nonsense from both points of view,—from that of Eastern idealism and of Western science. But if it is as real, the doctrine is sound sense in the eyes of Eastern idealism; and though Western science cannot countenance it, it is equally certain that it cannot reject it, for the matter is one which necessarily eludes its grasp.

Now, strange as it may seem, there is nothing in the Buddhist Scriptures to show that even those thinkers who are supposed to have declared war against the Ego regarded the identity between man and man, in a given line of Karmic succession, as less real than the identity between what a man is to-day and what he was twenty years ago, or will be twenty years hence. The author of the Milinda dialogues, for example, is supposed to have argued against the Ego. I doubt if he really did. It is quite possible, I think, that his dialogues have a different aim and admit of a different interpretation. But let us assume that, in theory at least, he denied the Ego, and that in this respect he falls into line with the modern votaries of metaphysical atomism. What then? I cannot find anything in any of his dialogues to show that his belief in individual re-incarnation was other than real. I cannot find anything to show that he regarded the identity between A, who is living now, and B, the future inheritor of his Karma, as in any way different from the identity between the A of to-day and the A of twenty years ago or twenty years hence. 1 Thoroughgoing denial of the Ego destroys the identity of a man from moment to moment as effectually as from life to life. But—to quote Pascal's words—"la nature soutient la raison impuissante et l'empêche d'extravaguer jusqu'à ce point." Even Dr Paul Carus, whose intense antipathy to the Ego makes him the protagonist of the metaphysical atomists, would probably admit, as a working hypothesis, that he was the same being as Dr Paul Carus of twenty years ago, just as he would speak of self-culture, self-development, self-control, though all the while he regards the sense of self as entirely delusive. And, in like manner, the author of the Milinda dialogues would have accepted, as a working hypothesis, the identity of himself with the next inheritor of his Karma, even though he regarded (according to our provisional assumption) the sense of self as entirely delusive. But between these two concessions, which seem to have so much in common, there is a great gulf fixed,—the very gulf which separates Western from Eastern thought. Dr Paul Carus, who is steeped in the science of the West, would never admit, even as a working hypothesis, that A, who is living now, was the same being as a certain B, who appeared on earth one hundred years ago (or whatever the number of intervening years might be). The idea of one man inheriting all the Karma of another man is one which he could not possibly entertain. The author of the Milinda dialogues might well have said, "I have lived on earth many times already, and shall probably live many times more, but of course there is no I in the case at all." But Dr Paul Carus could not say this, though he might well say, "I have lived on earth for so many years, and may possibly live for so many more, but of course there is no I in the case at all."

There is nothing, then, to show that the Buddhist of the anti-Ego school is not as sure of his identity from life to life as Dr Paul Carus is of his identity from year to year, or from day to day. In each case the sense of assurance sinks in theory to zero, but in practice it is strong enough for all the practical purposes of life. In other words, the denial is in each case academic (or "notional") whereas the belief is practical (or "real"). But the difference between the respective ranges of the "real" belief of a Buddhist and the "real" belief of Dr Paul Carus is immense, and has far-reaching consequences. Within the limits of his own earth life, Dr Paul Carus combines academic denial with "real" belief; but the moment those limits are passed, the denial ceases to be academic and becomes intensely "real." The Buddhist, who is much more logical, sees no reason for drawing a hard and fast line at either birth or death. Backward and forward, as far as the eye of his thought can reach, his denial of the Ego, however sweeping and uncompromising it may be, is always "notional," whereas his belief in it is always "real." We shall presently learn that the monk Yamaka, who identified Nirvâna with annihilation, was persuaded to abandon this "wicked heresy" by a fellow-monk, who reminded him that the arguments against the reality of the Nirvânic life of the "Saint" were not a whit stronger than the arguments against the reality of the true life of the "Saint" whilst on earth. The moral of this story is surely obvious and significant.

I have spoken at some length on this point because I wish to make it clear that, if denial of the Ego is real, if its meaning is fully pressed home, the doctrine of re-incarnation, which is undoubtedly the keystone of the whole arch of Buddhist thought, becomes pure nonsense. The essence of the doctrine is that B inherits the whole of A's Karma, C the whole of B's, and so on. Unless the identity of A with B, of B with C, and so on, is as real as the identity, within the limits of each earth life, of the child with the youth and the youth with the man, the doctrine loses its meaning, and the arch of thought which it holds together becomes a ruinous heap. We must therefore either assume that the arch of Buddhist thought and doctrine had no keystone, or that the Buddhist denial of the "Ego" was "notional" rather than "real." Of these alternative assumptions, reason and common sense alike demand that we should adopt the latter.

Whichever assumption we adopt, we are at liberty to say that the attempts which Dr Rhys Davids, Dr Paul Carus and other Western interpreters of Buddhism make to bring the doctrine of re-incarnation into line with the scientific doctrines of heredity, of physical causation, and the like, are sophistical and inconclusive. I have not made an exhaustive study of the eschatology of the modern "religion of science"; but I understand that it recognizes three kinds of immortality. The first is that of living in the lives of our direct descendants,—an immortality which one can enjoy, while still on earth, down to the second or third of the after generations (for a man may live to see his great-grandchildren), but which bachelors, old maids, and other persons who die without issue are not allowed to share. The second is the immortality of fame (or notoriety)—the immortality of a Marcus Aurelius (or a John Lackland)—an immortality which few persons are privileged to enjoy, and which, with very rare exceptions, is of brief duration. The third is the immortality of living in the consequences of one's actions, so far as these affect for good or for evil the lives of other men. The immortality to which Buddha taught his disciples to look forward has nothing in common with any of these. The immortality of living in the ever-widening consequences of one's conduct is real enough, and the contemplation of it may give satisfaction to certain minds. But the immortality which the law of Karma makes possible is wholly different from this. The Karmic consequences of action are in the main inward and spiritual,—the effect on the doer of what he habitually does. Hence it is that the doctrine of re-incarnation, when divorced from the doctrine of a re-incarnating soul or Ego, loses its meaning and its value, and becomes as wildly fantastic as Western thought too readily assumes it to be. It stands to reason that, if there is no Ego, the inward consequences of a man's conduct will end abruptly at his death. What then? Are we to suppose that the outward consequences of his conduct, which have diffused themselves far and wide during his lifetime, will after his death—perhaps long after his death, for the return to earth may be long delayed—be reunited in the channel of a single human life? The supposition is not merely incredible, but absolutely unthinkable. The alternative supposition that B, the inheritor of A's Karma, will be rewarded (or punished)—presumably by an omnipotent magician—for A's conduct while on earth is worse than unthinkable. It does violence to one's sense of law on every plane of thought. But when the doctrine of Karma is supported and elucidated by the conception of a re-incarnating soul or Ego, it at once becomes intelligible, even from the point of view of denial of the Ego. To say that conduct always re-acts upon character, and that the departing soul will therefore take away with it from earth the inward consequences of its action and bring these back to earth, with all their possible ulterior consequences, at its next incarnation, is to say what is certainly disputable and perhaps untrue but at any rate has the merit of making coherent sense.

The inherent unreasonableness of the doctrine of Karma, as Western orientalists choose to interpret it, will become more apparent when we consider it in its relation to the motives which Buddha set before his followers. The paramount motive was the prospect of escaping from the "whirlpool of rebirth" and attaining to the bliss of Nirvâna. That this goal should be won within the limits of a single earth-life, however virtuous, was not—we may rest assured—contemplated by Buddha, or by any of those thinkers who carried on the tradition of his teaching. This is a general statement which admits of isolated exceptions. A man of abnormal spiritual development, like Buddha himself—a man whom a long series of virtuous lives had brought to the threshold of Nirvâna—might conceivably cross that threshold before he died, and return to earth no more. But for the rank and file of mankind the goal of deliverance was a "far-off divine event" to which the journey was in any case long and toilsome, though it might be materially shortened if the Path which Buddha pointed out to mankind—the path of sympathy and self-control—was resolutely entered and faith-fully followed. "The Buddhist," says Dr Rhys Davids, "hopes to enter, even though he will not reach the end of, the Path in this life; and if he once enters therein, he is certain in some future existence, perhaps under less material conditions, to arrive at the goal of salvation, at the calm and rest of Nirvâna." "He is certain." But is it he who will arrive at the goal, or someone else? Why does the life of sympathy and self-control tend to shorten the journey to Nirvâna? Obviously, because it makes for the spiritual development of the man who leads it; because it strengthens his character, deepens his insight, expands his consciousness, purifies his soul. But what if there is to be no identity between A, who is now walking in the Path, and B, the next inheritor of his Karma? From the point of view of the goal which Buddha set before men, the inward consequences of A's conduct—the reaction of what he does on what he is—are of supreme importance. But if there is no self, no Ego to return to earth, the inward consequences will, as I have lately pointed out, end abruptly at A's death, and there will be no character—developed, expanded, purified—for A to transmit to B, his new self. We must at any rate assume, if we are to see any meaning in Buddha's appeal to mankind, that the identity between A and B is as real as the identity between the A of this year and the A of next year, however real (or unreal) that identity may be. And this, I think, is what the accredited exponents of Buddhism, including those who may have denied the Ego in theory, have always taken for granted. There is nothing to show that, when Buddhism expounds and enforces the doctrine of natural retribution, it has any doubt as to B inheriting the inward consequences of A's conduct. But the inward consequences of A's conduct are summed up in his character; and if he transmits his character to B, he transmits himself.

It is here that Buddhism parts company with those Western interpreters of it who try, like Dr Paul Carus, to affiliate it to the (so-called) "religion of science." Whatever theory Dr Paul Carus may hold as to the identity 1 (or non-identity) of the man of sixty or seventy years with the same man (as we must call him) at the age of twenty or thirty, he would admit, without hesitation, that it was both reasonable and just that the old man should suffer because the young man had sinned. Similarly, whatever theory the author of the Milinda Dialogues may have held as to the identity (or non-identity) of B with A, he would have admitted, without hesitation, that it was both reasonable and just that B should suffer because A had sinned. But Dr Paul Carus could never bring himself to admit this: he could never in any way recognize individual re-incarnation.

Let us, however, suppose that Buddha and his followers were in full accord with Dr Paul Carus. Let us suppose that their denial of the Ego, as an entity which survives death, was not academic, but practical and real. In that case what would become of the paramount motive which they set before their fellow-men? If it were possible for each man, in his own lifetime on earth, to attain to Nirvâna, there would be a meaning, even for those who denied the Ego, in the promise of deliverance, though in that case the fulfilment of the Buddhist Law would involve the early extinction of the whole human race. But as, apart from a few isolated cases, the possibility of a man attaining to Nirvâna in his own earth-life has never been contemplated by Buddhism, the promise of deliverance, when coupled with an authoritative denial of the Ego, must be regarded as the hollowest of mockeries. What sense is there in telling me to live virtuously now in order that, if my successors in that line of earth-lives to which I happen to belong are equally virtuous, someone who would otherwise appear on earth 100,000 years hence (let us say) may not be born; and in order that someone else—his immediate predecessor in the given line of lives—may enjoy the evanescent bliss of Nirvâna? To tell A to be virtuous in order that, somewhere in the remote future, Y may be supremely happy for a few years and Z may not be born, is to set him a meaningless task. It is difficult to say which sense is the more deeply outraged by such a doctrine of moral retribution,—one's sense of justice or (for the chain of cause and effect is obviously broken at each successive death) one's sense of natural law.

I will now set forth as briefly as possible my reasons for calling the current interpretation of Buddha's ideas a "misreading of Buddha."

The antecedent improbability of a great Teacher breaking away completely from the highest and deepest thought of his nation and his age, is very great. The great Teacher is always a reformer as well as an innovator; and to reform is to go back to an ideal which had been forgotten, or otherwise obscured. The chances are, then, that Buddha, who was unquestionably one of the greatest of all moral teachers, went back from what was corrupt and degenerate in the thought and the consequent practice of his age to what was pure and spiritual. This much we may say before we begin to study his scheme of life.

But when we study that scheme, and find, as we certainly do, that it is the practical application and embodiment of the great ideas of Indian idealism—so much so, indeed, that we may actually deduce from those ideas (given a practical aim on the part of their votary) the leading features of the Buddhist "Law"—we cannot but feel that the probability of the Founder of Buddhism having been an idealist (in the truest sense of the word) at heart—at the heart of his own deep silence—is raised to a very high degree.

And when, having for argument's sake assumed the opposite of this, assumed that the teaching of Buddha was directly and fundamentally subversive of the ideas which found utterance in the Upanishads, we find that the whole system falls to pieces and the wisdom of it becomes unthinkable nonsense, then what has hitherto been probability of a very high degree seems to approach the level of certainty. At any rate, if we may not yet say that the creed which Buddha held but did not openly profess, was the spiritual idealism of ancient India, we may say that the counter-hypothesis—that Buddha's creed was the direct negation of that lofty faith—can easily be disproved. The efforts that are made to bring the teaching of Buddha into line with the negative dogmatism of the "religion of science" would be ludicrous if they were not, in a sense, pathetic. For, in truth, they prove nothing except the depth of the abyss that separates Eastern from Western thought.

The Silence of Buddha

IT is the silence of Buddha which has misled so many of his commentators. The teacher who, while pointing out to us the ultimate issues of life, keeps silence as to its ultimate realities and ultimate principles, must be prepared for his philosophy—the philosophy that is at the heart of his silence—to be misunderstood. It is not merely that he gives us no clue to the labyrinth of his deeper thoughts, and so leaves each of us free to explore that labyrinth for himself. There is another and a graver danger to which he exposes the faith of his heart. Of those who take a speculative interest in his ideas, few will be content to regard his silence as purely agnostic. The majority will see in it either the negation or the confirmation of their own philosophical prejudices. The positive dogmatist, who has made up his mind that the ultimate realities of existence are such and such, will regard it as a challenge and a defiance, and will apply to it the epithets which he reserves for denial of his own creed. The negative dogmatist will insist that it is a polite concession to the weakness of the "orthodox," and that behind it is a conception of life as fundamentally negative as his own. In either case the silence of the Master will be construed as equivalent to denial and revolt.

This is the fate which has befallen Buddha. Because he said nothing about God he is held—by the "orthodox" as well as by the "unbeliever"—to have "denied the divine." Because he said little about the "Self," and because that little was mainly negative, 1 he is held to have denied the Ego. And he is credited with all the consequences of these tremendous denials. He who on principle kept silence about what is, ultimate is supposed to have elaborated a complete system of negatively ultimate thought.

There is nothing in the history of human thought more dramatic or more significant than the silence of Buddha. Let us try to fathom its depths. That there is a deep spiritual meaning, that there was a deep spiritual conviction, at the heart of it can scarcely be doubted. It was not from indifference that Buddha, of all men, became and remained to the end an apparent agnostic. And, apart from indifference, though there may be silence about "great matters," there can be no agnosticism (in the sense of metaphysical neutrality) in the thinker's inner life. A state of perfect mental equilibrium is incompatible with living interest in the deeper problems of existence. The silence of Buddha seems to have been the deliberate fulfilment of a self-imposed vow. At any rate there was a strong purpose behind it; and that purpose must have been the outcome, not of philosophical indifference, but of some master theory of things.

The more closely I study the stories in which Buddha answers the over-curious with silence and gives his reasons for doing so, and the more freely I surrender myself to the subtle influence of their atmosphere, the stronger does my conviction become that Buddha kept silence, when metaphysical questions were discussed, not because he had nothing to say about great matters, but because he had far too much, because he was overwhelmed by the flood of his own mighty thoughts, and because the channels of expression which the riddle-mongers of his day invited him to use were both too narrow and too shallow to give his soul relief. As it is on the plane of spiritual emotion, so it is on the plane of spiritual thought. "Silence," says one of Shakespeare's characters,

> "is the perfectest herald of joy:
> I were but little happy if I could say how much."

The babbling river, as another poet reminds us, is overwhelmed and silenced by the flow of the tide-wave from the unfathomed sea. This simile has the beauty of truth. The mind that is visited by world-encompassing waves of thought (or of emotion) has more to say than words can express, or than other minds can receive. There are, indeed, some gifted souls for whom the channel of poetry provides an overflow (rather than an outflow) for their flooding thoughts. For the rest of us (as Buddha saw clearly) there is but one available outlet,—that of action, conduct, life; and life will have a stronger purpose and a larger scope when silence is behind it than when its motive force is a flux of words. So eloquent and so significant is Buddha's own silence, that it seems at last, when one becomes familiar with it, to give a clearer insight into the secrets of his soul than any formulated confession of words could ever have done.

Let us now hear the reasons which Buddha himself (or those who spoke in his name) gave for his silence. Let us study the three stories which Dr Oldenberg has selected as indicative of his attitude towards the questions with which the thinkers of his day perplexed themselves. The first runs thus:

"Then the wandering monk Vacchagotta went to where the Exalted One was staying. When he had come near him, he saluted him. When saluting him, he had interchanged friendly words with him, he sat down beside him. Sitting beside him the wandering monk Vacchagotta spake to the Exalted One, saying: 'How does the matter stand, venerable Gotama, is there the Ego?'

"When he said this, the Exalted One was silent.

"'How then, venerable Gotama, is there not the Ego?'

"And still the Exalted One maintained silence. Then the wandering monk Vacchagotta rose from his seat and went away.

"But the venerable Ânanda, when the wandering monk Vacchagotta had gone to a distance, soon said to the Exalted One:

"'Wherefore, sire, has the Exalted One not given an answer to the questions put by the wandering monk Vacchagotta?'

"'If I, Ânanda, when the wandering monk Vacchagotta asked me: "Is there the Ego?" had answered: "The Ego is," then that, Ânanda, would have confirmed the doctrine of the Samanas and Brahmanas who believe in permanence. If I, Ânanda, when the wandering monk Vacchagotta asked me: "Is there not the Ego?" had answered: "The Ego is not," then that, Ânanda, would have confirmed the doctrine of the Samanas and Brahmanas who believe in annihilation. If I, Ânanda, when the wandering monk Vacchagotta asked me: "Is there the Ego?" had answered: "The Ego is," would that have served my end,

Ânanda, by producing in him the knowledge: all existences are non-Ego?'

"'That it would not, sire.'

"'But if I, Ânanda, when the wandering monk Vacchagotta asked me: "Is there not the Ego?" had answered: "The Ego is not," then that, Ânanda, would only have caused the wandering monk Vacchagotta to be thrown from one bewilderment into another: "My Ego, did it not exist before? but now it exists no longer!"'"

In this story Buddha gives two reasons for refusing to answer Vacchagotta's question. He is asked to answer Yes or No. Whichever answer he may give, some school of metaphysicians is sure to claim him as its own. And whichever answer he may give, he is sure to bewilder Vacchagotta.

That Buddha had no patience with the metaphysicians is made clear by this and by other stories. He had many quarrels with them. He objected to them for playing with words, with the result that on the one hand they drew people away from the main business of life and on the other hand profaned by the inadequacy of their symbols the deep mysteries which they professed to explore. He objected to the misconception of knowledge, of truth, of reality, which underlay their shallow dualism, and made it possible for them to assume that all the problems of existence could be brought to the issue of a simple Yes or a simple No. Above all, he deplored the loss of temper which the very futility of their wordy wrangling rendered inevitable,—the loss of charity, the loss of serenity, the loss of self-control, the loss of all the qualities which he had called upon men to cultivate. "The theory that the world is eternal, the theory that the world is infinite, the theory that the soul and the body are identical"—of each of these and of all kindred theories he says the same thing—"this theory is a jungle, a wilderness, a puppet show, a writhing and a fetter, and is coupled with misery, ruin, despair and agony and does not tend to aversion, absence of passion, cessation, quiescence, knowledge, supreme wisdom and Nirvâna."

But we shall the better understand his antipathy to the metaphysicians if we consider the second of his reasons for remaining silent,—his fear of either misleading or bewildering Vacchagotta. Dr Oldenberg thinks that in giving this reason he came very near to saying that there was no Ego, and that it was only regard for Vacchagotta's susceptibilities which kept him silent. This criticism is, I think, based on a misconception of Buddha's mental attitude. Buddha saw clearly enough that the answer to Vacchagotta's question, as to all similar questions, was "Yes and No,"—"Yes" from this point of view, "No" from that. The words that are ascribed to him—words which may well have been his—suggest that some such thoughts as these were passing through his mind: "The Ego is real beyond all reality, but I cannot hope to make Vacchagotta understand this. If I tell him that the Ego is, he will assume that I mean by the word what he does, and so be led astray. If, foreseeing this, I tell him that the body is not the Ego, the sensations are not the Ego, the consciousness is not the Ego, and so forth,—if, in my desire to bring home to him the transcendent reality of the Ego, I refuse to allow him to identify it with any of those things which he has been accustomed to regard as real,—he will come to the conclusion that there is no Ego, that the word is an empty name. If, on the other hand, I tell him that, as he understands the word, there is no Ego, that the sense of individuality, of separateness, which seems to him to be of the essence of the sense of self, is delusive (separateness being the very negation of true selfhood), he will be equally bewildered. In either case he will feel that he has been living in a dream. What can I do, then, but keep silent?

Had Buddha shared Dr Paul Carus' fundamental antipathy to the Ego—to the whole idea of selfhood—he would, I think, without hesitation have answered the monk's question with an uncompromising No; for metaphysical atomism, like every other development of materialism, is very easy to explain, the strength of materialism lying in this, that it is the precise system of thought which the average man, who had forgotten his mother's teaching and silenced the questionings of his heart, would—if he took to thinking—construct for himself. Had Buddha believed in the Ego, as the pious Christian believes in it, as a something (to use Dr Rhys Davids' words) "which flies out away from the body" and retains its individuality for all time, he would have answered the monk's question with an unqualified "Yes"; for he would have known that the monk's conception of the Ego coincided with, or at any rate approximated to, his own. That he said neither "Yes" or "No" suggests that he neither believed in the Ego, as the pious Christian believes in it, nor disbelieved in it, as the votary of the "religion of science" disbelieves in it; and leaves us free to conjecture that his conception of the Ego, whatever form it may have taken, transcended the range of ordinary thought and would not suffer itself to be translated into intelligible speech.

The second story has been thus epitomized for us by Dr Oldenberg:

"The venerable Mâlukya comes to the Master, and expresses his astonishment that the Master's discourse leaves a series of the very most important and deepest questions unanswered. Is the world eternal or is it limited by bounds of time? Does the Perfect Buddha live on beyond death? Does the Perfect One not live on beyond death? It pleases me not, says the monk, that all this shall remain unanswered and I do not think it right; therefore I am come to the Master to interrogate him about these doubts. May it please Buddha to answer them if he can. 'But when anyone does not understand a matter and does not know it, then a straightforward man says: I do not understand that, I do not know that.'

"We see: the question of the Nirvâna is brought before Buddha by that monk as directly and definitely as could ever be possible. And what answers Buddha? He says in his Socratic fashion, not without a touch of irony, 'What have I said to thee before now, Mâlukyaputta? Have I said, Come, Mâlukyaputta, and be my disciple; I shall teach thee whether the world is everlasting or not everlasting, whether the world is finite or infinite, whether the vital faculty is identical with the body or separate from it, whether the Perfect One lives on after death or does not live on, or whether the Perfect One lives on and at the same time does not live on after death, or whether he neither lives on nor does not live on?'

"'That thou hast not said, Sire.'

"'Or hast thou,' Buddha goes on, 'said to me: I shall be thy disciple, declare unto me, whether the world is everlasting or not everlasting, and so on?'

"This also must Mâlukya answer in the negative.

"'If a man,' Buddha proceeds, 'were struck by a poisoned arrow, and his friends and relatives called in a skilful physician, what if the wounded man said: "I shall not allow my wound to be treated until I know who the man is by whom I have been wounded, whether he is a noble, a Brahman, a Vaiçya, a Çûdra"—or if he said: "I shall not allow my wound to be treated until I know what they call the man who has wounded me, and of what family he is, whether he is tall or small or of middle stature, and how his weapon was made with which he has struck me." What would the end of the case be? The man would die of his wound.'

"Why has Buddha not taught his disciples, whether the world is finite or infinite, whether the saint lives on beyond death or not? Because the knowledge of these things does not conduce to progress in holiness, because it does not contribute to peace and enlightenment. What contributes to peace and enlightenment, Buddha has taught his own: the truth of suffering, the truth of the origin of suffering, the truth of the path to the cessation of suffering. 'Therefore, Mâlukyaputta, whatsoever has not been revealed by me, let that remain unrevealed, and what has been revealed, let it be revealed.'"

In this story Buddha claims to have taught his disciples all that they need to know and can be made to understand. More than this he cannot and will not teach them. He may know more about the deeper realities of existence than he chooses to reveal. Mâlukya suggests that he should make open confession of his ignorance, but he makes no response to this. His reason for keeping silent is that, if men are to wait till Mâlukya's questions have been adequately answered, they will have to wait for ever, and meanwhile the main concerns of life—the pursuit of peace and enlightenment, the practice of self-control, the cultivation of sympathy—will be forgotten and neglected. The average man may either ask the "Doctors" to answer those great questions for him, or he may try to answer them for himself. The result will be the same in either case. The questions will never be answered; the Path will never be entered; and, what is worse, the evil passions which are generated by verbal controversy will poison the springs of spiritual life.

When we read this dialogue we seem to have travelled far from the Indian idea that knowledge of reality is the first condition of "salvation." But, in truth, we have never really quitted it. The metaphysical path to knowledge was one which Buddha looked upon with distrust and aversion; but knowledge itself—the knowledge which has its counterpart in inward enlightenment, the knowledge of reality which makes for peace and deliverance—was the very goal to which the Path was intended to lead. The truth of things, as Buddha conceived of it, could not be set forth in a series of formulæ, for (to go no further) the laws of language would make that impossible; but it could be lived up to and lived in to: and so he bade men control their passions and desires, and cultivate kindness and good-will, that the consequent growth of their souls might be rewarded by the expansion of their consciousness and the deepening of their insight, till it became possible for them to know (in the truest sense of the word) the fleeting from the abiding, the phantasmal from the real. The propositions which Mâlukya challenged Buddha to answer had but little meaning for him. This we may take for granted. But he might conceivably have waived them aside, and tried to disclose to his disciples the inner faith of his own heart. That he made no attempt to do so does not prove that there was no master theory of things behind his formal teaching. When we read the words "whatsoever has not been revealed by me let that remain unrevealed," we cannot but feel that what "remained unrevealed" was something well worth revealing. What the silence of Buddha does prove, or at least suggest, is that the creed of his heart was too deep for words,—that the realities which it sought to encompass and co-ordinate far transcended the normal range of human thought.

What the first story left us free to conjecture, the second has suggested to us as a plausible hypothesis,—namely, that Buddha's silence was the outcome, not of the hollowness of his creed, but of the very abundance of his spiritual faith. The third story falls into line with the first and second, but brings us nearer to the same conclusion.

"King Pasenadi of Kosala, we are told, on one occasion on a journey between his two chief towns, Sâketa and Sâvatthi, fell in with the nun Khemâ, a female disciple of Buddha, renowned for her wisdom. The King paid his respects to her, and inquired of her concerning the sacred doctrine.

"'Venerable lady,' asked the King, 'does the Perfect One exist after death?'

"'The Exalted One, O great King, has not declared: the Perfect One exists after death.'

"'Then does the Perfect One not exist after death, venerable lady?'

"'This also, O great King, the Exalted One has not declared: the Perfect One does not exist after death.'

"'Thus, venerable lady, the Perfect One does exist after death, and at the same time does not exist after death?—thus, venerable lady, the Perfect One neither exists after death, nor does he not exist?'

"The answer is still the same: the Exalted One has not revealed it. . . .

"The King is astonished. 'What is the reason, venerable lady, what is the ground, on which the Exalted One has not revealed this?'

"'Permit me,' answers the nun, 'now to ask thee a question, O great King, and do thou answer me as the case seems to thee to stand. How thinkest thou, O great King, hast thou an accountant, or a mint-master, or a treasurer, who could count the sands of the Ganges, who could say: there are there so many grains of sand, or so many hundreds, or thousands, or hundreds of thousands of grains of sand?'

"'No, venerable lady, I have not.'

"'Or hast thou an accountant, a mint-master, or a treasurer, who could measure the water in the great ocean, who could say: there are therein so many measures of water, or so many hundreds, or thousands, or hundreds of thousands of measures of water?'

"'No, venerable lady, I have not.'

"'And why not? The great ocean is deep, immeasurable, unfathomable. So also, O great King, if the existence of the Perfect One be measured by the predicates of corporeal form: these predicates of the corporeal form are abolished in the Perfect One, their root is severed, they are hewn away like a palm tree and laid aside, so that they cannot germinate again in the future. Released, O great King, is the Perfect One from this, that his being should be gauged by the measure of the corporeal world: he is deep, immeasurable, unfathomable as the great ocean. "The Perfect One exists after death," this is not apposite; "the Perfect One does not exist after death," this also is not apposite; "the Perfect One at once exists and does not exist after death," this also is not apposite; "the Perfect One neither does nor does not exist after death," this also is not apposite.'

"But Pasenadi, the King of Kosala, received the nun Khemâ's discourse with satisfaction and approbation, rose from his seat, bowed reverently before Khemâ, the nun, turned and went away."

Supreme reality—the ideal object of all high thinking, of all knowledge, of all wisdom—is here symbolized by the Perfect One's existence. And that existence, we are told, is "deep, unfathomable, immeasurable as the great ocean." "When such a reason," says Dr Oldenberg, "is assigned for the waiving of the question as to whether the Perfect One lives for ever, is not this very giving of a reason itself an answer? And is not this answer a Yes? No being in the ordinary sense, but still assuredly not a non-being; a sublime positive, of which thought has no idea, for which language has no expression, which beams out to meet the cravings of the thirsty for immortality in that same splendour of which the apostle says: 'Eye hath not seen, nor ear heard, neither have entered into the heart of man, the things which God hath prepared for them that love Him.'"

The nun Khemâ had caught the spirit of her Master's teaching. The explanation that she gave of his teaching harmonizes so well with those which he himself is reported to have given, when challenged with probing questions by Vacchagotta and Mâlukya, that we must needs regard it as at least provisionally true. Buddha kept silent because his heart was overfull, because he had too much to say.

What other explanations of his silence can be given?

Three, and three only, suggest themselves to my mind.

The first is that he was a pure and consistent agnostic, an indifferentist not only in the presence of the wrangling dogmatists, but also in the depths of his own soul. Had he been this, had he been what no man is who feels and thinks deeply, he would have told his disciples that he regarded all the statements and all the solutions of the ultimate problems with equal indifference, and in telling them this would have explained and justified his silence.

The second is that his own attitude towards great matters was one of helpless bewilderment. Had it been this, had the light of his clear and authoritative teaching been the reflection of an impenetrable fog of doubt, he would have openly said so, for such a confession would have added force and weight to his contention that men must win deliverance, not by trying to guess metaphysical riddles, but by walking in the Path.

Thus the bare fact of Buddha's silence makes the first and the second explanations of it untenable.

The third is that he was a negative dogmatist, who refrained, for fear of scandalizing his disciples and paralyzing their spiritual energies, from openly formulating his sweeping negations. This is the hypothesis which Dr Rhys Davids, Dr Paul Carus, and others are disposed to accept. I have already given my reasons for rejecting the first part of it. I will now consider the second. Had Buddha been a negative dogmatist, would he have refrained from formulating his nihilistic creed? I think not. So sincere was he and so deeply in earnest, that he would have kept nothing back from his disciples—this we may assume at the outset—which it would have been possible for him to communicate to them. Now it happens that a creed whose formulæ are all negations is, of all creeds, the easiest to expound; and the fact that Buddha made no attempt to expound his creed is therefore a convincing proof that the faith of his heart was not the "religion of science." When he expounded his scheme of life, he gave such reasons as he could for inviting men to adopt it. That he kept other reasons in reserve can scarcely be doubted. Had these occult reasons admitted of being stated, he would surely have stated them. That he would have played the opportunist in a matter of more than life and death, that he would have kept silence about the master problems of human thought when it was possible and even easy for him to set forth his solution of them, is to my mind incredible.

The question which confronts us admits of being discussed on other than a priori grounds. There are stories which bear on it. Just before he died Buddha is reported to have said, "I have preached the truth without making any distinction between exoteric and esoteric doctrine; for in respect of the truth, Ânanda, the Tathâgata has no such thing as the closed fist of a teacher who keeps some things back." The inference which Dr Rhys Davids draws from these words—that there is nothing esoteric in Buddhism—is not warranted by the premises, and is inconsistent with Dr Rhys Davids' own contention that, in his reply to the two young Brahmins who asked him to show them the way to union with God, Buddha "adopted the opportunist position"and gave his sanction to beliefs which in his heart of hearts he disowned. There is always, in the nature of things, something esoteric in the faith of a man who has thought deeply and sincerely. There are many thoughts which he cannot communicate—the intervening barriers are insuperable—to the rank and file of mankind. There are some thoughts which he cannot communicate even to those who are in close sympathy with his general attitude towards the deepest of all problems. There are a few thoughts which he is compelled to keep back even from those whose inner life is very near and dear to his own. And, behind and beyond all these, there are movements of his own inner being which will probably some day shape themselves into thoughts, but which meanwhile remain—unformulated and unformulable—below the threshold of his own conscious life. When Buddha told Ânanda that he had kept nothing back from his disciples, he was doubtless contrasting in his mind his own methods with those of the Brahmanic teachers of his day,—teachers who kept everything back from their disciples, who sought to regulate the lives of the people down to the minutest details of conduct, yet gave no reason for what they prescribed, and so crushed down the spiritual life of India under the deadly burden of an apparently meaningless ceremonialism. And he doubtless meant that he had told his disciples everything which it was possible for him to disclose to them. More than that he did not mean: or the stories of his silence are all untrue.

But whatever his words to Ânanda may have meant, it is certain that he who spoke them was not an opportunist: it is certain that, if he had been in possession of a creed as clear, as intelligible, and as easy to formulate as the (so-called) "religion of science," he would have disclosed it to all who came to him for guidance. Dr Rhys Davids makes no attempt to harmonize the ultra-candour of the man who claimed to have kept nothing back from his disciples, with the shiftiness of the man who kept back from the two young Brahmins, while he responded to their demand for spiritual guidance, his disbelief in the fundamental dogma of their creed. But the attempt deserves to be made. There is surely a mean between the complacent opportunism which allows a man to simulate complete sympathy with beliefs which he has long outgrown, and the aggressive candour which makes him blurt out, or try to blurt out, whatever is in his mind, with the result that he misleads and deceives his neighbour in the sacred name of Truth. "Il y a des choses," says Joubert, "que l'homme ne peut connaître que vaguement: les grands esprits se contentent d'en avoir des notions vagues; mais cela ne suffit point aux esprits vulgaires. Il faut, pour leur repos, qu'ils se forgent ou qu'on leur offre des idées fixes et determinées sur les objets même où toute précision est erreur. Ces esprits communs n'ont point d'ailes; ils ne peuvent se soutenir dans rien de ce qui n'est que de l'espace; il leur faut des points d'appui, des fables, des mensonges, des idoles. Mentez leur donc, et ne les trompez pas." It is certainly better to "lie" to men than to "deceive" them. But Buddha did not lie to the "esprits vulgaires" of his day. He kept silence in their presence.

Having rejected as untenable three plausible explanations of Buddha's silence, we are left face to face with the only theory which takes account both of the fact of his silence and of the reasons which he gave for it,—the theory that he had a creed of his own, a creed which went to the root of all great matters, but which, in some sort, bound him to silence. Such a creed was, as it happens, already in existence. The deeply spiritual philosophy which had inspired the authors of the Upanishads was, in its essence, esoteric. The conception of God—the Supreme Reality—as, on the one hand, the soul or inner life of the Universe, and, on the other hand, the true self of each individual man, is one in the presence of which thought becomes an impertinence and speech a profanation. The feelings which arise in the soul in response—if there happens to be any response—to an idea which is at once overpoweringly vast and elusively subtle, do not suffer themselves to be systematized or formulated, but pass in an instant, in the first pulsation of their mighty movement, far beyond the limits of any tabulated creed. This the sages of India instinctively felt, and feeling this they "let their words be few." Even in the Upanishads, which were composed, not for the world at large but for an inner circle of sages and recluses, the language used is that of paradox and negation. That in which all their thinking centred—the Divine in man—was not to them an object. of scientific curiosity, a being whose nature could be exhaustively analyzed or whose attributes could be set forth in a series of formulæ. They habitually spoke of him 1 as "That." They shrank from applying any name to him which might suggest either that he was a member of a class, or that he had a distinct individuality of his own. If they predicated anything of him, they at once predicated its opposite. He is swifter than the mind, yet he moves not: he is far and near: he is at once innermost and outermost: and so forth. The moment of apprehension, as thought strives to grasp him, is also the moment of discomfiture and recoil. Speech, thought, sight, hearing,—each of these in turn is made possible by him, and therefore each in turn fails to reach him. He is beyond sight, beyond speech, beyond mind, beyond the known, beyond the unknown. He is veiled from thought by the excess of his own inward light. Dwelling at the heart of man, as the "unbeholden essence" of all things,—gathering into his infinite inwardness all the outermost boundaries of the Universe,—he is at once too subtle to be grasped by any effort of mental analysis, and too vast to be encompassed by any flight of imaginative thought. "He thinks of it, for whom it passeth thought; who thinks of it doth never know it."

Men who had to use such language as this within the narrow limits of an esoteric circle, had no choice but to become silent when those limits were passed. For "those who understand," the language of paradox and negation has a meaning; but paradoxes bewilder the uninitiated, and the language of negation is apt to be mistaken for the language of denial and revolt. This, then, was the tremendous problem that confronted the sages of the Upanishads. Possessed with a spiritual idea, so deeply, so inexhaustibly true that, if it could but be assimilated by the heart of man, it would in the fullness of time "redeem the world,"—they were debarred, on the one hand by the fundamental laws of thought and language, on the other hand by the very depth and truth of their cherished idea, from revealing it—as an idea—to mankind. How, then, were they to bring it home to the hearts and lives of their fellow-men? The ceremonial solution of the problem, which they adopted as a counsel of despair, proved to be no solution; and the problem remained unsolved till Buddha himself solved it—whether consciously or unconsciously, is the question that now confronts us—by transferring it to the plane of practical life.

That Buddha's ethical scheme was a practical interpretation, an exposition in terms of human conduct and human life, of the paramount idea of the Upanishads, I have already attempted to show. Was the coincidence—at every vital point—between the scheme and the idea an accident, or was it deliberately planned? That the latter is by many degrees the more reasonable hypothesis, is too obvious to need demonstration. If we hesitate to adopt it, the reason is that Buddha, though he worked out the idea, as a principle of action, with consistent thoroughness and consummate skill, not only made no attempt to expound it, but even turned back, on the threshold of their inquiry, all who sought to go behind the scheme to the philosophy that it embodied. But this difficulty will vanish when we remind ourselves that if Buddha, who made it his life's work to preach the gospel of deliverance to all men, had accepted the paramount idea of the Upanishads and made it his own, he would have been bound by the very strength and depth of his faith in it to wall it round with inviolable silence.

Link by link, the chain of proof has been forged which connects the inmost soul of Buddha with the spiritual idealism of ancient India. It is true that, in such a matter as this, demonstration is not to be looked for; but it is also true that each new link adds strength and elasticity to the chain as a whole. Τ μὲν ἀληθε πάντα συνᾴδει τὰ ὑπάρχοντα. The theory that Buddha was at heart a spiritual idealist has received confirmation from many quarters. The last of the arguments that support it—the last and not the least weighty—is that it, and it alone, accounts for and justifies his silence.

The Secret of Buddha

THE creed which I am trying to interpret is that of Buddha himself. With the creed of the Buddhist world, with the creed of this or that Buddhist Church, I have no direct concern. Dr Paul Carus is gratified because the South Buddhist Church has sent him a certificate of orthodoxy. Would it give him equal pleasure to know that his interpretation of the creed of Christ (let us say) had been officially endorsed by some Presbyterian Synod, or even by the Vatican? I doubt it. Distance may lend enchantment to the "dogmatics" of a Buddhist church; but when one looks nearer home one begins to see things in their true proportions. It is not in the doctrine of any church or sect that the spirit of the Master's teaching is to be found. For good or for evil, churches and sects are under the control of the average man. On the one hand, they owe their existence to the secret demands of his better nature. On the other hand, they reflect in their theology his secret weaknesses,—his spiritual indolence, his intellectual timidity, his lack of imagination, the essential vulgarity of his thought. Hence it is that the faith which has been officially formulated is as salt which has lost its savour. If we are to hold intercourse with the soul of a great teacher, and so renew in our own souls the springs of his spiritual life, we must be prepared to go far behind and far beyond the formularies of the religion that calls itself by his name.

It follows—to revert to the case of Buddha and Buddhism—that in considering the meaning of this or that passage in the Buddhist "Scriptures," one must have recourse to the general impression of Buddha—the man, the thinker, and the teacher—which has been generated by careful study of all the available sources of evidence, including (as perhaps the most important of all) the spiritual atmosphere of the age in which he lived, rather than to the particular interpretation of the passage in question which has conic to be regarded as "orthodox" by the Buddhist world. Even the fact that there was an apparent agreement with regard to the meaning of the passage between Eastern "dogmatics" and Western scholarship, would count for little in one's eyes, in the event of the given interpretation conflicting with one's general impression of the spirit of Buddha's teaching; for, in the first place, the agreement between Eastern and Western thought would probably prove to be wholly superficial; and, in the second place, scholarship, as such, is debarred by its own aims and interests and by the special preparation which it presupposes, from making that wide survey and that deep and sympathetic study of all the available evidence, which would be needed if the inner meaning of the passage was to be wrested from it.

I have convinced myself that faith in the ideal identity of the individual with the Universal Soul was the hidden fountain head of Buddha's practical teaching. I will now test the worth of this conclusion by applying it, as a provisional hypothesis, to the solution of some of the many problems that perplex the student of Buddhism. The best way to handle those problems is to consider the grave charges which have been brought against Buddha and Buddhism,—charges which have been so often reiterated that they are now openly endorsed by the "man in the street."

Five of these are of capital importance.

We are told that Buddha denied the Soul or Ego; in other words, that his teaching was materialistic.

We are told that there was no place for God in his system of thought; in other words, that his teaching was atheistic.

We are told that he regarded all existence as intrinsically evil; in other words, that his teaching was pessimistic.

We are told that he taught men to think only of themselves and their personal welfare; in other words, that his scheme of life was egoistic.

We are told that after Nirvâna—the inward state of him who has lifted the last veil of illusion—comes annihilation; in other words (since what is behind the last veil of illusion is ex hypothesi supremely real), that Buddha regarded Nothing as the Supreme Reality, and that therefore his teaching was nihilistic.

Can these charges be substantiated? If they can, we are confronted by the most perplexing of all problems. How comes it that a religion which has such vital defects has had such a successful career? That Buddha won to his will the "deepest heart" of the Far East is undeniable. Was it by preaching the gospel of materialism, of atheism, of pessimism, of egoism, of nihilism, that he achieved this signal triumph? This is the problem into which all the other problems that beset the path of the student of Buddhism must ultimately be resolved."

Let us now consider, by the light of the hypothesis which I am seeking to verify, each of the capital charges that have been brought against Buddha.

(1) The materialism of Buddha.

Let us assume that, far from denying the Ego, Buddha believed in it, in his heart of hearts,—believed in it with the depth and subtlety of belief which are characteristic of Indian idealism,—believed in it as the "unbeholden essence" of all things, as the all-generating, all-sustaining life which individualizes itself in every human breast, yet is what it really is at the heart of the Universe, and nowhere else. What would be the attitude of one who so conceived of the Ego towards the popular belief—popular, one may safely conjecture, in Buddha's day as in ours—in the intrinsic reality of the individualized Ego, or individual soul? That the Ego is not real, in the fullest sense of the word, till it has become one with the Universal Soul, is the postulate on which all his philosophy, both as a whole and under each of its aspects, would be hinged. On its way to the goal of union with the Divine, the individual soul must needs pass through many stages of unreality. So long as it retains its sense of isolation, its mistaken sense of I-ness, it is, comparatively speaking, unreal. What is real in it is its potential universality. What is unreal is what it regards as of its very essence,—its individuality, its sense of separateness from all other things. Had Buddha looked at the problem of selfhood from the standpoint of Indian idealism, he would have seen that the popular belief in the intrinsic value of the individual Soul is fundamentally false, not on the plane of metaphysical speculation only, but on every plane of human life; and he would have set himself to combat it in each of its many forms. Of the many forms that it takes I need not speak at length. The materialism of him who identifies his soul (his "self") with his body, or who conceives of it as the "totality" of his own sensations, perceptions, or other states of consciousness; the semi-materialism of him who (like the pious Christian) regards the soul as "something which flies out away from the body at death," or as one of many parts or organs of a complex being; the sentimental clinging to individuality; the metaphysical clinging to individuality;—these may be mentioned as typical forms of that reluctance to regard the Universal Soul as the only true self, which is so characteristic of popular thought in all the stages of its development, and against which Buddha, if I have not misread his philosophy, must have waged a relentless war. If I am asked why Buddha, who eschewed metaphysical controversy, should have thought it necessary to combat a belief which seems to be primarily metaphysical, my answer is that the belief is not primarily metaphysical, that on the contrary it is the reflection in consciousness of a deep-seated instinct which has vital ethical consequences—the instinct to affirm the ordinary self, to accept it, minister to it, magnify it, rest in it—in a word, the egoistic instinct, the hidden root of every form of spiritual evil, and the first and last of moral defects. As the suppression of egoism was the very end and aim of Buddha's scheme of life, and as in this matter the distinction between theory on the one hand and sentiment, desire, and impulse on the other, is hard to draw and easy to efface, it was but natural that Buddha should wage war against the egoistic instinct even when it disguised itself as a semi-philosophical theory. But he waged that war, as he did everything else that he took in hand, within the limits prescribed by his own "sweet reasonableness" and exalted common-sense. Leaving it to the metaphysical experts to wrangle over the more abstract aspects of the problem of selfhood, he contented himself with combating on quasi-popular grounds the popular delusion that the individual Ego is real, permanent, self-contained.

Let us assume this much; and we shall see a new meaning in each of the many passages on which Western criticism has based its theory that denial of the Ego was the cardinal article of Buddha's creed. We shall see that, whenever he seems to be denying existence to the Ego as such, what he is really doing is to deny reality to the individual Ego, to the ordinary surface self.

Let us first consider a dialogue in which the principal speaker is the venerable Sâriputta, but in which the arguments advanced may well have been devised by Buddha himself, coinciding as they do with arguments which he is reported to have used in one of his early discourses. A monk, named Yamaka, had convinced himself, as many modern interpreters of Buddhism have done, that the "doctrine taught by the Blessed One "amounted to this, "that on the dissolution of the body the monk who has lost all depravity is annihilated, perishes, and does not exist after death." His fellow-monks urged him to abandon what they regarded as a "wicked heresy," but to no purpose. At last they besought the venerable Sâriputta to "draw near" to Yamaka and try to convert him to a truer view of the Blessed One's teaching.

"And the venerable Sâriputta consented by his silence. Then the venerable Sâriputta in the evening of the day arose from meditation, and drew near to where the venerable Yamaka was; and having drawn near he greeted the venerable Yamaka, and having passed the compliments of friendship and civility, he sat down respectfully on one side. And seated respectfully at one side, the venerable Sâriputta spoke to the venerable Yamaka as follows: 'Is the report true, brother Yamaka, that the following wicked heresy has sprung up in your mind: Thus do I understand the doctrine taught by the Blessed One, that on the dissolution of the body the monk who has lost all depravity is annihilated, perishes, and does not exist after death?'

"'Even so, brother, do I understand the doctrine taught by the Blessed One, that on the dissolution of the body the monk who has lost all depravity is annihilated, perishes, and does not exist after death.'

"'What think you, brother Yamaka? Is form permanent, or transitory?"

"'It is transitory, brother.'

"'And that which is transitory—is it evil, or is it good?'

"'It is evil, brother.'

"'And that which is transitory, evil, and liable to change—is it possible to say of it: This is mine—this am I—this is my Ego?'

"'Nay, verily, brother.'

"'Is sensation . . . perception . . . the predispositions . . . consciousness, permanent, or transitory?'

"'It is transitory, brother.'

"'And that which is transitory—is it evil, or is it good?'

"'It is evil, brother.'

"'And that which is transitory, evil, and liable to change—is it possible to say of it: This is mine; this am I; this is my Ego?'

"'Nay, verily, brother Yamaka.'

"'Accordingly, brother Yamaka, as respects all form whatsoever—as respects all sensation whatsoever—as respects all perception whatsoever—as respects all predispositions whatsoever—as respects all consciousness whatsoever, past, future or present, be it subjective or existing outside, gross or subtle, mean or exalted, far or near, the correct view in the light of the highest knowledge is as follows: This is not mine; this am I not; this is not my Ego.

"'Perceiving this, brother Yamaka, the learned and noble disciple conceives an aversion for form, conceives an aversion for sensation, conceives an aversion for perception, conceives an aversion for the predispositions, conceives an aversion for consciousness. And in conceiving this aversion he becomes divested of passion, and by the absence of passion he becomes free, and when he is free he becomes aware that he is free; and he knows that rebirth is exhausted, that he has lived the holy life, that he has done what it behooved him to do, and that he is no more for the world.

"'What think you, brother Yamaka? Do you consider form as the Saint?'

"'Nay, verily, brother.'

"'Do you consider sensation . . . perception . . . the predispositions . . . consciousness as the Saint?'

"'Nay, verily, brother.'

"'What think you, brother Yamaka? Do you consider the Saint as comprised in form?'

"'Nay, verily, brother.'

"'Do you consider the Saint as distinct from form?'

"'Nay, verily, brother.'

"'Do you consider the Saint as comprised in sensation? . . . as distinct from sensation? . . . as comprised in perception? . . . as distinct from perception? . . . as comprised in the predispositions? . . . as distinct from the predispositions? . . . as comprised in consciousness? . . . as distinct from consciousness?'

"'Nay, verily, brother.'

"'What think you, brother Yamaka? Are form, sensation, perception, the predispositions and consciousness united the Saint?'

"'Nay, verily, brother.'

"'What think you, brother Yamaka? Do you consider the Saint as a something having no form, sensation, perception, predispositions or consciousness?'

"'Nay, verily, brother.'

"'Considering now, brother Yamaka, that you fail to make out and establish the existence of the Saint in the present life, is it reasonable for you to say: Thus do I understand the doctrine taught by the Blessed One, that on the dissolution of the body the monk who has lost all depravity is annihilated, perishes, and does not exist after death?"

"'Brother Sâriputta, it was because of my ignorance that I held this wicked heresy; but now that I have listened to the doctrinal instruction of the venerable Sâriputta, I have abandoned that wicked heresy and acquired the true doctrine.'"

Mr H. C. Warren, from whose translation of the dialogue in his learned work, "Buddhism in Translation," I have made this extract, heads each page in the dialogue with the significant words, "There is no Ego." That is how he interprets the teaching of Sâriputta. But surely what Sâriputta intended to teach was the exact opposite of this. The monk Yamaka believed that at the death of the "Saint"—at the moment when his cycle of earth-lives had come to an end—he ceased to be. This belief, we are expressly told, was regarded as a "wicked heresy"; and Sâriputta disabused Yamaka's mind of it by showing him that it was as difficult for him to "make out and establish" the existence of the "Saint" in the present life as in the life beyond death (and beyond rebirth). He reminds him, in words which, according to tradition, had been used by Buddha himself, that the Ego is not to be identified with form, with sensation, with perception, with the "predispositions," with consciousness, since each of these is transitory and therefore evil, and "of that which is transitory, evil and liable to change it is not possible to say 'This is mine; this am I; this is my Ego.'" "The ignorant unconverted man . . . considers form in the light of an Ego, considers sensation . . . perception . . . the predispositions . . . consciousness in the light of an Ego," and therefore clings to those apparent "selves" though they are all transitory and evil. "The learned and noble disciple does not consider form, sensation, etc., in the light of an Ego," and he therefore detaches himself from each of those delusive "selves." Not a word is said, in any part of the discourse, in disproof of the existence of the Ego. The point of the argument is that each of the apparent Egos—the Ego of form, the Ego of sensation, and the rest—is unreal; and that the man who regards the Ego of the "Saint" as non- existent after death, because it will then be finally detached from form, sensation, etc., is bound by the logic of his own delusion to regard the Ego of the "Saint" as non-existent while on earth, since, if the "Saint" has indeed won deliverance, he will have finally detached himself, even while on earth, from each of those phantom Egos, and in doing so will have found his true self.

From this point it is possible to advance to two conclusions. As disbelief in the after-death existence of the "Saint" is a "wicked heresy," it stands to reason that it is also a "wicked heresy" to regard the "Saint"—the true Ego—as non-existent now. This is the first conclusion, which the Western critic who seeks to father upon Buddha his own denial of the Ego will do well to bear in mind. The second seems to have been tacitly drawn by both Sâriputta and Yamaka, and to have carried conviction to the latter's mind. As it is obviously absurd to say that the "Saint" is non-existent now, it stands to reason that it is also absurd to say—as Yamaka had said—that the "Saint" will cease to be after death. The whole discourse is directed nominally against Yamaka's "wicked heresy," but really against the erroneous belief that the individual Ego, the Ego which is associated with form, with sensation, and the rest, is the true Ego,—a belief which had generated in Yamaka's mind the "wicked heresy" that "on the dissolution of the body" the Saint "is annihilated, perishes, and does not exist." Indeed it is no exaggeration to say that in this discourse disbelief in the reality of the Ego—the true Ego which transcends the limits of the transitory, and therefore passes beyond the reach of thought and language—is authoritatively condemned.

Dr Rhys Davids lays great stress on a discourse in which various attempts to conceive of the existence of the Ego after death are condemned as heresies. Here, as in the dialogue which has just been considered, the Ego is that of the man who has won deliverance while still living on earth, and whose cycle of earth-lives is therefore coming to an end. The prying attempt to follow the liberated Ego into the life beyond death, into the unimaginable bliss of Nirvâna, is repelled as impertinent and delusive, and every form that it takes is condemned as a "heresy." The discourse ends with these words: "Mendicants [Monks], that which binds the Teacher 1 [the Saint, the Perfect One] to existence is cut off; but his body still remains. While his body shall remain he will be seen by gods and men, but after the dissolution of the body, neither gods 2 nor men will see him." "Would it be possible," asks Dr Rhys Davids, "in a more complete and categorical manner to deny that there is any soul—anything of any kind, which continues to exist, in any manner, after death?" This criticism (so characteristically Western) is as wide of the mark as is Mr Warren's headline comment on the dialogue between Sâriputta and Yamaka. What the preacher is trying to enforce is what Sâriputta had impressed upon Yamaka, that the Ego of the "Saint"—the true Ego, for the "Saint" is one who has found his true self does not exist after death in any form or mode which is comprehensible by human thought. Far from denying the existence of the Ego, the preacher is insisting on its transcendent reality. "Neither gods nor men" will see the "Saint" after death, not because he will then be non-existent, but because his being will have out-soared all the categories of human thought.

In these and other such discourses Buddha falls into line with the thinkers of the Upanishads, who described by a series of negations what they regarded as the true Ego,—the Divine in man. The coincidences between his teaching and theirs are so significant that the only way to account for them is to assume that his faith—the deepest faith of his heart—was in its essence identical with theirs. If the account that he gave of the Ego was purely negative, if he abstained from positive statements (even in that paradoxical form which was dear to the thinkers of the Upanishads), the reason was that he wished men to find out for themselves, by following the Path of soul-expansion, what the Ego really is. He said to them, in thought if not in words: "The Ego is not this thing or that; it is not any of the things with which you are used to identify it. If you wish to know what it is, enter the Path and follow it to the end. Your question will then be answered, for it will have transformed itself into a burning thirst for the ideal and the divine; and in the bliss of Nirvâna that thirst will be eternally slaked and eternally renewed."

Dr Rhys Davids is confirmed in his belief that Buddha denied the Ego, by the fact that the "heresy of individuality" is one of the three "Fetters" which have to be broken on the very threshold of the new life. But here, as elsewhere, Buddha is denying the reality, not of the Ego as such, but of the individual Ego; in other words, he is condemning by implication the blindness of him who regards the limitations which his individuality imposes upon him as the essential conditions of his existence. So, too, when he names among the fetters which have to be broken in the later stages of the Eight-fold Path, the desire for life in the worlds of form, and the desire for life in the formless worlds, he is thinking, not of the desire for life as such but of the desire for separate life, for the continuance of individuality,—the hydra-headed desire which is ever tending to counteract the centripetal energy of love.

There is one set of discourses on which those who regard Buddha as a negative dogmatist lay great stress,—the so-called Milinda dialogues, or conversations between the Greek King, Menanda, of Baktria, and Nâgasena, the Buddhist teacher. Nâgasena seems to have been an acute controversialist who loved argument for its own sake almost as much as Buddha disliked it, and who, had he lived in Europe in the Middle Ages, would probably have nailed theological or metaphysical theses to church-doors. That he had caught the deeper spirit of the Master's teaching is, to say the least, improbable; but that his discourses present to us an interpretation of that teaching, which had gained currency in his day, can scarcely be doubted. I have elsewhere allowed, for argument's sake, that he may have had an academic antipathy to the Ego. If he had, his discourses do less than justice to their theme. The arguments by which a merely academic belief (or disbelief) is sustained are in the nature of things ineffective. The spiritual atmosphere of his age, the words that he finds himself compelled to use, even his own subconscious convictions—are all against the thinker. In the well known Chariot dialogue, Nâgasena is supposed to have proved conclusively that "there is no Ego." I cannot see that he has done this, and I am by no means sure that he has attempted to do it. What he has proved is that, just as the name chariot belongs to the vehicle as a whole and not to any of its parts, so the name Nâgasena belongs to the living being as a

whole and not to any of his organs or faculties. If the dialogue is directed
against anything, it is directed against the vulgar belief that the Soul is a
quasi-material something (like the babe of vapour in mediaeval art) which can
be separated from the rest of the man, just as a wheel can be separated from the
rest of the chariot; or again that the soul is one among many faculties which go
to make up the whole man. The flame simile, which is also supposed to be
directed against the soul-theory of the Brahmanic philosophy, is one which that
theory, far from rejecting, would accept as singularly apt. For just as fire uses
up fuel, and in doing so manifests itself as flame (that is, as burning fuel), so the
Soul, in its journey through the earth-life, continually uses up physical matter,
and in doing so manifests itself as a living body (that is, as physical matter
fused and vitalized by the Soul-fire). When the Soul retires from the physical
plane, the body, deprived of its vitalizing influence, disintegrates into dust, just
as fuel, when its fire is extinct, turns to ashes; but the Soul itself (if we may
follow its progress through the intervening stages of existence) continues to use
up matter, though, as the matter used is now impalpable, the Soul-flame
becomes invisible till the time comes for it to feed again on the fuel of physical
nature,—in other words, to appear again on earth. Even when Nâgasena's
hostility to the Ego is unmistakable, his belief in re-incarnation causes his
arguments to miscarry. He may flatter himself that he has disproved the
identity between A (who is living now) and B (the future inheritor of his
Karma); but, as a believer in re-incarnation, he must needs take pains to prove
that B will justly be held responsible for what A has done or left undone; and
in his attempt to make good this point he has to admit (or rather insist) that the
relation between A and B is exactly analogous to that between a "young girl"
and the same girl "when grown-up and marriageable."

Dr Rhys Davids has truly said that Buddha's "whole training was
Brahmanism; and that he probably deemed himself to be the most correct
exponent of the spirit as distinct from the letter of the ancient faith." If this is
a true statement of Buddha's attitude towards Brahmanism, it surely behoves
the student of Buddhism to seek initiation into the deeper mysteries of the
"ancient faith," before he attempts to interpret the creed of one who, while
breaking with the letter of that faith, "deemed himself to be the most correct
exponent of its spirit." This, however, is what the Western critic, with his
instinctive contempt for alien modes of thought, is extremely reluctant to do.
What he does, in nine cases out of ten, is to carry with him to the study of
Buddhism the prejudices and prepossessions of Western thought—foremost
among which is the assumption that nothing exists, in the order of nature,
except what is perceptible by man's bodily senses—and to insist that the
teaching of Buddha shall conform to these, and be measured by their standards.
Hence arise misconceptions and misunderstandings which might have been
avoided. If Buddhism seems to our Western minds to abound in errors and
anomalies, the reason is that we insist on looking at it through a distorting
medium. One who had steeped himself in the spirit of the Brahmanic
philosophy before he began his study of Buddhism, would see that wherever
Buddha seems to be denying existence to the Ego, what he is really doing is to
deny reality to the apparent Ego or superficial Self, so that he may thereby
clear the way for the exposition, not in words but in the unwritten language of

conduct, character, and life, of the profound conception which is the very quintessence of the "ancient faith,"—the conception "that Brahma and the Self—the true Self—are one."

(2) The Atheism of Buddha.

The Christian critics of Buddhism call Buddha an atheist, nominally because he said nothing about God, really because his conception of God differs from their own.

I have already attempted to show that the silence of Buddha about God—the Supreme Reality—was quite compatible with a sublimely spiritual conception of God and a deeply spiritual faith in him. I have shown that such a conception and such a faith were in the air that Buddha breathed, and that, if he had accepted them and made them his own, the very reverence which they would have generated would have bound him to silence in the presence of his audience,—the rank and file of mankind. I have shown that his own ethical teaching was the practical exposition of this unformulated theology,—the revelation of it, not as a theology but as a scheme of life, to those who would have been bewildered by it, and who would therefore have misunderstood and misapplied it, had any attempt been made to expound it to them in words, I have inferred from this that Buddha did believe in God, not as the West believes in him, but as the Far East, at the highest level of its imaginative thinking, has ever believed in him,—as the Supreme Reality which is at the heart of the] Universe, and which is at once the life and soul of Nature and the true self of Man.

But the fact remains that Buddha, though he preached the gospel of deliverance, said nothing about God. To us, with the Jehovah-virus in our veins, to us who for many centuries have been content to believe that the Universe is under the direct rule of that national deity whose sayings and doings are recorded in the Hebrew Scriptures, it seems the height of impiety to keep silence about God. It is well for us to remind ourselves that in the Far East, in the days of India's spiritual greatness, it was deemed the height of impiety to talk freely about God. We call the silence of the East atheistic. The sages of India, though they would have thought it discourteous to say so, would have regarded our loquacity as profane. To unveil to the mind of the average man ideas which are in the nature of things so large, so deep, and so subtle that, without mental power of a very high order, it is impossible to grasp their initial—let alone their final—meaning, is to expose the most sacred of all truths to the risk (the certainty, one might almost say) of being misinterpreted and misused. From such a risk the sages of India shrank as from blasphemy against the Divine. It may be difficult for us to enter into this feeling, but it is well that we should know that it did (and does) exist.

The silence of the Far East has another aspect, and one which is equally repugnant to the "orthodox" thought of the West. In itself, in the eloquence of its dumbness, it is an abiding protest, not merely against the profane loquacity of Western dogmatism, but also against its deadly despotism. To tell men that they must, under pain of eternal damnation, believe such and such things about God—or rather accept as divinely true such and such theological formulæ, whether they see any meaning in them or not—is to quench in their breasts that spark of spiritual freedom which is also the germ of spiritual life. It is true that the symbolical presentation of religious truth, which official Brahmanism adopted in preference to the doctrinal, may develop, as it certainly did in India, into a ceremonial despotism as oppressive as any that the creeds of the West have ever exerted. But Buddha's own silence was agnostic, in the deeper sense of the word, to the very core. We could imagine him saying to his disciples: "I have given you my reasons for urging you to enter the Path. If those reasons commend themselves to you, enter the Path and see to what goal it will lead you. But do not ask me to explain my own explanation. Do not ask me for deeper reasons than those which I have given you. Do not ask me to tell you what I, for one, believe about the greatest of all great matters. The words that make sense to me would ring as nonsense in your ears. The thoughts that bring light to me would dazzle you to the verge of blindness. And I should but deepen your perplexity if I tried to give you the guidance that you seek. But the Path itself will enlighten you if you will trust yourself to it; and when you have followed it far enough you will be wise with a wisdom beyond that of the wisest sage." The idea which underlies the whole of Buddha's teaching—underlying what he said and also what he left unsaid—the idea that knowledge of divine truth must be evolved from within, instead of being imposed from without, is the direct negation of that idea of a supernatural revelation, which underlies all the creeds of the West.

After all, it is not so much the silence of Buddha that the West regards as atheistic, as the creed which that silence hints at and seems, in a sense, to shadow forth,—a creed which seals the lips of those who see deepest into the heart of its hidden truth. The orthodox Christian, who believes that to give assent to a series of formulæ is to enter into possession of divine truth, and who therefore regards intolerance as a virtue and self-assertion as a sacred duty, feels instinctively that a creed which will not suffer itself to be formulated, and which therefore makes no attempt to impose its yoke upon human thought, is the hereditary enemy of his faith. His instinct has not misled him. Between the "Higher Pantheism" of India and the Supernaturalism of the Western World there is, in the region of ideas, a truceless war. Had Buddha tried to expound the creed of his heart, it would assuredly have been branded as atheistic by those who now apply that epithet to his silence. "Such divinity," said the late Canon Liddon, "as Pantheism can ascribe to Christ is, in point of fact, no divinity at all. God is Nature, and Nature is God; everything indeed is Divine, but also nothing is Divine; and Christ shares this phantom divinity with the universe,—nay with the agencies of moral evil itself. In truth, our God does not exist in the apprehension of Pantheistic thinkers; since, when such truths as creation and personality are denied, the very idea of God is fundamentally sapped, and . . . the broad practical result is in reality neither more nor less than Atheism." The writer of this passage proves nothing by his arguments but his fundamental inability to understand a creed which belongs to a plane of thought on which his mind has never learned to move: and, having misrepresented that creed beyond recognition, he brands it with a title which he regards as in the highest degree opprobrious and offensive. "Men become personal," says Dr Newman, "when logic fails; it is their mode of appealing to their own primary elements of thought and their own illative sense, against the principles and the judgment of another." When A calls B an atheist, he does not necessarily mean that B denies the existence of God. What he does mean is that B's conception of God differs fundamentally from his own, and that he cannot by any effort of thought place himself at B's point of view.

On the whole, then, I incline to the opinion that Christianity calls the teaching of Buddha atheistic, chiefly because it suspects that behind his scheme of life and at the heart of his silence dwells a rival conception of God. If this is so, Christianity has misplaced its censure; for if trust is of the essence of faith, there is no conception of God to which the term atheistic is so strangely inappropriate as to that which sealed the lips of Buddha. Curiosity and doubt are the foster-mothers of theology; but he who has once convinced himself, as Buddha must have done, that light and love are at the heart of the Universe, ceases to be curious about God. In the glow of his radiant and all-embracing optimism the petty theories by which man seeks to justify to himself the ways of God and his own timid faith in God, are seen to be worthless and vain. The sceptics who pride themselves on their "orthodoxy" are startled and alarmed by his silence. But out of its depths comes forth, whenever one listens for it, a message, not of atheistic denial but of whole-hearted trust in God,—trust so full, so firmly rooted, and so sure of itself, that silence alone can measure its strength and its serenity.

"And I say to mankind, Be not curious about God,
For I who am curious about each am not curious about God,
(No array of terms can say how much I am at peace about God and about death)."

(3) The Pessimism of Buddha.

In each of the charges that it brings against the teaching of Buddha, the West delimits with precision the range of its own thought. When it attempts to prove that Buddha denied the Ego, what it succeeds in proving is that its own conception of the Ego is as narrow and commonplace as that of the materialists and semi-materialists of Buddha's day. For the only reason that it gives for ascribing to Buddha denial of the Ego is that he refused to identify it with any of the things—form, sensation, and the like—of which the "ignorant, unconverted man" says, "This is mine; this am I."

So, too, when the West accuses Buddha of atheism, it tells us, by implication, how crudely anthropomorphic is its own conception of God. Buddha, who refused to individualize the Ego, would have been false to his deepest convictions had he allowed himself, in any respect or degree, to individualize the Supreme Reality. But because he kept silence about God rather than use words which might seem (however figuratively) to individualize him, he is held to have "denied the Divine." This means that if the West may not worship the Jewish Jehovah or some kindred deity, it will reject as untenable the whole idea of God.

Let us now consider the charge of pessimism which is so often brought against Buddha. In formulating this charge, the West defines with precision the limits of its own conceptions, first of happiness and then of the Universe. The true pessimist—who is also the true atheist—is he who sees darkness, and darkness only, at the heart of the Universe. Was Buddha a pessimist in this sense of the word? That he regarded the earth life as full of sorrow is undeniable. Does this convict him of pessimism? Not unless the earth-life is the only life, and the visible world the "all of being."

The impermanence of everything earthly seems to have impressed itself deeply on Indian thought. In the West we live, and are content to live, from year to year, and even from day to day; and we regard as permanent things that will last unchanged for a few generations, or even for a few years. But the far-sighted Indian mind, looking backward and forward through vast stretches of time, saw that sooner or later everything outward, however secure of life it might seem to be, must change and fade and pass away. To the Brahmanic thinkers the impermanence of things was a proof of their unreality. But Buddha, who made his appeal, first and foremost, to the "general heart of man," saw that impermanence reveals itself to the many, not as unreality but as sorrow. He saw also that the connection between impermanence and sorrow is the outcome of the widespread tendency to mistake the impermanent for the real. Men cling to shadows and lean on reeds. The shadows fail them, and so cause disappointment and disillusionment. The reeds "pierce their bosoms," "and then they bleed." Seeing that this was so and must be so, Buddha did what he could to make men realize that this life, as they conceived it, was full of suffering. But he did this, not because he despaired of Nature, but because he had unbounded trust in her. Far from teaching men that life was intrinsically evil, he taught them that the evil in it, the suffering which seemed to be of its essence, was in large measure the result of their own ignorance—their "ignorance of the true being and the true value of the Universe"—and that those who could detach themselves from whatever was impermanent and changeable might, even while on earth, enjoy a happiness higher and purer than any that the soul of man could consciously desire. So far was he from being a pessimist, in the deeper and darker sense of the word, that at the heart of Nature he could see nothing but light. If that light dazzled his eyes and blinded him to the lesser light that plays over the surface of life, his blindness was a proof, not of the despair of his soul, but of the very excess of its optimistic faith.

There are passages in the "Imitation of Christ" which might have been written by the Sages of the Upanishads. Such are "Amor ex Deo natus est; nec potest nisi in Deo requiescere." "Fili, ego debeo esse finis tuus supremus et ultimus, si vere desideras esse beatus." "Omnia vanitas præter amare Deum et isti soli servire." If Indian idealism is pessimistic, so is the outlook on earth and on life which finds expression in these inspired aphorisms. But surely it is not pessimism but abounding optimism which makes a man pitch his standard of happiness immeasurably high, and yet believe that the resources of the Universe are more than equal to any demand that the aspiring heart may make upon them. He who could say to his followers: "What you deem happiness is unworthy of the name. There are better things than this in store for you. There are treasures of happiness in store for you,—pure, perfect, imperishable, real. These will be given to you freely if you will but win them for yourselves":—he who could say this (or the equivalent of this) had reached the highest conceivable level of optimism. To accuse him of pessimism is to make confession of one's own lack of imagination, of insight, and of faith. Those who believe that the surface life is the only life and that its pleasures are the beginning and end of happiness, and who assume that Buddha's faith coincided with their own, may well regard him, when they yearn that he saw nothing but sorrow and suffering in the surface life and its pleasures, as the gloomiest and most uncompromising of pessimists. But the charge that they bring against him recoils upon themselves. If the surface life is the only life, and if its pleasures are the beginning and end of happiness, then indeed there is darkness—the darkness of death—at the heart of the Universe. But Buddha's conception of life, if he was true, as he believed himself to be, to "the spirit of the ancient faith," was the exact opposite of this; and what he saw at the heart of the Universe was, not the darkness of death, but the glory of Nirvâna.

(4) The Egoism of Buddha.

On this point the Western critics of Buddhism are divided. Some of them, including Dr Rhys Davids, Dr Paul Carus, and other enemies of the Ego, contend that Buddha's teaching was ultra-stoical, in that he bade men do right for right's sake only, the sole reward which the doer was allowed to look forward to being the enjoyment of inward peace during that twilight hour which should precede the final extinction of his life. 1 Others, including the critics who seek to depreciate Buddhism in the supposed interest of Christianity, contend that Buddha was an egoistic hedonist, who taught each man in turn to think of himself and his own welfare only, and whose conception of happiness had so little in it of idealism or aspiration that it scarcely rose above the level of providing for humanity an early escape from sorrow and pain.

The answer to those who regard Buddha as ultra-stoical is that, as a matter of plain historical fact, what he set before men, when he bade them enter the Path, was the prospect, not of doing right for right's sake (he would probably have seen no meaning in those words) but of winning release from suffering—the suffering of those who struggle in the whirlpool of rebirth,—and of entering into bliss—the bliss of those who will return to earth no more.

In giving this answer I may seem to justify the critics who brand Buddha's scheme of life as egoistic. But no. Buddha's scheme of life was as far from being egoistic as from being ultra-stoical. It is the word self that misleads us. With the doubtful exception of the word Nature, there is no word in which there are so many pitfalls. When we ask whether a given scheme of life is egoistic or not, our answer will entirely depend on the range of the self for which the scheme in question makes provision. To get away from self is impossible; but it may be possible to widen self till it loses its individuality and becomes wholly selfless. Long before that ideal point has been reached, long before the individual has become one with the Universal Self, the word egoistic will have lost its accepted meaning.

That Buddha's teaching was entirely free from the cant of altruism may be admitted without hesitation. Accepting as a fact, which can neither be gainsaid nor ignored, that every man naturally and instinctively seeks his own happiness, and that therefore in the last resort the desire for happiness is the only motive to which the moralist can appeal, Buddha took upon himself to teach men to distinguish the semblance of happiness from the reality, to detach themselves from the former and to win their way to the latter. "Tous les hommes," says Pascal, "recherchent d'être heureux: cela est sans exception. Quelques differents moyens qu'ils y emploient, ils tendent tous à ce but. C'est le motif de toutes les actions de tous les hommes, jusqu'à ceux qui vont se pendre." It is impossible for me to prefer my neighbour's happiness to my own; for if I am asked why I take such pains to make him happy, I can but answer (in the last resort) that it makes me happy to do so.

Buddha's teaching is equally free from the cant of Stoicism. To bid men do right for right's sake "in the scorn of consequence," is as though a doctor should order his patients to eat the right sort of food for the sake of its rightness, and without regard to its effect on the health of the eater. What is it that constitutes rightness in food,—and in conduct? The right food (from a doctor's point of view) is presumably the food that ministers most effectively to the health of the patient; and it is in the interest of his health, and not of any abstract conception of rightness, that the patient is advised to eat it. It is the same, mutatis mutandis, with right conduct. The exhortation to do right for right's sake is saved from being meaningless only by the tacit assumption that right doing makes, on the whole and in the long run, for the happiness of the doer. Indeed, it is because such and such courses of action make for the true happiness of him who follows them, and for no other reason, that we call them right. In other words, the epithet right, as applied to conduct, withholds its meaning from us until we define it in terms of happiness. That being so, it is surely better that the moralist should make his appeal (as Buddha openly did) to man's unquenchable desire for happiness than to a motive which would be utterly ineffective were it not that its air of sublime disinterestedness is, in the nature of things, a hollow sham.

But, while Buddha steered clear of the quick-sands of altruism and pseudo-stoicism, he took care not to wreck his scheme of life on the less dangerous, because more plainly visible, rock of egoism. It is when we begin to study the details of the scheme, that we see how little it deserves to be called egoistic. Based as it is on the conviction that the Ego—the real self—is not to be identified with "form," with "sensation," with "perception," or with anything else that is impermanent and changeable, it keeps one aim steadily in view,—to detach man, by a course of self-discipline which may last through many lives, from each of his apparent or lower selves, and to help him to find his true self. As it is attachment to the apparent or lower self—that tendency to identify oneself with what is impermanent and changeable, which makes one say of this thing and of that, "This is mine: this am I: this is my Ego"—as it is this clinging, grasping, self-asserting frame of mind which is the root of all selfishness] (to use a homelier word than egoism), it is clear that Buddha's scheme of life, far from, being egoistic or self-regarding, was in its essence a scheme for the extirpation of "self."

Buddha did not say to his disciples, what the altruist professes to say, "Thou shalt love thy neighbour better than thyself." He did not even say to them in so many words, "Thou shalt love thy neighbour as thyself." But he bade them enter a path which, if faithfully followed, would lead each man at last to love all men as himself. For if one is to escape from the impermanent, one must take refuge in the Eternal; and the Eternal and the Universal are the same fundamental reality looked at from different points of view. Every precept that Buddha gave has one positive aim in view,—to help the soul to expand its life or, in a word, to grow. But to the process of soul-growth there are no assignable limits. The soul has not attained to maturity, has not fulfilled its destiny, has not found its true self, until (according to the sublime conception which is at the heart of the "ancient faith") it has become one with the Universal Self, and in becoming one with it has become one with all men and all things. When that stage has been reached, when the Ego has become all-embracing, the last trace of "egoism" will have vanished, and the precept, "Thou shalt love thy neighbour as thyself" (the real meaning of which will not till then have been apprehended) will at last have been fulfilled. So, too, will the desire of the heart for happiness.

It is by the Christian, the professed follower of Christ, that the charge of egoism is most frequently brought against the teaching of Buddha. It is strange that such a charge should come from such a quarter. Will the Christian consent to brand as egoistic the teaching of his own Master? The conception of life which underlies Christ's searching question: "What is a man profited if he shall gain the whole world and lose his own soul?" is, according to the view that we are able to take of it, either ignobly selfish or sublimely self-forgetful. On this point opinions may differ. What is certain is that the gospel of Buddha is neither more nor less "egoistic" than the Gospel of Christ. For at the heart of each gospel is the same overmastering conviction that it is better for a man to find "his own soul"—his own true self—than to "gain the whole world."

In conclusion. The desire for unreal happiness—the Protean desire which Buddha sought to extinguish—leads us into all the highways and byways of selfishness, and into every haunt of error and delusion; and the phantom which is ever flitting before us ends by eluding our grasp. But the desire for real happiness—the desire which Buddha at once appealed to and strove to foster—is the desire (self-justifying and self-fulfilling) for oneness with the All; nor will that "egoistic" desire have found final fulfilment till it has provided an escape for the soul from the prison-house of "self" into the boundless ether of love.

(5) The Nihilism of Buddha.

The supreme end of Buddhist endeavour, the last term in its ascending "series," is Nirvâna. When the Path has been followed to its goal, when the victory over self has been fully won, when the prize of victory has been fully earned, the emancipated soul (if I may use that word "without prejudice") passes away from earth, passes beyond the vision of "Gods and men" and enters the bliss of Nirvâna. What does this mean? The "Perfect One" has disappeared from the eye of thought behind the veil of human experience. What is there behind that veil? What is there behind the last of the many veils which life (as we who are living on earth understand the word) hangs before our eyes? The question as to the destiny of the Perfect One and the question as to the real life of those who are now on earth are (as Sâriputta saw clearly) one and the same. What is the answer to them?

The answer which the learned criticism of the West ordinarily gives, and which the popular criticism of the West faithfully echoes, is, in a word, Nothing. "Tout se réunit," says Barthélemy Saint-Hilaire, "pour démontrer que le

Nirvâna n'est au fond que l'anéantissement définitif et absolu de tous les éléments qui composent l'existence." According to Eugène Burnouf, "Le Nirvâna est l'anéantissement complet, non seulement des éléments matériels de l'existence, mais de plus et surtout du principe pensant." These statements are typical, and I need not add to them.

The word Nirvâna means "going out" or "extinction." But, as Dr Rhys Davids explains with force and clearness, what is extinguished, when Nirvâna is won, is not existence but passion and desire. In support of this thesis Dr Rhys Davids appeals to some verses in one of the Sacred Books of Buddhism, in which "we have an argument based on the logical assumption that if a positive exists its negative must also exist; if there is heat, there must be cold; and so on. In one of these pairs we find existence opposed, not to Nirvâna, but to non-existence; whilst in another the three fires [of lust, hatred and delusion] are opposed to Nirvâna." But, though Dr Rhys Davids is careful to distinguish Nirvâna from annihilation, he is bound by his own assumption, that Buddha denied the Ego, denied "that there is anything of any kind which continues to exist, in any manner, after death," to regard Nirvâna as the prelude to annihilation. For him, then, and for those who think with him, Nirvâna, on which the Buddhist writings have ever "lavished" "awe-struck and ecstatic praise," is the twilight hour that precedes the night of Nothingness,—an hour in which the "Perfect One," having at last extinguished the fires of lust, hatred and delusion, enjoys the bliss of perfect peace. "Death, utter death, with no new life to follow, is a result of but it is not Nirvâna."

It matters little whether Nirvâna is itself the night of Nothingness, or the twilight hour which precedes that night. The goal of the Path is, in either case, the premature annihilation of him who walks in it. When the Perfect One has lifted the last veil of illusion and passed behind it into the reality which it hides from thought, he becomes absorbed into Nothing. It follows that the self-existent] Reality which underlies all appearances and which is therefore at the very heart of the Universe is, in a word, Nothing.

Did Buddha really believe this? Was it in the strength of this supreme negation that he devoted his life to the enlightenment and emancipation of his fellow-men, and won to his will the hearts of all who listened to his teaching? The hypothesis which we are invited to accept as an established conclusion, is so wildly improbable, that we have a right to ask those who formulate it to bring forward strong documentary evidence in support of it. As it happens, no such evidence is forthcoming. On the one hand, the passages in the Buddhist Scriptures on which the hypothesis has been based all admit of an entirely different interpretation,—namely, that after the death of the body the Perfect One ceases to exist, not absolutely, but only in the sense which "the ignorant, unconverted man" attaches to the word existence. On the other hand, there are passages in the Buddhist Scriptures in which the hypothesis is directly or indirectly traversed; such as the dialogue between Yamaka and Sâriputta, in which the belief that "on the dissolution of the body the monk who has lost all depravity is annihilated" is first condemned as a wicked heresy and then conclusively refuted; or, again, as the dialogue between King Pasenadi and the nun Khemâ, in which the question as to the existence of the Perfect One after death is shown to be unanswerable, not because the Perfect One will then have ceased to be, but because he will have passed beyond the reach of human thought.

It is worthy of note (though the point seems to have escaped the notice of the Western students of Buddhism) that the question "What becomes of the ordinary, unemancipated man when he dies?" is never asked in any Buddhist dialogue. Why is this? Evidently because the doctrine of re-incarnation is the accepted answer to the question. What interests King Pasenadi, the monk Yamaka, and others is not the general question "What comes after death?" but the particular question, "What becomes of the Perfect One when he finally passes away from earth?" The answer to this question is always the same. "Do not ask. The question is unanswerable. The Perfect One passes, when he dies, beyond the remotest horizon of human thought; and when thought fails, words can do nothing but perplex and mislead."

The truth is that here, as elsewhere, when the West seems to be passing judgment on Buddhism, it is really delimiting the range of its own thought. To the consideration of the problem of the Perfect One's final state, as of all kindred problems, Western thought carries with it the metaphysical assumption which has obsessed it for two thousand years,—the assumption that nothing exists, in the order of Nature, except what is perceptible by man's bodily senses. The religious thought of the West has always taken refuge from the consequences of this assumption in the dream-world of the Supernatural. But the dualism of Nature and the Supernatural was (and is) entirely foreign to Indian thought. Seeing, then, that Buddha transported the Perfect One beyond the vision of Gods and men, and yet provided no asylum for him in any Supernatural heaven, the Western exponents of Buddhism find themselves driven to conclude, with the monk Yamaka, that "on the dissolution of his body" the Perfect One "is annihilated, perishes, and does not exist after death." But it is Western, not Indian, thought which creates the vacuum that receives the Perfect One's emancipated soul. When Dr Rhys Davids, after quoting Buddha's words, "While his body shall remain he will be seen by Gods and men, but after the termination of life, upon the dissolution of the body, neither Gods nor men will see him," asks: "Would it be possible in a more complete or categorical manner to deny that there is any soul—anything of any kind which continues to exist, in any manner, after death?" there is an obvious answer to his triumphant challenge. It is by assuming that Buddha, too, believed in the intrinsic reality of what is perceptible and the non-existence of what is imperceptible, that he proves his point. But has he any right to make that assumption? Is not Buddha's attitude towards the problem of reality the very question which is really (though not ostensibly) in dispute? And inasmuch as Buddha devoted his life to teaching men that the perceptible is the unreal, is it not rash, to say the least, to assume offhand that his mind was ruled by the fundamental postulate of Western thought? Yet, unless his mind was ruled by that postulate, the words on which Dr Rhys Davids lays so much stress can be shown to have another meaning than that which he ascribes to them, and the conclusion—that Buddha regarded death as the end of life—instead of being obviously true, becomes demonstrably false. What Buddha meant (if we may argue from the general tenor of his teaching) when he said that, upon the dissolution of the Perfect One's body, neither Gods nor men would see him, was not that the Perfect One would then pass into non-existence, but rather that then at last he would attain to absolute reality. For the perceptible world, as Buddha conceived of it, is the world of dreams and shadows; and it is therefore clear that, until the Perfect One has passed, wholly and irrevocably, beyond the horizon of perception, 1 he has not found rest in the Real.

Let us now attempt, in defiance of Buddha's express prohibition, to penetrate the mystery of Nirvâna. The mystery is, in a sense, final. The Path ends—for good and all—in Nirvâna. The Western hypothesis that Nirvâna is not the final state of the Perfect One, but the prelude to that state, is wholly gratuitous. Not a word is said in any of the passages with which the students of Buddhism have made us familiar, which might seem to suggest that the Nirvânic state ends with the death of the Perfect One's body, or that there is any state of existence (or non-existence) beyond it. 2 That Buddha, who turned the prying mind back on the hither brink of Nirvâna, should have looked beyond Nirvâna and told men what was awaiting them on its farther shore, is in the highest degree improbable. The progress of the Perfect One is followed till Nirvâna begins:

> "But there sight fails. No heart may know
>   The bliss when life is done."

The question, then, which we have to ask ourselves is this: What goal would he be likely to reach who followed the Path to the end? This question suggests a second: What is the Path supposed to do for him who walks in it? The answer to this question is embodied in Buddha's scheme of life. The Path detaches him who walks in it from the impermanent, the changeable, the phenomenal. But it does this, not by the ascetic curtailment of the range of his life, but by the progressive expansion of his consciousness. It will be remembered that Buddha told his disciples in the earliest of his discourses that they were to steer a middle course between the "unworthy and unreal" paths of pleasure on the one side, and mortification on the other. It will also be remembered that the precepts which he gave them aimed, to make a general statement, at the cultivation of two faculties,—self-control and sympathy. The function of self-control is, on the one hand, to train the will for the task that awaits it,—the task of directing the process of soul-growth; and, on the other hand, to prevent the lower and narrower self from becoming so aggressive as to arrest the outgrowth of the higher and larger self. And the function of sympathy, which carries a man out of himself into the lives of others, is to promote the outgrowth of the higher and larger self, by raising the level and widening the range of one's life. Thus the Path detaches men from the phenomenal, not by cutting it out of their lives or otherwise blinding them to its existence, but by giving them the power (through the expansion of their consciousness) of seeing it in its true proportions and its true light. It is possible for one who walks in the Path to take an interest and a pleasure in the ephemeral concerns of life, and yet to hold on to them by the very lightest of threads. There is nothing of Puritanical gloom or sourness in the teaching of Buddha. The foreglow of Nirvâna falls on the Path and throws its rays on either side of it, till those who walk in it learn at last to take an innocent delight even in the things which they know to be phantasmal.

Now the goal of the Path is the natural consummation of it,—not a reward which will be given by an omnipotent onlooker to those who have kept to the Path and obeyed its commandments, but the end to which the Path naturally and inevitably leads; an end which is not merely pre-figured by the Path, even in its earlier stages, but is also, in some sort, present in promise and potency in those earlier (and all subsequent) stages, just as the full-grown oak is present in promise and potency in the acorn and the sapling, or the ripened peach in the fruit-bud and the blossom. And inasmuch as the function of the Path is to detach men from the phenomenal by expanding their consciousness, and to expand their consciousness by fostering the growth of their souls, it seems to follow that the goal of the Path will be the ideal perfection of him who walks in it, and that when this ideal state has been reached the consciousness of the Perfect One (as we may now call him) will have become all-embracing, and his detachment from the phenomenal complete. We are now in a position to give this tentative and provisional answer to the question, What is Nirvâna? Nirvâna is a state of ideal spiritual perfection, in which the soul, having completely detached itself—by the force of its own natural expansion—from what is individual, impermanent, and phenomenal, embraces and becomes one with the Universal, the Eternal, and the Real. In other words, the essence of Nirvâna is the finding of the ideal self, in and through the attainment to oneness—living, conscious oneness—with the All and the Divine.

It is true that Buddha spoke of consciousness as one of the five things from which the "learned and noble disciple" must strive to detach himself; but he obviously meant by consciousness what his audience, composed for the most part of ordinary unenlightened men, would have understood the word to mean,—that sense of selfhood which is based on the sense of difference from other things, In the Nirvânic consciousness the sense of selfhood is based on the sense of oneness with other things, or rather of oneness with the vital essence of all things,—with the living Whole. 'When we predicate consciousness of him who has passed into Nirvâna, what we mean is that the Nirvânic state of being is on the farther, not on the hither, side of consciousness; that it enormously transcends what we, with our limited range of perception and thought, understand by consciousness, but that it is reached by the continuance of the same process of growth by which consciousness itself has been evolved. The Western mind, which is dominated, even in its seasons of speculative activity, by mathematical and mechanical conceptions, understands by oneness with the Divine a quasi-material absorption into the Whole, which involves the complete extinction of consciousness in him who

"Slips into the shining sea."

The Indian conception of oneness with the Divine is the polar opposite of this. If soul is to mingle with soul it must do so as soul, preserving, yet raising to an infinite power, all the characteristics of soul life,—its freedom and self-compulsion (which it now realizes as infinite energy), its thought (which it now realizes as infinite wisdom), its desire (which it now realizes as infinite love).

Such, in shadowy outline, is the conception of Nirvâna which my study of Buddha's teaching, from the standpoint of Indian idealism, has forced upon my mind. That I carried the conception with me is undeniable, and that I should eventually work round to it was no doubt pre-ordained. But the curve of thought which I have completed has helped me to enrich and deepen the conception, for it has enabled me to trace the steps by which the genius and practical wisdom of one gifted Teacher could transform a philosophical idea into a master principle of action, and so make it available for the daily needs of mankind. To the Sages of the Upanishads re-union with the Divine was the goal of meditative aspiration,—a goal which few could hope to reach, for the path to it was one which few could find and fewer still could follow. Buddha saw that it was also the goal of spiritual growth, and that as such it could be reached—in the fullness of time—by the lowliest and most ignorant of men. But he saw also that, as the goal of spiritual growth (and therefore of spiritual endeavour), it must be pursued unconsciously; that the path to it must be clearly defined, but that of the goal itself nothing was to be predicated except that it was the home of happiness and peace.

Dr Oldenberg complains that Buddha's teaching is a "fragment of a circle to complete which and to find the centre of which is forbidden by the Thinker." But if we place at the centre of the circle the sovereign dogma of Indian idealism, if we assume that Nirvâna, the admitted end of Buddhist desire and endeavour, is a state of self-realization through union with the Divine or Universal Soul, the circle will complete itself: for we shall see a meaning in every precept that Buddha gave, and in every argument that he used; we shall see a meaning in every discourse and dialogue which Western thought has (on this hypothesis) misunderstood; we shall see a meaning in the Western misunderstanding of Buddha's teaching; we shall see a meaning in Buddha's mysterious silence; and we shall see that his scheme of life was a "perfect round,"—a coherent and consistent whole. Nor are we making a random guess when we fix that particular centre for Buddha's circle of thought. "Of all plane figures the circle alone has the same curvature at every point." If Buddha's ethical teaching was indeed a fragment of a circle, then it is possible for those who care to do so, both to complete the circle and to find its centre. But we must be allowed to assume, before we undertake this task, that the fragment which is before us is part of a circle and not of any less perfect curve. The conception which Western critics, in their desire to claim Buddha as of their own school of thought, place at the centre of his philosophy, has the grave demerit of turning what is supposed to be the fragment of a circle into a fragment, or series of fragments, of one of the wildest and most lawless of curves. But if we assume that Buddha's scheme of life, as it existed in his mind, was a "perfect round," and that what he chose to formulate was a fragment of that "perfect round," we shall find that there is only one possible centre to it,—the conception which history, psychology, and common-sense unite in suggesting to us as central,—the conception that the Universal Self is the true self of each one of us, and that to realize the true self is the destiny and the duty of man.

The Bankruptcy of Western Thought

THE higher thought of the West is bankrupt, in the sense that it can no longer meet its obligations. When I say this I do not merely mean that its liquid assets are less than its liabilities. It is desirable that the liabilities of thought should at all times far exceed its liquid assets, and it would point to a lamentable lack of speculative enterprise if they did not. What I do mean is that the liabilities which Western thought has incurred are greatly in excess of its resources,—of its realizable as well as its liquid assets.

Let us see how this has come to pass. The function of high thinking is to provide working capital for the speculative enterprises of the soul. The speculative enterprises of the soul take the form of spiritual desires. The working capital which thought provides takes the form of philosophical ideas,—tentative and provisional theories of things. As it seldom happens, in the commercial world, that an enterprise which is thoroughly successful does not ask, from time to time, for fresh capital in order that, without departing from its original aim, it may widen the field of its operations and reach a yet higher level of success,—so in the inner life of man, whenever the desires of the heart receive genuine satisfaction, the proof of this lies in the fact that, in response to a fresh influx of ideas, new desires arise which are really new developments of the old, or, in other words, that the old desires, stimulated and modified by thought, become deepened, widened, purified, and otherwise transformed.

Sometimes, however, it happens that the "ideals" which thought provides, in response to the demands of spiritual desire, become stereotyped into systems of "dogma," and as such are accepted by the heart as fully and finally true. When this happens the development of spiritual desire ceases, or, in the language of commerce, the soul becomes so unenterprising that its liabilities, now brought within a very narrow compass, are fully met by its liquid assets. In this state of ignoble solvency, the soul, having ceased to grow—for its desires are its growing pains—has begun to degenerate and to turn its face towards death. Then comes the inevitable reaction. The expansive energies of Nature, which triumphant dogmatism had long held in check, force at last a new outlet for themselves, and in doing so stimulate the deeper desires of the heart into new activity and direct them into new channels. In such an epoch the need of the soul for fresh capital—for new ideas—is stronger than it has ever been, but the difficulty of finding it is greater. For as the soul has long since closed its capital account, the sources of supply, which are fed by the very demands that are made upon them, will have long since ceased to flow. The old stereotyped ideas have satisfied the soul for so many years that the organs of spiritual thought, atrophied by disuse, have at last become incapable of supplying new ideas,—the negative dogmas which man formulates in his season of reaction and revolt being, if anything, narrower and more rigid than the positive dogmas of the churches and sects. What happens, then, when the old order changes, is that the soul, carried by its outburst of speculative enterprise far beyond the limits of the ideas which had so long sufficed for its needs, takes upon itself obligations for which its working capital—its spiritual philosophy—is wholly inadequate. The end of this is that it drifts into a state of insolvency, in which it pays the penalty of having so long been ignobly solvent. Or, rather, it is the thought of the age which goes bankrupt, for thought is under a permanent obligation to supply the soul, in its adventurous moods, with the capital which it needs for its enterprises.

This is what has happened in the West. And if we ask ourselves why this has happened, we can but answer that Western thought has, from the beginning of things, allowed itself to be dominated by the ideas of the "average man." The philosophy of the average man is simplicity itself. He begins, as all men necessarily do, with the apparent antithesis of himself and the outward world. While his philosophy is in its sub-conscious stage, he is content to ascribe reality to both the terms of the antithesis. But when he begins to reflect, in his crude way, on "great matters," his standpoint changes. Utterly incapable of subtle thinking, his mind instinctively relapses into the vulgar dualism of the existent and the non-existent. The aphorism, "Seeing is believing," dominates his thought; and the naïvely egoistic assumption that what the Universe seems to be to his bodily senses that it is in itself, and that therefore nothing exists, in the order of Nature, except what is perceptible by the bodily senses, becomes the cardinal article of his faith. But the consequences of this materialistic assumption are repugnant to his heart. And so, in response to the demands of his heart, his mind devises a supplementary theory of things,—the conception of a world above Nature in which the higher realities of which his bodily senses can take no cognizance, may find an asylum. Foremost among these higher realities are those towards which his religious instincts direct themselves,—supreme, or, as he calls it, divine goodness, divine wisdom, divine power.

Thus instead of one Universe the average man must needs have two,—Nature and the Supernatural World; and between these two a great gulf is fixed in his thought, a gulf of nothingness which makes natural intercourse between the two worlds impossible. But, as always happens in a dualism, the intervening gulf of nothingness drains into itself the reality of both worlds; draining away from Nature her inwardness, her spirituality, and, in the last resort, her life; draining away from the world above Nature its substance, its actuality, and all of it that is convincingly real.

The fatal influence of this dualistic cosmology will make itself felt long after the idea of the Supernatural has lost its hold upon human thought. Meanwhile, the ascendency of the idea is fraught with serious danger to the spiritual development of mankind. It is not enough that a supernatural world should be evolved by thought in response to the demands of the heart. Intercourse with that world must somehow or other be opened up and carried on. And as natural intercourse between the two worlds is impossible, supernatural inter-course must take its place. The gulf cannot be passed by man; but God, who dwells beyond it, can pass it at his own good pleasure and in his own good time. Hence comes the general idea of supernatural revelation, with all its sub-ideas,—the idea of divinely selected peoples, of divinely commissioned teachers, of divinely inspired scriptures, of divinely guided churches, and the rest. We need not follow the idea into all these details, but we shall do well to follow it into some of its inevitable consequences. What is revealed to man from the supernatural world, by whatever means the intercourse between the two worlds may be carried on, is obviously "the Truth." As such, if it is to be made available for man's needs, it must admit of being formulated and. taught. In other words, the dogmatic 1 standpoint and the dogmatic temper are necessary corollaries to the general idea that the truth of things can be revealed to man by the Supernatural God. Between dogmatism and free-thought there is, in the nature of things, a truceless war. The conception of truth as an un-attainable ideal, the quest of which is "its own exceeding great reward," is wholly incompatible with the dogmatic standpoint. The exercise of speculative thought is indeed permitted by dogmatism, but under conditions which make the concession a mockery. Not only must its enterprises be carried on within narrow and strictly defined limits, but they must also lead it to pre-ordained conclusions. This means that "high thinking," the thought which makes what is defined and accepted the starting-point of its enterprises, is not merely discountenanced by dogmatism, but rigorously repressed. But the repression (or restriction) of speculative thought means the repression (or restriction) of spiritual desire. For thought both indicates the general direction in which desire is to operate, and provides it with the working capital for its bolder ventures. It follows that, when the working capital which thought is allowed to provide is strictly limited in amount, and when that limited amount is accepted by desire as entirely adequate to its needs, desire itself is bringing its speculative operations to a standstill. In other words, dogmatism limits the scope of desire in the very act of limiting the sphere of thought; and so far as it is successful in imposing those limits, it tends to arrest the growth of the soul.

These are general conceptions. Let us return to the history of Western thought. It is to the genius of one small nation that the West owes, for good or for evil, its spiritual standpoint. Jehovah, the God of Israel, is accepted as the Lord Paramount of the Universe by the greater part of the Western World, those who are in rebellion against his authority being unable to find any rival claimant to his throne. Whatever may be one's own attitude towards the ideas which Israel evolved and formulated, one cannot but admire the strenuousness and force of character which enabled a small, remote, and politically feeble nation to force its conception of God and Man and Nature upon the thought and the conscience of the Græco-Roman world. But admiration of Israel's character and achievements must not blind us to the fact that his astonishing success as a propagandist was due to his weakness, not less than to his strength. The genius of Israel was essentially practical. In his seasons of spiritual expansion it became poetical; and his poetry, which reflected the intensity as well as the narrowness of his nature, was (at its highest level), in the fullest sense of the word, sublime. But he easily fell, as we all do, below the level of poetic rapture; and when he began to fall, he dropped to ignominious depths. For he had no philosophy, in the deeper sense of the word, to sustain him. Singularly destitute of "ideas," he was incapable of effective self-criticism (though abundantly capable both of self-exaltation and self-depreciation); and he followed his quasi-commercial conception of religious duty into the most meticulous details of legalism, fully believing that in doing so he was working the will of God. For intellectual meditation, for sustained and concentrated reflection, for the depths and the subtleties of thought, he had no turn whatever. His philosophy was that of the average man, and his triumph has been, in part at least, the triumph of the average man's ideas. Addressing himself to ordinary people—the people who believe that the visible world is the real world, and yet are unwilling to accept the logical consequences of that belief—he won their whole-hearted support by meeting them on their own intellectual level, by speaking to them in their own language, by expounding to them their own theory of things. His explanation of the Universe, with all its subsidiary conceptions: the conception of a personal and supernatural God, made in the image of Man; of the creation of the visible world by the fiat of God's will; of the disobedience of Man to God's commandments, and his consequent fall from innocence and bliss; of the selection of a certain people as the depository of the truths which God chose to reveal to fallen Man; of the formulation of God's will in a code of law; of the promise of God's favour to those who should obey that law, and of his wrath to those who should disobey it;—all this, as far as it goes, is just such an explanation as the average man, if his curiosity was thoroughly awakened, would, in his attempt to account for the more striking facts of existence and at the same time to give satisfaction to the master desires of his heart, be likely to evolve for himself. What wonder that when, through the magnetic influence of Christ's gracious and commanding personality and through the self-sacrificing devotion of the high-souled Jews who transmitted that influence to the Gentiles, the Jewish scriptures became known far and wide, the Jewish scheme of things—crowned and completed by the conception of Christ as the mediator between God and Man and the redeemer of fallen Humanity, and so made available for all believers, irrespective of race—should have been accepted as an authoritative explanation of all the mysteries of existence?

It is true that, along with his own philosophy, systematized and dramatized for him by Israel, the average man received some fragments of the spiritual teaching of Christ. But he accepted that teaching, not for its own sake, not for the sake of the philosophy that was behind it—of that he knew nothing, and had it been revealed to him he would have shrunk from it with suspicion and alarm—but for the sake and on the authority of Christ. His own interpretation of it was, as might have been expected, at best one-sided and inadequate, at worst literal and mechanical; and so disquieting were its precepts, owing to his inability to enter into their spirit, that an instinctive regard for his own mental balance and sanity led him in nine cases out of ten to ignore them completely. But the fact remains that, in a sense and in a manner, he did receive the spiritual teaching of Christ, and that from then till now the ferment of it has been at work in his heart. As, however, it was through the example rather than the words of his Master that the spiritual ideas which have been the leaven of his inner life were transmitted to him, it is not to be wondered at that his reception of them has been in the main a subconscious process, and that they have not materially modified the movement of his conscious thought. 1 For many centuries, indeed, his acceptance of his own philosophy was complete. Those who offered to shake his faith in it—Gnostics, Arians, Albigenses, and the like—fared ill at his hands. Through his Agent-General, the Pope, and in the Councils which were dominated by his "collective wisdom," he waged relentless war against heretics and schismatics; and at last things came to such a pass that whoever sent even a faint ripple of doubt over the stagnant lagoon of his (so-called) faith, whoever said or did anything which might conceivably give him the trouble of turning over in his orthodox slumber, was liable to be burned at the stake.

This triumph, in the region of speculative thought, of the average over the exceptional man, was a misfortune for the human race. For it involved the suppression of high-thinking, which is in its very essence a departure from the commonplace and the average; and the suppression of high-thinking involves, in the last resort, the suppression of spiritual desire. Not, indeed, that it is possible for spiritual desire to be finally suppressed. The expansive forces of Nature, the expression of which in man's inner life constitutes his spiritual desire, may be dammed back for centuries, but sooner or later they will find a new outlet for themselves. This is what happened in the West. The revival of classical learning, the invention of printing, the discoveries of distant lands, and other influences which need not here be considered, all working in unison with the secret leaven of Christ's spiritual teaching, combined to generate a new life in the soul of man. Long heralded and long delayed, the day of liberation dawned at last. In the age (or ages) of the Renascence there was a remarkable lateral expansion of desire. In the age (or ages) of the Reformation there was an equally remarkable purification and elevation of desire. The triumph of the average man had been too complete, and its inevitable Nemesis had duly come. The soul of man, which had long lain in a comatose slumber and which had made many abortive efforts to arouse itself, was now at last alive and awake, and ready for new speculative ventures. Full of energy and enterprise, it turned to thought for the working capital that it needed,—for the help and guidance which large ideas alone can supply.

But there was no response to its appeal.

Before the Western mind could begin to think, it had to vindicate its right to think. In other words, it had to fight for freedom. That fight is still in progress, and the end of it is not yet in sight. Meanwhile, the speculative achievements of Western thought have been, in the nature of things, inconsiderable. Of its triumphant success in the sphere of physical science I need not speak. Physical science is not philosophy. Nor need I pause to consider that metaphysical movement which is supposed to have been initiated by Descartes. The successive idealistic ventures which have been one of the distinguishing features of that movement, have all been "apparent failures." The truth is that high-thinking had been so long and so rigorously suppressed that, even in the efforts which the Western mind has made to free itself from bondage to the average man's ideas, it has shown at every turn the baneful effect of his ascendency. It is a mistake to suppose that the struggle for freedom which has been in progress for five centuries has been wholly, or even in large measure, conducted by men of exceptional mental gifts. It was pre-ordained, one might almost say, that the average man should himself take a leading part in it. Whenever the average man is allowed, as he has been in the West, to control the larger movements of thought, however carefully his philosophy may be formulated by the theologians and guarded by the Churches, the day will surely come when, in his individual capacity, he will rise in revolt against himself in his corporate capacity, and range himself, in his attempt to vindicate the right of private judgment, by the side of the exceptional men whom, in his corporate capacity, he is only too ready to burn. But, in entering into this anomalous alliance, he illogically claims, and half-unconsciously exercises, the right to impose the fundamental assumption of his philosophy on the minds of his allies. And though he is at one with them in their demand for freedom of conscience, he leaves them, and leaves himself, but little room for the exercise of that sacred right.

This is one among many reasons why the average man's fundamental assumption—that the physical plane is the whole of Nature—still dominates Western thought. In the deadly shade of that assumption his spiritual ideas wither almost as soon as they are born. In his own philosophy materialism is still modified by supernaturalism. But, in rejecting the old theologies which formulated and systematized his belief in the Supernatural, and the old organizations which guarded it from criticism, he has exposed it to the danger of being undermined by speculative thought. Indeed, it is no exaggeration to say that the one solid achievement of critical thought in the West, in recent years, has been to undermine the belief in the Supernatural and to discredit the whole theory of things which was built on that insecure foundation. The immediate consequences of this achievement have been and will long be disastrous. Take away from the philosophy of the average man the conception of the Supernatural,—and materialism, pure and simple, remains.

It is sometimes said that in the present age there is a feud, with regard to "great matters," between the "heart" and the "head." The feud is also, though less correctly, spoken of as one between Religion and Science. Strictly speaking, the parties to the quarrel are two rival theories of things—Supernaturalism, which seems, for the time being, to satisfy the "heart," and Materialism, which seems, for the time being, to satisfy the "head." To identify religion with supernaturalism is as unfair as to hold science responsible for materialism. The religious instinct invented supernaturalism, as an antidote to the materialism of popular thought; and the spread of scientific habits of thought discredited supernaturalism, and so re-habilitated materialism as the philosophy of the average man in his seasons of "free-thought." But the hypothesis of a world above Nature is as little of the essence of religion, as is the materialistic degradation of Nature of the essence of science.

That there is, in the present age, a feud between the "head" and the "heart"—between "reason" and "faith"—is, I think, undeniable. The churches and sects denounce "rationalism" as vehemently as the Free-thinkers and Agnostics (to give them the titles which they have appropriated, but to which they have no claim) denounce "superstition." The very platform on which the head and the heart meet in their controversy, is the tacit assumption that their respective philosophies are the only possible solutions of the problem of the Universe. "Quit the fold of the Church," says the votary of "faith," "and you will sink deeper and deeper into the quagmire of materialism, till you end by denying God, denying the soul, denying the life beyond the grave." "Cease to believe in God," says the "Free-thinker," "cease to believe in the soul, cease to dream of a life beyond the grave, or you will find yourself committed to all the assumptions of supernaturalism, and, sinking deeper and deeper into the quagmire of superstition, you will end by surrendering your conscience to the casuist and your freedom to the priest." It is a significant fact that in France, where the average man is more logical and clear-headed than in any other country, there are (when all is said and done) two parties and two only,—Catholics and "Free-thinkers." Between these two there is a deep-seated and far-reaching feud. It might almost be said that every Frenchman is bound to range himself on one side or the other in that deadly quarrel, bound to subscribe to all the positive dogmas of Catholic theology or, failing that, to all the negative dogmas of what miscalls itself "Free-thought,"—a creed which centres in the dogmatic denunciation of "the deplorable superstition of a life after death." Between ecclesiastical supernaturalism and secularistic materialism there seems to be no middle term. But if in France every man is either a Catholic or a "Free-thinker," in other countries, where men are less logical, it not unfrequently happens that the same person passes and re-passes between the two hostile camps. Again and again one sees the young man who has been nurtured in the ancient faith, reject supernaturalism as an irrational hypothesis, and go forth, exulting in his freedom, in quest of a truer and deeper philosophy; and sometimes one sees the same man, weary of a creed which authoritatively tells him, while the shadows are lengthening on his path, that death is the end of life, creep back in his old age to the fold which he had quitted in his youth, and justify himself for his second apostasy by arguing that, as an interpreter of the deeper mysteries of existence, the heart is, in all probability, more to be trusted than the head.

Assuming that there is a feud between the head and the heart, let us ask ourselves how the feud has originated, what it indicates, and how it is to be healed. We mean by the "heart" the headquarters of desire,—by the "head" the headquarters of thought. The function of the head is to supply the heart with the working-capital that it needs for its speculative enterprises, in other words, with the "ideas" that it needs for the due evolution of its spiritual desires. It sometimes happens that the heart goes to the head for ideas, and is sent empty away. But these are exceptional cases. As a rule, when there is a complete dearth of ideas, the reason is that there has been no demand for them, the soul having become so un-enterprising that the unexpended balance of its original capital proves to be more than sufficient for its needs. But Nemesis waits, as we have seen, on this ignoble solvency. Sooner or later the soul will awake from its orthodox slumber, and make itself ready for new speculative ventures. Then there will be an immense expansion of desire, and a corresponding need for new ideas. For a time, indeed, that need will not be acutely felt. A sustained attempt will be made to pour the new wine into the old bottles, to finance the new enterprises with the old capital. But after a time the inadequacy of the old ideas will be realized; and the heart will go to the head for the new ideas that its expanding desires imperatively demand. But the head, having had no call made upon it, will have long since ceased to enlarge its own capital; and when the heart goes to it, it must either confess itself insolvent, or try to dissuade the heart from committing itself to enterprises which it (the head) is unable to finance. In self-defence it will take the latter course. It will say to the heart: "These enterprises for which you ask financial help are mad and impossible, and will end in your utter ruin. Abandon them, one and all, and limit your desires to what is measurable and attainable. For that I will provide you with the limited amount of capital that you will need, but on one condition,—that I am allowed to become a partner in your business."

How will the heart receive this advice? The new desires for which it needs working capital are not revolutionary ventures, but natural and necessary developments of its old desires. To tell it that these new desires are mad and impossible enterprises is to tell it, by implication, that the whole of its business is unsound. Both the head and the heart will feel instinctively that the former's response to the latter's demand for ideas amounts to this. Were it possible for the head to say, in response to the heart's appeal: "Your business has contracted and otherwise deteriorated owing to your having, through indolence and timidity, neglected to expand it: but the business itself—the fundamental desires which you seek to exploit—is sound enough; all that is needed is that you should enlarge your capital and develop your business in new directions and on a bolder scale":—were it possible for this stimulating answer to be given to the expectant heart, the inner life of man would be quickened into new activity, and a new season of soul-growth would be begun. But it is not possible. Were the head to tell the heart that what the latter needs, above all things, is fresh capital, it would thereby make open confession of the emptiness of its own coffers. What it will find itself driven to do is to discountenance the enterprises of the heart,—not its new ventures only, but the spirit of enterprise which is and has ever been the breath of its life; to tell the heart that spiritual desire—the desire which directs itself towards the far-off and mysterious—is in the nature of things a vanity and a delusion; in fine, to invite it to wind up the business which it lives to transact, and to embark on a new career which bears the same relation to the old that the till of a village grocer bears to the counting-house of a merchant prince. What will happen when the heart, in its hour of expansive energy, receives this chilling rebuff? Who shall blame it if it resolves hence-forth to forswear its alliance with the head; if it abandons its dream of finding new ideas to match the new desires that had begun to renew its life; if it recoils from the new desires, as from phantoms which are luring it to destruction; if it goes back at last to the old discredited ideas and the old devitalized desires, determined at whatever cost to patch up its dwindling business and carry it on as best it may?

That I may make my meaning clear, let me trace in outline the history of one of the master desires of the heart,—the desire for immortality. I select this desire for consideration because, of all spiritual desires, it is at once the most popular and the most profound; and I call it a spiritual desire because it unquestionably directs itself towards the far-off and the mysterious. When it was still in its infancy, the crude conceptions of supernaturalism were sufficient for its needs. The pious Christian was content to believe that on a certain day in a not very distant future his body, which he found it difficult to distinguish from his real self, would rise again from the dead; that he would then appear before the judgment-seat of Christ; that if he had lived well while on earth he would be rewarded with eternal happiness; that if he had lived ill he would be punished with eternal misery. This theory of things was provided by the head in response to the demands of the heart; but when once the theory had been accepted and formulated by the Christian Church, the head was forbidden to criticize it, forbidden to modify it except in unessential details, forbidden even to think about it except within the clearly defined limits which Catholic theology had marked out. The consequence was that thought (in the deeper sense of the word) got out of touch with the idea of survival, lost all interest in it, held entirely aloof from it. For a time the desire for immortality was satisfied with the doctrines of a bodily resurrection and a future judgment; but satisfaction is the grave of desire; and as the heart, like the head, was forbidden to speculate (in its own way) about the destiny of the departed spirit, it too lost interest in the problem, and instead of moving onward, as desire should always do, it began to oscillate between two ignoble feelings,—callous indifference and superstitious fear. When the tyranny of dogmatism was relaxed, and some measure of freedom was restored both to the head and to the heart, the former began to criticize the current eschatology and to turn away from it as irrational, while the latter began to turn away from it as ignoble and inadequate.

So far, so good. Had it then been possible for the head to supply the heart with larger and deeper conceptions of what is vulgarly called "the future life," the heart would have begun to discover new depths and new developments in its desire for immortality; and, in its attempt to interpret these, the head would have begun to discover new depths and new developments in its theory of immortality; and in this way man's whole conception of Nature would have been expanded and enriched. But 1,000 years of forced inaction had atrophied the constructive energies of thought, and its critical power alone remained. Even the critical power of thought, which cannot be dissociated from the constructive, had suffered from the despotism which confined it, so far as any freedom was allowed it, to the study of physical phenomena, and forbade it to meddle with "spiritual things." For criticism, in the truer and deeper sense of the word, it had no capacity. Its growing power of analytical criticism enabled it to under-mine the foundations of supernaturalism. But when it had done this work, it had gone as far as it was possible for it to go. The dreamland of the Supernatural had vanished, and "Nature" remained. But it was the Nature of the average man. The philosophy of the average man, with its central assumption that the outward and visible world is the whole of Nature, was still in the ascendant; and now that the corrective influence of supernaturalism had been withdrawn, the latent materialism of that commonplace philosophy began to resume its sway. To free itself from that sway was beyond the power of thought. Incapable of constructive criticism, it could do nothing but bow its neck to the yoke of the very assumption which the heart had instinctively rejected as intolerable, and in its effort to free itself from which it had, in conjunction with the head, devised the theory of the Supernatural. To expose the unsoundness of that provisional theory was (and is) within the power of thought. To devise a better theory was (and is) beyond its power and, for the time being, beyond its aim.

What will happen, then, when the heart, no longer able to rest in the old doctrines of Resurrection and Judgment, of Heaven and Hell, but still cherishing the desire for immortality, goes to the head for light and guidance? It will be told that not only are the old ideas about immortality false and hollow, but that there are no ideas which can take their place. It will be told that the desire for immortality is itself a delusion—the primary delusion, of which the fables of the theologians are a fitting interpretation,—and that it must be sur-rendered if the heart is to find peace. And if the head is asked to justify these sweeping negations, it will give reasons for them which strike at the root, not of this desire only but of spiritual desire as such. That it may the better prove how entirely it is under the control of the average man, it will appeal to his primary assumption—that the visible world is the only world—as to a self-evident truth; and if the authority of its favourite axiom is questioned, it will support it with many arguments, each of which is a mere re-statement of the axiom under a more or less transparent disguise; and, having thus established its authority, it will draw inferences from it which prove, as it contends, that not the idea of immortality only, but the idea of spiritual life, the idea of spiritual freedom, the whole "soul-theory" (as it contemptuously calls it), is baseless as a dream. And that it may the better prove how incapable it is of interpreting a genuinely spiritual desire, such as the longing for immortality, it will take upon itself to scold the heart for cherishing a desire which, besides being demonstrably delusive, is base, selfish, and unmanly,—a "lust for positive happiness," which poisons morality at its fountain-head.

The desire for immortality may or may not be delusive—demonstrably delusive it certainly is not—but it is the very cant of pseudo-stoicism to say that it is base and selfish. For, after all, what is the desire for immortality? Is it not the desire, which man shares with all other living things, to grow—to continue to grow—to ripen—to move towards the goal of natural perfection?

"We feel that we are greater than we know."

We feel that the scale of our life and the scope of our work are great beyond measure, and that it would be as reasonable to expect an oak tree to make the full measure of its possible growth in a single season as for the soul to make the full measure of its possible growth in a single life. It is the soul's belief in itself which makes it desire immortality, just as it is the oak tree's belief in itself which makes it wait expectantly for the warmth and moisture of another spring; but the soul's desire for continued growth is entirely redeemed from selfishness by the fact that, in the higher stages of its development, the soul can continue to grow only by becoming selfless. It is true that in the quasi-concrete forms which the desire takes, in the pictures which man makes for himself of the "future life," he shows the limitations of his undeveloped nature,—the materialism of his unimaginative mind, the selfishness of his unexpanded heart. But the desire itself is unselfish, with all the unselfishness of a cosmic force.

Rebuffed and rebuked by the head, the heart recoils upon itself; and as the head cannot provide it with the illuminating ideas about immortality for which it asks, and as it cannot surrender a desire which is a part of its very life, it has no choice but to revert to the old ideas, to accept these as of Divine authority, and to confine the desire (which had struggled in vain for freedom and expansion) within the narrow channel which they provide. This means that, owing to lack of working capital, its speculative enterprise has failed; and this again means that thought, which is bound by its charter to supply the heart with "ideas," is unable to meet its obligations, and is therefore, in a word, bankrupt..

Neither the head nor the heart is to be blamed for this fiasco. The scale of the catastrophe is so large, and the forces which have combined to produce it are so complex and have been so long in operation, that it is impossible to say where the responsibility for it is to be laid. Also, it may be admitted that for the heart to be at open feud with the head is better than for the two to work together, as they have sometimes done, in chains. To that extent one may regard the quarrel between them with something of fatalistic complacency. But it is a mistake to say, as is sometimes said, that the quarrel is a necessity of. Nature, and to suggest that there are two kinds of truth—truth for the head and truth for the heart—and that these have nothing in common. Truth, like Nature, is in the last resort one and indivisible. So is the soul. The division of the soul into the head and the heart may be a necessity of thought, so far as thought comes under the control of its instrument, language; but it is not a necessity of Nature. If the distinction between the two is to be maintained, it must be on the understanding that one of the most vital functions of each is to co-operate with the other, and that neither can do its own special work effectively except in alliance with the other.

The heart is like a woman. Its intuitions are sound, but its attempts to justify them are fallacious and inconclusive. "Le cœur," says Pascal, "a ses raisons que le raison ne connaît pas: on le sait en mille choses." This is quite true; but the heart, left to itself, will not only fail to discover its hidden reasons, but will insist on giving other reasons—quite wrong reasons—for its fundamentally right conclusions. For if the heart takes upon itself to interpret some strong and true desire which possesses it, the chances are that it will fall a victim, in its search for an explanation, to the first commonplace theory that comes in its way, or, failing this, will revert to some old worn-out theory which in its own secret recesses it has already discarded; with the result, in either case, that the evolution of the desire will be arrested, and its pent-up energies put to some baser use. In other words, the right conclusions of the heart, being obscured by wrong reasons, will recede into the background; and the heart will end by substituting for these its own misinterpretations of them,—misinterpretations which are wholly due to its perverse attempt to understand and explain what it sees and feels.

It is true that in the medium of poetry—which never argues, never apologizes, never explains itself—the conclusions which the heart reaches by the divination of instinctive desire, may find a safe retreat. But to sustain life in that fluid medium, in which no problem is ever solved but all reasons and all conclusions are held in solution, is to the full as difficult as to breathe the rarefied air of abstract thought. Reasons for its intuitive conclusions, ideas to justify and direct its spiritual desires, the heart must have: but to discover those reasons, even if they be locked up in the heart itself, to discover the meaning, the function, and the purpose of the heart's desire is, after all, the business of thought; and the home of thought is what we call the head.

Here we come to a paradox from which there seems to be no escape. If we ask in what court the case between the head and the heart is to be tried, we can but answer: In the court of reason, the court which is presided over by the head. This shows how fundamentally fallacious—how unreal and unnatural—is the dispute in question. When the heart takes upon itself to anticipate or reverse the ruling of the head, it violently usurps the function of the latter, and gives a verdict in its own favour in a court whose authority it has refused to recognize. The heart should go into the court of reason, not as a suitor against the head—that feud is, I repeat, fundamentally fallacious—still less as a judge, but as a witness who is deeply interested in a case which is ever on trial, and whose evidence deserves to be received and weighed. When the head refuses to accept the depositions of the heart, and then makes light of the heart's protest, it is, in its judicial capacity, deliberately ignoring evidence which bears directly on the matter in dispute. In thus ceasing to be impartial, it abdicates its judicial functions, and takes a side in the very case which it has undertaken to try. This is equivalent to closing its court; and when the court of reason is closed, a state of chaos ensues, in which there is not even the semblance of order, until might becomes right and cuts the knots which cannot otherwise be loosed.

In the West, then, we have the strange spectacle of the head, which ought to be judicial and impartial, playing in its own court the rôle of a partisan and an advocate; while the heart, which is and ought to be an interested witness, finding that the Presiding Judge refuses to accept its evidence, takes forcible possession of the judicial bench and gives judgment on the case in dispute, using arguments the insufficiency of which it had fully recognized in the very act of entering the court. For it is this, and nothing less than this, which happens when reason gives judgment against "faith," having from the outset refused to listen to its evidence; and when "faith," in revenge, claims, on rational grounds, the right to reverse the rulings of reason.

The feud between the head and the heart is at once an abiding proof of the ascendency of dualism in Western thought, and a practical example of the working of that fatal fallacy. Spirit or matter, life or machinery, inward or outward, faith or reason, the heart or the head,—again and again we are invited to make our choice between what are supposed to be mutually exclusive alternatives, though they are really aspects—at once antithetical and correlative—of the same fundamental reality. In the order of Nature there is no abiding feud between the head and the heart. When we say that there is such a feud, what we mean is that for the time being the head and the heart—thought and desire—are unable to co-operate, the result of this being that neither is fulfilling its true function, and that the whole machinery of the inner life is deranged. The readiness of the Western mind to accept this state of things as normal, shows how deep-seated is the evil and how urgent is the need for a remedy. It is also equivalent to an admission that the title of this chapter is justified, and that Western thought is no longer solvent. When thought is solvent, when it is able to supply the ideas that desire needs, not for its ignoble satisfaction but for its expansion and development, the head and the heart cease to be enemies, and become what Nature intends them to be,—fellow-workers and friends.

Light from the East

UNABLE to meet its obligations, unable to supply the soul with the ideas that it needs for the due interpretation and evolution of its desires, Western thought can save itself from hopeless insolvency only by borrowing ideas from some other source. If it will condescend to do this, and if, having enriched its treasury with these new ideas, it will put them to a profitable use, by bringing them into harmony with what is true and of lasting value in its own theory of things, it will not only extricate itself from its embarrassments, but will be able in due course to pay back its debt with more than compound interest.

But the ideas that are borrowed must be those which the soul really needs. Now the soul needs, above all things, to be allowed to believe in itself. Belief in oneself is the supreme motive force in Nature, the power which is behind every desire, every enterprise, every effort, to grow, every "instinct to live." What we call the feud between the heart and the head is really the soul's indignant protest, on the plane of instinct and desire, against a theory which satisfies it, for the time being, on the plane of conscious thought,—the theory that the material world is the whole world, that all phenomena, up to and including the spiritual life of man, admit of being stated and explained in terms of physical force and physical law, and that therefore the soul itself is not a reality but an empty name. In other words, the heart's revolt against the head is the soul's protest against its own disparagement of itself. The first, and in a sense the last, desire of the soul is to be allowed to believe in itself; for all faith, all hope, all joy, all that makes life worth living, is present in embryo in that one belief.

The soul, then, must be allowed to believe in itself; and if this, its fundamental act of faith, is to be really effective, if it is to give the soul the stimulus and the guidance that it needs, if it is to make an end of the intestine strife that tears the soul asunder, it must be free from any suspicion of doubt. This means that no attempt should be made to prove the reality of the soul. For if its reality were provable, it would obviously not be final or complete. Proof implies the unprovable. To prove reality is to build, in the last resort, on the rock of what is unprovably real. How do I know, for example, that the outward and visible world is real, in any sense or degree? Because my senses and my reason assure me (provisionally and within limits) of its reality. But what is the value of this assurance if I, whose reality is unprovable, am other than real? And because my reality is unprovable, it stands to reason that, just so far as the reality of the outward world is provable, it is to that extent provisional and incomplete. It is my secret doubt as to the intrinsic reality of the outward world, which makes me attempt to prove it; and when the process of proof has reached its conclusion, its very conclusiveness becomes the measure of its failure; for it is only by postulating a higher and more intrinsic reality (in myself) that I am able to prove that the outward world is real in any sense or degree. For most men, indeed, the proof of the reality of the outward world is a process which gives satisfaction long before it has reached its final term,—in other words, long before the appeal to the soul's guarantee has become necessary. From this we may infer, if we please, that the average man's instinctive and sub-conscious belief in the solvency of the guarantor is complete, though he is incapable of the sustained effort of thought which might enable him to realize the significance of this belief, or even to become conscious of its existence. But what distinguishes the soul from all other objects of speculative thought, is that any attempt which may be made to prove its reality is, in the nature of things, foredoomed to miscarry at the very outset. This fact is deeply significant; but it is on its vital rather than its metaphysical significance that I wish to dwell. Belief in its own reality is the very root of the soul's life: to prove or attempt to prove its reality is to undermine and otherwise weaken its roothold; and to weaken its roothold is to retard the process of its growth.

But to allow the soul to believe in itself is to make faith, instead of reason, the basis of one's philosophy of life. The answer to this possible protest is that the highest function of reason (as the word is understood by those who oppose it to faith) is to prove; and that, inasmuch as proof implies the unprovable, the philosophy that is based on reason hangs in mid-air instead of resting on the solid earth. This means that no philosophy is or can be based on reason, and that every philosophy, including materialism itself, is based on an act of faith. But as every act of faith resolves itself into faith in the source of all faith, the soul (even the materialist's belief in the intrinsic reality of the outward world being resolvable, in the last resort, into belief in his own self as the guarantor of its reality), it seems to follow that the soul's belief in itself is the only belief which is self-sanctioned, and therefore the only philosophical postulate which allows the thinker to proceed at once on his way.

If the soul is to believe in itself, it must break away, finally and completely, from Western standards of reality, or rather—for the Western mind does not think in the category of the real and the unreal —from Western criteria of existence. While it is engaged in freeing itself from these fetters, its conception of Nature will undergo a profound and far-reaching change. Vast possibilities will begin to dawn upon its vision. No longer bound by the crude assumption that the palpable is the real and the impalpable the non-existent, it will begin to use its long-pinioned wings; and as it ascends from height to height, and discovers horizon beyond horizon, it will begin to suspect that, after all, the normal limits of human vision may not be the limits of the Universe. It will begin to wonder whether there may not, after all, be other worlds than that which the bodily senses reveal to us; other planes of being than the physical; other senses in man than those which he shares with the lower animals; other forces than those of material Nature. In the light of this dawning conception, the postulate of a supernatural order of things, which has done so much to narrow and debase man's conception of Nature, will become finally discredited by being justified and explained. The idea of the Supernatural cannot be wholly illusory. However erroneous, however mischievous may be its mode of expressing itself, we must needs believe that at the bottom of an idea which has ruled the lives and swayed the hearts of men in many lands and many ages, there is a real experience and a real desire. The supernatural world is the impalpable side of Nature, including all that is "inward and spiritual," expressed in a semi-materialistic notation. It follows that, when the soul is allowed to believe in itself, the supernatural world will be re-absorbed into Nature by a quasi-spontaneous process, for the inward side of Nature will then be seen to be the real side,—the substance of which the outward world is the shadow, the vital essence of which the outward world is the expression and the form. Nor is it only the soul's conception of Nature which will expand indefinitely when the conventional criterion of existence becomes discredited. It is also the soul's conception of itself. Allow the soul to believe in itself, and it will try to discover what its self really is. This means that it will wander far and wide, wander to the uttermost ends of the world, in quest of its own boundaries; and as these will never be discovered, it will not rest till it has absorbed all things into itself. In other words, it will not rest till it has spiritualized Nature,—spiritualized her so completely that the very things which it once regarded as the only substantial realities will begin to pass before it as moving shadows, and the material world, which it once regarded as the Alpha and Omega of Nature, will begin to melt into a dream.

Two things, then, will happen when the soul has learned to believe in itself. Its conception of Nature, freed from the limits which the popular criterion of existence imposed upon it, will be raised to an infinite power. So will its conception of itself. And these two parallel conceptions, meeting at last "at infinity," will become one.

Thus the first idea that the soul needs, if it is to be restored to a state of spiritual solvency—the idea that the soul itself is real—will give an immense stimulus to its flagging vitality, will rekindle the flame and widen beyond measure the range of its desire, will revive its dormant spirit of enterprise, will dispose it for new and daring ad-ventures. But if these adventures are to be properly equipped and directed, further ideas will be needed; and these, too, must be provided by thought. The general idea of the soul's intrinsic reality must be supplemented by speculative ideas of large import,—ideas as to the law of the soul's life, as to its inward standard of reality, as to its origin and its destiny, as to the relation between its individual and its universal self. In evolving these ideas, thought will half lead and half follow desire, and will thus both guide and stimulate it. But if the ideas are to be effective, they must remain ideas, and not be allowed to degenerate into formulæ. To go far into detail, to map out a complete chart for the soul on the eve of its voyage of discovery, would stultify its spirit of enterprise; and to stultify its spirit of enterprise is to damp down the very flame of its life. If the chart which thought provides is both complete and correct in all its details, it must needs be that the far-off world of mystery which draws to itself the soul's desires has already been fully explored and surveyed, and that there is nothing left in it to discover. It is by desire, even more than by thought, that the blighting influence of dogmatism makes itself felt; and desire is the soul's instinctive effort to grow. The very basis of dogmatism is the false assumption that ultimate truth is communicable from without—as "theological information"—instead of being the inmost life of the soul, a life which the soul must win—or rather, evolve—in and for itself. When the soul realizes that it is real—and, if real at all, then supremely real—it will also realize that truth, which is the subjective counterpart of reality, is intimately its own; and it will instinctively reject all teaching which does, or pretends to do, for it what it ought to do and must do for itself.Thus the primary idea that the soul is real will automatically protect the soul from the cramping and warping pressure of·dogmatism, and, while disposing it to welcome all sub-ideas which give it stimulus and guidance, will strengthen it to reject the teaching that is merely formal, and that does not reveal to it what is and has ever been its own.

This leads me to say again that, whatever spiritual ideas the thought of the West may borrow from whatever quarter, it must be able to assimilate these, if they are to rescue it from its present state of insolvency, and make them its own. I mean by this, first, that it must learn at last to recognize them as belonging to that inner life of the soul which it is the function of thought to interpret; and, next, that as they come to it—nominally from without, but really from within—it must meet them along its own line of approach, and give them the particular expression which is in keeping with its own criticism of life. For just as the individual soul, in the course of its development, should prove its individuality by universalizing itself in its own particular way, so if the soul of the West is to make the ideas which it borrows really productive, it must transform them by processes of its own till it has made them available, first for the special needs of the West, and then for the more general needs of Humanity. In this, and in no other way, will it be able to pay them back in due season, enriched and expanded by the use that it has made of them.

Four things, then, are needed if the bankruptcy of Western thought is to come to an end. In the first place, the idea that the soul is ultimately real—an idea which the heart imperatively needs, but which the head is unable to supply—must be borrowed from some other source. In the second place, the idea must be accepted on its own evidence, and therefore without any shadow of reserve or doubt. This means that the source from which the idea is borrowed must be one in which, having always been regarded as demonstrably indemonstrable, it has the force and authority of an axiom,—not of a mere assumption, still less of a logical conclusion. In the third place, with this master idea the soul must borrow the subsidiary ideas by which it has been interpreted and otherwise supported in the land of its origin; but it must take care that these subsidiary ideas, while giving it stimulus and guidance, do not in any way cramp or deaden its life, or impede the free play of its thought and its desire. In the fourth place, it must make the ideas that it borrows its very own; for until it has done this it will not be able to trade with them to advantage; and it is only by trading with them to advantage that it can hope to pay them back, with the generous interest which is due for so timely a loan.

In asking the West to adopt this heroic remedy, I can appeal to a precedent which Christendom at least will regard as authoritative,—to the example of Christ. Nearly 2000 years ago, when the ideals of Paganism had exhausted their influence, and when, as a consequence of this, the soul of the West was sinking deep into the mire of materialism—a materialism of thought as well as of desire—Christ renewed its failing strength, and drew it back to firm ground, by borrowing from the Far East the master idea of the soul's intrinsic reality and the derivative ideas that revolve round this central orb, and by making these his own. As regards the source to which he went, the ideas that he borrowed, and the use that he made of them, we who revere Christ as our Lord and Master, shall do well to follow his lead.

To the pious Christian, who believes that Christ brought his ideas—or shall I say, his store of "theological information"?—down to earth from the supernatural Heaven, the suggestion that he borrowed ideas from India, or any other terrestrial land, may possibly seem profane. Yet Theology itself admits, or rather insists, that Christ was (and is) "very man" as well as "very God"; and if he was "very man," if he was open to all human influences, we may surely take for granted that his pure and exalted nature was peculiarly sensitive to the spiritual ideas of his age. That Christ had come under the influence of the spiritual ideas of the Far East is a hypothesis which explains many things, and for which therefore there are many things to be said. To attempt to prove in detail the indebtedness of the "Gospel" to the "Ancient Wisdom" would carry me far beyond the limits which the aim of this work has imposed upon me. But I would ask anyone who can approach the question with a genuinely open mind to make the following simple experiment. Let him first saturate himself with the spiritual thought of India,—with the speculative philosophy, half metaphysical, half poetical, of the Upanishads, and with the ethical philosophy of Buddha. Let him then study the sayings of Christ, making due allowance for the distorting medium (of Jewish prejudice and Messianic expectation) through which his teaching has been transmitted to us. He will probably end by convincing himself, as I have done, that the spiritual standpoints of the Sages of the Upanishads, of Buddha, and of Christ were, in the very last resort, identical.

With this hypothesis to guide us, let us study some of the more characteristic sayings of Christ. What is the "Sermon on the Mount" but a systematic and strenuous attempt to revolutionize human life by giving men a new ideal and a new standpoint,—by substituting, in accordance with the central trend of Indian thought, an entirely inward for an entirely outward standard of moral worth? The sayings in it which seem to be violent and paradoxical, when we interpret them literally, disclose their meaning and their purpose directly the light of this conception is turned upon them. To say that "every one that looketh upon a woman to lust after her hath committed adultery with her already in his heart" is, one would think, to disparage by implication the self-control which arrests lawless desire on the threshold of lawless action; but the words had to be spoken in order that the reality of the inward standard might be emphasized, and the hollowness of formal rules, when divorced from the spiritual principles that are behind them, might be brought home to his hearers. The words, "if thy right eye cause thee to stumble pluck it out and cast it from thee" are, as they stand, a hard saying. But when he spoke them, Christ was but expressing in his own language the profound truth which Indian thought had long insisted upon,—that the outward self (form, sensation, perception and the rest) is unreal and valueless, in comparison with the overwhelming reality and incalculable value of the inward life. His stern and terrible command is in its essence the echo of what Buddha had said, centuries before, in quite other words: "The material form is not the self: the sensations are not the self: the perceptions are not the self: the conformations [predispositions] are not the self: the consciousness is not the self."

The "Kingdom of Heaven," which figures so prominently in Christ's discourses, is obviously the kingdom of soul-life;—a kingdom which is ever at hand, ever in the midst of us; which immingles itself with "the world," or kingdom of the surface life, as the eternal immingles itself with the transitory, the real with the phantasmal, truth with illusion, light with darkness; or, again, which waits with divine patience at the heart of "the world," as "perfect peace" waits at the heart of fever and strife. To enter this inward Kingdom is to enter "the Path" into which Buddha led his disciples. To become (in the fullest sense of the words) a naturalized citizen of the Kingdom is to pass into Nirvâna. When Christ says, "Lay not up for yourselves treasures upon the earth, where moth and rust doth consume, and where thieves break through and steal; but lay up for yourselves treasures in heaven, where neither moth nor rust doth consume and where thieves do not break through nor steal; for where thy treasure is there will thy heart be also," he is but harping on the theme, so familiar to Indian thought, of the impermanence of outward things and the permanence of the inward life. When he likens the kingdom of heaven to the "hidden treasure" or the "pearl of great price," to win which a man will sell all that he has, he is but echoing the teaching of the Indian sages that the Self within the self is alone real, and that all the things which we prize must be surrendered in order that He may be won.

Even the words which Christ is reported to have used about his own kinship to and oneness with "the Father"—words on which all the fantastic structures of Christian theology have been based—are but the expression, in a new notation, of the sublime Indian doctrine that "He is the true self of every creature,"—that "Brahma and the self are one."

Lastly, the great question in which the whole of Christ's spiritual teaching is summed up and typified—"What shall it profit a man if he gain the whole world and lose his own soul; or what shall a man give in exchange for his soul?

with its implicit assumption that the soul is greater and more precious than "the whole world," is the very question which India had again and again asked herself, and in which all her meditations on great matters had centred.

The ideas which dominated Christ's teaching, and which, according to my hypothesis, had come to him from the Far East, were not wholly new to the Græco-Roman world of his day. Xenophanes, Parmenides, Pythagoras and (above all) Plato had expounded them, each from his own point of view and in his own language, to esoteric circles of disciples. But no popular exposition of them had been attempted in the West till Christ came ender their influence and was captivated by their truth and beauty. Whether they were consciously or unconsciously adopted by Christ matters little. The broad fact confronts us that the ideas which he expounded coincide, at every vital point, with ideas which were current in India many centuries before the Christian era. Had India, through all those centuries, been entirely walled off from Western Asia and Southeastern Europe, the coincidences between the teaching of Christ and the teaching of Buddha and his forerunners might conceivably be regarded as purely fortuitous. But never, before the establishment of British rule in India, had the opportunities for intercourse between East and West been so numerous or so favourable as in the centuries which immediately preceded the birth of

Christ. For during a part, at least, of that period a chain of partially Hellenized kingdoms stretched from India to the Mediterranean, forming a broad highway along which the spiritual ideas of India travelled, slowly but surely; Westward. We need not lay much stress on the inscription which records the intention of the Buddhist Emperor, Asoka, to send missionaries from India to Syria, Egypt, and other Hellenized lands, in order to preach the gospel of deliverance; for we have no evidence that those missionaries were ever sent. But the migration of a spiritual idea is not dependent, wholly or even mainly, on the labours of its accredited agents. The decadence of religion and philosophy in the Græco-Roman world during the centuries which intervened between the death of Alexander and the birth of Christ, had created a spiritual vacuum which was waiting to be filled; and the westward set of the current of Indian ideas was as natural a movement as that of the Trade Winds or the Gulf Stream.

But if we may not say that Christ originated the ideas which he expounded, we may—and must—say that he was grandly original in the use that he made of them. The inspired teacher is not he who invents new ideas—for great ideas are never invented—but he who having received them, from whatever quarter, is able to assimilate them and make them his own. It is because he did this to the largest and most luminous ideas that have yet dawned upon the human spirit, that Christ must take rank with Buddha as one of the foremost teachers of mankind. What Buddha had done to the ideas of the Upanishads, Christ did to the same ideas when they had come to him, as they probably did, through the medium of Buddha's ethical teaching, he made them available for the daily needs of ordinary men.

But the method by which Christ worked was entirely his own. To graft the spiritual idealism of India on the stem of Hebrew poetry, and so to bring it home to the heart, rather than to the mind or the conscience, was the work of his life. Leaving it to thinkers, like Plato, to develop the idea of soul-growth through the medium of abstract thought,—leaving it to moralists, like Buddha, to develop it through the medium of a scheme of life,—Christ was content to develop it through the medium of poetic emotion. Out of the rival conceptions of God which were symbolized by Brahma and Jehovah respectively, he devised a third—the "resultant" of their respective forces—the idea of the All-Father who loves and is loved by his children, men. Setting before men, as Plato and Buddha had done, the finding of the soul or true self as the goal of their life's endeavour, he neither gave them reasons for pursuing that goal (as Plato had done) nor directions for pursuing it (as Buddha had done), but he gave them instead of these a motive for pursuing it—of all motives the strongest and the purest—the quasi-personal love of the All-loving God. Where Plato and where Buddha were strong, each in his own way, Christ was by comparison weak; but he had a strength which was all his own. Plato reasoned about God. Buddha kept silence about God. Christ made him the theme of his poetry. Each of these modes of dealing with the idea of the Divine has its own merits and its own defects. The defects of Christ's treatment of the idea are obvious. The teacher who tries to popularize spiritual truth by formulating it in terms of poetry, may almost be said to invite men to literalize and despiritualize his teaching. Christ took this risk and paid the penalty of his daring. But though the penalty was a heavy one, yet when he had paid it in full there was a substantial balance in his favour. As a speculative thinker he does not compete with Plato. As a systematic teacher he does not compete with Buddha. But as a source of spiritual inspiration he has no rival.

With Christ's example before us, we need not hesitate to go for spiritual ideas to the only land in which they have ever (as far as we know) been indigenous,—to Ancient India. In the India which gave birth to the Upanishads, belief in the soul grew on its own stock and sprang from its own roots. No attempt was made to prove the reality of the soul, or to apologize for the belief in it. So far as any reason was given for the "soul-theory," it was a reason which proved—if I may be allowed the paradox—that the reality of the soul is unprovable.

> "Only by soul itself
> Ts soul perceived.—when the Soul wills it so!
> There shines no light save its own light to show
> Itself unto itself."

The idealistic ventures of the West have all suffered shipwreck on the rock of the average man's "common-sense,"—an euphemistic title for his spiritual indolence, his lack of imagination, and his inability to think clearly or coherently. But the spiritual thought of India, in the days when her soul was awake and active, was, at its highest level, strictly esoteric. In the teaching of Buddha we have the nearest approach to popularizing it that was ever made; but what Buddha submitted to the average man were, not the conclusions of Indian idealism, not the reasons for those conclusions, but their practical consequences. That the average man was deeply interested in the soundness of Buddha's scheme of life, was no reason (so its author seems to have thought) for allowing him to examine the philosophical conceptions that underlay it. The average man is deeply interested in the stability of the Forth Bridge; but had the engineers of that structure invited him to handle the profound mathematical problems which had to be solved before their designs could be completed, they would justly have been deemed insane. Not less insane would it have seemed to the Master Thinkers of India to allow the average man to handle the problem of reality, or any kindred problem.

It is true that to ignore the average man in the region of high thinking is a loss to the life of a nation as well as a gain; and that India has paid heavily for having ignored him. But the gain to her thought, while her spiritual life was at or near its zenith, was immense. Serenely indifferent to the verdict of the market place, Indian idealism never explains itself, never gives account of itself, never even for a moment distrusts itself. This means that under its ægis the soul's belief in itself is complete. And this again means that the soul is not curious about itself, or about .the worlds of which it is at once the centre and the circumference; that it is content with ideas and impatient of formulæ; that high thinking is neither the master nor the servant of spiritual desire, but its peer and its other self; that the head is ready to give the heart the guidance that it really needs,—the guidance that stimulates to fresh endeavour, not the guidance that blinds the vision and paralyzes the will.

It is to India then—the India of the Upanishads and of Buddha—that the

West must go for the ideas, both central and subordinate, which shall rescue it from its embarrassments and restore it to a state of spiritual solvency. The central idea for which it is waiting is that of the reality of the soul. Of the sub-ideas to which this idea is central it must select those which it will find most easy to assimilate. For if it is to put the ideas that it borrows to a profitable use, it must make them its own; it must, in a manner, re-create them by bringing them into harmony with the highest achievements of its own thought. Now the highest achievements of the Western mind are and have long been scientific. It is in the sphere of physical science that its most successful work has been done, and that its most characteristic qualities have been developed. There are obvious reasons—in the West, where for centuries men have been authoritatively taught to identify the impalpable with the supernatural, there are special reasons—why the physical or palpable side of Nature should have been the first for Science to explore. But there is no reason why Science should confine her operations to that particular sphere. To be immersed in physical matter is not of the essence of Science. What is of her essence is the secret faith which is the mainspring of all her energies,—the faith of the soul of man in the intrinsic unity of Nature, its latent belief that the Universe is "not an aggregate but a whole." The aim of science—an aim which is not the less real because it is seldom consciously realized—is to discover one all-pervading substance, one all-controlling force, one all-regulating law. Subordinate to, but vitally connected with, the belief in the unity of Nature is the belief in law,—the belief of the soul in the veracity of Nature, in the stability and self-identity of the Universe. These two beliefs (if we are to call them two) constitute the true creed of Science. They are beliefs, be it observed, not disbeliefs. Each of them has its counterpart in what I may call a cosmic desire,—in the instinctive response of the soul to a message from the heart of the Universe. What passes in certain quarters for the creed of Science is a series of dogmatic negations or disbeliefs. But the true creed is a faith, a hope, and an aspiration; and, sooner or later, it will find expression for itself in action, in conduct, in life.

Such being, in its essence, the creed or secret faith of Science, it is a shock to the scientific thought of the West, when it asks philosophy to give it the ground plan of the Universe, to find itself face to face with the dualism of popular thought. The very raison d'être of Science is to prove that the Universe is an organic whole; and it is therefore an insult and a mockery to the mind which has long been living in an atmosphere of scientific effort and achievement, to be told that there are two worlds or spheres of being in the Universe, not one; that these two worlds are parted by an unfathomable abyss of nothingness which makes natural intercourse between them impossible; and that the Supreme Power which is supposed to have fashioned the world of Nature, and which now dwells apart from it in the supernatural Heaven, reveals itself at its own good pleasure to the dwellers in Nature by suspending the laws which are (one must believe) the expression of its own being,—in other words, by stultifying its own work and thwarting its own will. What wonder that the Western mind, in the violence of its re-action from so irrational a philosophy, should surrender itself to a theory of things which it regards as the only possible alternative for dualism,—to a materialistic monism in which unity is achieved by suppressing the impalpable, and therefore by despiritualizing and devitalizing the Universe? And what wonder that it should be unable to realize, owing to the poison of dualism being still in its veins, that a monism which is based on a comprehensive negation is not an alternative for dualism, but a new version of it;—the attempt to escape from dualism, by suppressing one of the terms of a given antithesis, leading one of logical necessity into the toils of a deadlier fallacy,—the fundamental dualism of the existent and the non-existent?

If the "advanced" thought of the West desires, in general, to convince itself of the unity of the Universe, it desires, more particularly, to bring the life of the soul—to bring the moral and spiritual worlds in which the life of the soul expresses itself—under the reign of natural law. This desire, which is 'both legitimate and salutary, is systematically thwarted by the dogmatic teaching of those who pose as the champions of the soul. For twenty centuries the "soul-theory" has been presented to the consciousness of the West in the notation of the Supernatural. As so presented, it outrages at every turn man's sense of law and his cognate (and virtually identical) sense of justice. To teach man that sin entered the world because his "first parents" violated an arbitrary command of the supernatural God; that because of this one original act of disobedience the whole human race stands condemned to eternal death; that the death of Christ on the cross has made it possible for men to escape from the terrible consequences of Adam's sin; that this one brief earth-life decides for all time the destiny of each individual soul; that either eternal salvation or eternal damnation awaits the departed spirit; that grace (the higher life of the soul) is a supernaturally communicated gift, a water of healing which (as some contend) is "laid on" at every priest-served altar, or (as others contend) takes possession of the "elect" in a sudden and irresistible stream,—to teach man such things as these is to make open mockery of his sense of law and order and justice, and to warn him at the outset that there can be no science of the inner life. To this mockery and this warning the scientific thought of the West has begun to reply with open defiance. Forbidden by supernaturalism to bring the life of the soul under the sway of natural law, it is being led by the secret logic of its faith (for it cannot but cling to its intuitive conviction that the realm of natural law is co-terminous with the Universe) to disbelieve in the life of the soul, to ask for proofs of its existence, and at last to relegate the whole "soul-theory" to the limbo of exploded superstitions. In thus abandoning the "soul-theory," the advanced thinkers of the West imagine that they are undoing the demoralizing work of supernaturalism. But in this matter, as in their treatment of the general problem of dualism, the remedy that they offer is worse than the disease. The West has never realized—so faulty has been its ethical training—that the inward consequences of moral action are regulated by one of Nature's most just and most inexorable laws; and the normal attitude of the average man towards the problem of moral responsibility is that, apart from legal and social considerations, it matters little how one acts. He still feels, however, that it matters some-thing; for the general idea that moral goodness makes for the well-being of the soul has always been formally countenanced by supernaturalism, and is still, in some degree, a restraining, if not an inspiring, influence in his life. But let him be fully convinced that he has no inward life, and that therefore his conduct can have no inward consequences,—and it will not be long before he feels his way to the logical conclusion that (again apart from legal and social considerations) it matters nothing how one acts.

We see, then, that the advanced thought of the West has, unknown to itself, a true and deep philosophy of its own,—a philosophy which centres in recognition of the essential unity of Nature and of the all-pervading supremacy of natural law. In virtue of this unformulated philosophy, it is the sworn enemy of dualism in general and of supernaturalism in particular; but it cannot yet realize what its hostility to dualism means, or where it is to find the remedy for the evil which it dimly discerns. The remedy for dualism is not the monism (if one must call it so) which suppresses one of the terms of a world-embracing antithesis, but the higher monism which recognizes that each term is the complement and correlate of the other; nay, that there is a reciprocal relation between the two in virtue of which each in turn owes to the other its meaning, its purpose, and (in the last resort) its very right to exist;—which recognizes, for example, that silence "implies sound," that failure is "a triumph's evidence," that the supernatural world is at the heart of Nature, that form is as truly the expression of spirit, as spirit is the soul and life of form.

Such a monism was once taught in the Far East. The Indian doctrine of the fundamental identity of the individual and the universal life, and, more especially, of the ideal identity of the individual with the Universal Soul, makes an end, once and for all, of the false dualism of the human and the Divine, 1 and provides for the return of the Lord and Giver of Life from his exile in the supernatural dreamland to his home at the heart of Nature. If Western thought will accept this doctrine as a provisional theory of things, and try to master its meaning, it will be able to extend the conception of natural law to the inner life of man and to all the worlds—moral, æsthetic, poetic, religious, and the rest—which the ferment of that life has generated; it will be able, in due course, to take in hand the task for which its special bent and special training are even now equipping it, the task of building up the science of the soul.

When it takes that task in hand, it will find that Buddha has anticipated it, to the extent of indicating the main lines on which it will have to work. An attempt has been made by some of the Western exponents of Buddhism to show that the teaching of Buddha falls into line with the anti-idealistic theories of the dominant school of Western thought. The attempt has not been successful; for it can be shown, I think, that Buddha based his scheme of life, not on rejection of the "soul-theory," but on whole-hearted acceptance of it. But those who contend that Buddha's philosophy is modern and Western, have come within a little of stumbling upon an important truth. Though he belonged to a far-off age and a far-off land, the founder of Buddhism was akin to us in the scientific bent of his mind, in his grasp of the idea of law. His teaching does not fall into line with our thought, for in truth he was far more "advanced" than we are; but it is possible that our thought, as it develops, will come into line with his teaching.

The scientific achievements of the West, so far as they have any philosophical significance, fall under two main heads, the discovery (if I may use the word), on the physical plane, that the Kingdom of Nature is under the reign of law (a conception of Nature which Science must have unconsciously brought with her to her work of investigation, and which has made that work possible); and the further discovery that all laws of Nature are subordinate to the master law of development or growth. 1 Both these discoveries were anticipated by Buddha; but they were made by him—or by the thinkers who sowed what he reaped—not on the physical plane, but on the spiritual, on the plane of man's inner life. Buddha realized, as no man before (or since) had ever done, that the soul is a living thing, and that, as such, it comes under the all-pervading, all-controlling law of growth. And he realized the practical bearing of this conception.

Physical science says to the husbandman, "Do such and such things, and your crops (taking one season with another) will be abundant: neglect to do them, and your crops will be poor;" or, in other words, "Bring your husbandry into harmony with certain laws of physical Nature, and you will fare well. Disregard those laws, and you will fare ill." What the science of the West is doing for the growth (and the development) of wheat and barley, Buddha did for the growth of the soul. He taught men that, if they would bring their lives into harmony with certain fundamental laws of Nature, their souls would grow—as well-tended crops grow—vigorously and healthily; and that the sense of well-being which accompanies successful growth, and which, when consciously realized, is true happiness, would be theirs. He taught them this; and, in teaching it, he made that appeal to their will-power which is his chief contribution to the edification, as distinguished from the instruction, of the soul. The husbandman must take thought for his plants if their lives are to be brought into harmony with the appropriate laws of Nature; but the plant which we call the soul must take thought for itself. Penetrated with the conviction that what a man does re-acts, naturally and necessarily, on what he is, and so affects for all time the growth of the soul and its consequent well-being; penetrated with the conviction that conduct moulds character, and that character is destiny,—Buddha called upon each man in turn to take his life into his own hands, and himself to direct the process of his growth.

This message was his legacy to the ages. It is for Western thought to take it up and repeat it, developing in its own way the mighty ideas that are behind it. Dr Rhys Davids seems to think that it is "unmanly" 1 to take thought for one's soul; and it is possible that care for the soul has at times taken forms which are open to this reproach. But when the idea of soul-growth is interpreted in the light of the idea of inexorable law, it loses the sickly savour which clings, in some slight measure, to the ideal of saintliness, and one begins to realize that to take oneself in hand and to make one's soul grow, by the constant exercise of initiative and self-control, is to rise to an even loftier level than that of manliness (which, after all, is but the virtue of a sex), to the level of true manhood. The scheme of life in which Buddha embodied his science of the soul is in the highest degree bracing and stimulating; and one of the chief sources of its tonic influence is the sternness with which it insists on the merciless majesty of Nature's laws. Just as physical science warns us that, if we drink polluted water (let us say), our health will suffer, and the elimination of the poison from our bodies will be a long and painful process, so Buddha warns men that wrong-doing is not less certain to work itself out of the soul as sorrow and suffering than is right-doing to work itself into the soul as health, and therefore as happiness and peace. That nothing can come between conduct and its inward consequences—between what we do and what we are and shall be—is the conviction on which the whole of his teaching is hinged. The ideas about God and Man and the Universe which have made possible the Christian belief in the forgiveness of sins, belong to a quarter of thought in which his mind never moved. Unlike Jehovah, who is angry and then repents and forgives, the power which is at the heart of Nature

"Knows not wrath nor pardon."

If we sow the seed of wheat we shall reap wheat, and reap it, if we have been wise husbandmen, in abundant measure. But if we sow the seed of thistles, we must know for certain that our crop will be thistles, not wheat.

These ideas are eminently congenial to the scientific tone of Western thought; and the day will come (I venture to predict) when the conception of life which they embody will be accepted in the West as the sanest and truest conception that the mind of man has yet devised, and as the only stable foundation on which to build—what will surely be the fittest monument to Buddha's greatness—the science of the soul. The task of building that monument, of interpreting in the light of modern experiences and adapting to modern needs the spiritual ideas of ancient India, will probably devolve upon the West (which is unconsciously preparing itself for the task by its arduous work in the field of physical science), rather than upon the East. Should that be so, and should the West rise to the level of its opportunity, it would at last find itself in a position to pay back the loan that had saved its credit; for it would have traded with its borrowed ideas to the best advantage, and would have duly enriched them with its own thought, its own labour, and its own life.

Before these things can come to pass one practical difficulty will have to be overcome. It is possible that the sentimental thought of the West will offer as strong an opposition to the idea of the life and destiny of the soul being regulated by inexorable law, as is now offered by the intellectual thought of the West to the root-idea of soul-life. But the advanced thinker of that distant day will be able to re-assure his weaker brethren. For he will remind them that the Universal Soul, which is the true self of each of us, and which the process of soul-growth will therefore enable each of us to realize, is the same for all men; and he will ask them to infer from this that the most inexorable of all Nature's laws is the law to which even the master law of growth is in a sense subordinate,—the law which makes the Universe one living whole, the law of centripetal tendency, the law of Love.

The Sayings of Lao Tzu
by Lao Tzu
Translated by Lionel Giles

Table of Contents

EDITORIAL NOTE

THE object of the Editors of this series is a very definite one. They desire above all things that, in their humble way, these books shall be the ambassadors of good-will and understanding between East and West—the old world of Thought and the new of Action. In this endeavour, and in their own sphere, they are but followers of the highest example in the land. They are confident that a deeper knowledge of the great ideals and lofty philosophy of Oriental thought may help to a revival of that true spirit of Charity which neither despises nor fears the nation of another creed and colour.

L. CRANMER-BYNG.
S. A. KAPADIA.
NORTHBROOK SOCIETY,
21, CROMWELL ROAD,
KENSINGTON, S.W.

INTRODUCTION

WITH rare modesty and intelligent self-appreciation, Confucius described himself as "a transmitter, not a maker, one who loved and believed in the ancients." This judicious estimate fairly sums up the position of China's most prominent teacher. Incalculable though his influence has been over millions of the human race, it is due rather to his sterling common sense backed by the moral strength of his character, than to any striking intellectual power or novelty in his ideas.

But some fifty years before the time of Confucius there lived another great Chinaman, who, besides being a lover of antiquity, takes high rank as a profound and original thinker. Apart from the thick crop of legend and myth which soon gathered round his name, very little is known about the life and personality of Lao Tzu, and even the meagre account preserved for us in the history of Ssu-ma Ch'ien must be looked upon with suspicion. All the alleged meetings and conversations with Confucius may safely be rejected, not only on account of chronological difficulties, but because they are exactly the sort of invention which would to likely to pass current in an early and uncritical age. We need not, however, go so far as those who impugn the very existence of Lao Tzu as an individual, and regard the book which passes under his name as a mere collection of scraps of ancient proverbial philosophy. Some colour, indeed, is lent to this theory by the uncertainty that attaches to the proper interpretation of the name Lao Tzu, which is variously explained as (1) Old Boy, because he is said to have been born with a white beard (but we may rather suspect that the story was invented to explain the name); (2) Son of Lao, this being the surname of the virgin mother who conceived him at the sight of a falling star; or (3) Old Philosopher, because of the great age at which he wrote his immortal book, the Tao Tê Ching.

The mention of this classic, or "Treatise of the Way and of Virtue" (as it may be translated for want of better English equivalents), brings us naturally to the vexed question as to whether the text which has come down to us can really be attributed to the hand of Lao Tzu, or whether it is not rather a garbled and unauthorised compilation of his sayings, or even the mere forgery of a later age. The Chinese themselves, it may be remarked, are almost unanimous in denying its authenticity. It has been urged that we must make allowance here for Confucian bias; but the internal evidence alone should suffice to dispel the notion, to which many eminent sinologues have clung, that the Tao Tê Ching in its present form can possibly represent the actual work of Lao Tzu. On the other hand, it is highly probable that much of it is substantially what he said or wrote, though carelessly collected and pieced together at random. Ssu-ma Ch'ien, who published his history in 91 B.C., and was consequently removed from Lao Tzu by a much longer period than we are from Shakespeare, tells us that the Sage wrote a book of five thousand and odd words; and, indeed, by that time the Tao Tê Ching may possibly have existed in something like its present shape. But anyone who reflects on the turbulent condition of China during the intervening centuries, and the chaotic state of primitive literature before the labours of Confucius, to say nothing of the Burning of the Books in 213 B.C., will find it hard to convince himself that Ssu-ma Ch'ien ever had before him the actual writings of the philosopher.

Arbitrary and confused though the arrangement of the Tao Tê Ching appears, it is possible to trace a coherent line of thought throughout the whole. And although no coiner of paradox on such an extensive scale as Lao Tzu could hope to achieve absolute and invariable consistency, it is easy to see that the Tao Tê Ching is something more than a mere jumble of stray aphorisms—that it is, in fact, the well-defined though rudimentary outline of a great system of transcendental and ethical philosophy. That this magnificent scheme of thought never reached its full expression in Lao Tzu's treatment is largely due to the fact that he was perpetually struggling to convey his ideas through the medium of a language still imperfectly developed, and forming an inadequate vehicle for abstruse philosophical conceptions. This, too, combined with an extraordinary conciseness of diction, is the cause of the obscurity which hangs over several portions of the text, and which the labours of innumerable commentators have done very little to clear away. To the wide scope thus afforded for the imagination we owe the startling discoveries, in the body of the work, of the Doctrine of the Trinity, and of the Hebrew word for Jehovah, thinly disguised in its Chinese dress. Sad to say, both of these once famous theories are now totally discredited.

The real value of the Tao Tê Ching lies not in such puerilities, but in its wealth of suggestive hints and pregnant phrases, each containing a world of thought in itself and capable of expansion into volumes. Whether Lao Tzu ever developed the germs of thought thrown out with such prodigality, we do not know. At any rate, no record of the development remains. And if Lao Tzu failed to work out his own system, the task was never satisfactorily accomplished by those who came after him. It is true that an enormous superstructure of Taoist literature has been raised upon the slender foundation of the Tao Tê Ching, but these Taoist writers soon forsook the austerity of Lao Tzu's way for the more attractive fields of ritual and magic. Lao Tzu was a Socrates who never found a Plato or an Aristotle to reap the goodly harvest he had sown; even Chuang Tzu, the greatest of his followers, whose exquisite literary style contrasts strangely with the rugged sentences of the Tao Tê Ching, scarcely seems to have caught the true spirit of his Master, and is apt to lose himself in the vague speculations of a dreamy mysticism.

Lao Tzu's work, however, was able to command attention on its own merits. It was first officially recognised as a "canon" or "classic" under the Emperor Ching Ti (B.C. 156-140) of the Han Dynasty, after which the study of Tao survived many vicissitudes, being now under a cloud, and now again in high favour at Court. One Emperor was in the habit of holding forth on the doctrines of Lao Tzu before his assembled ministers, and would forthwith degrade any one who stretched, yawned, or spat during his discourse. Another published an edition of the Tao Tê Ching, which is described in the preface as "the root of all things, the teacher of kings, and the most precious jewel of the public." The first Emperor of the later Chin dynasty asked if Tao was of any use in government. Chang Ch'ien-ming told him that "with Tao a corpse could govern the Empire." By successive edicts the Tao Tê Ching was made obligatory at the examination for graduates of the second degree, every one was required to possess a copy of the work, and it was cut on stone at both capitals. Later on, printed copies were distributed to all directors of education, and it was translated into the language of the Nü-chên Tartars. Finally, Kublai Khan ordered all Taoist books to be burnt, with the exception of the Tao Tê Ching, thus showing a just appreciation of the gulf separating Lao Tzu from the later writers on Tao.

In view of the disjointed and inartistic character of the work, and its antagonism to many of the principles of orthodox Confucianism, it is small wonder that native scholars, with true Chinese subordination of matter to form, seldom profess to hold it in great esteem; and, indeed, its qualities are not such as would strongly appeal to an essentially hard-headed and materialistic race. Yet, on reflection, it will certainly appear that the teaching of Lao Tel has not been barren of practical results. The great political lesson of laisser-faire is one that the Chinese people has well assimilated and perhaps carried to excess; it may even be said to impregnate their national life more thoroughly than any doctrine of Confucius. From two great evils of modern civilisation—the bane of over-legislation and the pest of meddlesome and overbearing officialdom—China is remarkably free; and in few other countries does the individual enjoy such absolute liberty of action. Thus, on the whole, the Chinese may be said to have adopted Lao Tzu's main principles of government, with no small success. It is hard to believe that a rigidly despotic Empire, encumbered with an irksome array of laws and statutes, could have remained homogeneous and intact throughout so lengthy a period. Who can doubt that the enormous bulk of China has managed to defy the disintegrating action of time by reason of its very inertness and placidity? It has been suggested that Lao Tzu may have reached this doctrine of non-interference by observing that the Supreme Power, Tao, governs the Universe by fixed laws, and yet leaves to man an apparently unrestricted freedom of will. Be this as it may, he was undoubtedly the first man to preach the gospel of peace and intelligent inaction, being in this, as in many other respects, far in advance of his age.

In those troublous times, when the land was torn by internecine feuds, and the spirit of militarism was rife, it is not a little remarkable to find him expressing unqualified abhorrence of war, though, to be sure, this was but the logical outcome of his system of quietism. Few can help being struck by the similarity of tone between the sayings of Lao Tzu and the Gospel enunciated six centuries later by the Prince of Peace. There are two famous utterances in particular which secure to Lao Tzu the glory of having anticipated the lofty morality of the Sermon on the Mount. The cavillers who would rank the Golden Rule of Confucius below that of Christ will find it hard to get over the fact that Lao Tzu said, "Requite injury with kindness," and "To the not-good I would be good in order to make them good." It was a hundred and fifty years later that Plato reached the same conclusion in the first book of the Republic.

It is interesting to observe certain points of contact between Lao Tzu and the early Greek philosophers. He may be compared both with Parmenides, who disparaged sense-knowledge and taught the existence of the One as opposed to the Many, and with Heraclitus, whose theory of the identity of contraries recalls some of our Sage's paradoxes. But it is when we come to Plato that the most striking parallels occur. It has not escaped notice that something like the Platonic doctrine of ideas is discoverable in the "forms" which Lao Tzu conceives as residing in Tao. But, so far as I know, no one has yet pointed out what a close likeness Tao itself bears to that curious abstraction which Plato calls the Idea of the Good. The function and attributes of this grandiose conception are not set forth quite so fully or clearly as those of Tao, but it certainly covers a great deal more than the ordinary moral connotation of our word "good." [1] It is at once the creative and sustaining Cause of the Universe, the condition of all knowledge, and the Summum Bonum or supreme object of man's desire. Being a metaphysical entity, it cannot be perceived by the eye or ear of sense, and is therefore ridiculed by the inferior man of little intelligence, while only the few can enter into close communion with it. Now, all of this might stand equally well as a description of Tao. On the other hand, the inactivity and repose which are so insisted on by the Chinese thinker as the primary characteristics of Tao, would have been less intelligible to the Greek, and seem to bring us nearer to Buddhism.

The lack of reliable information about Lao Tzu is very disappointing. One cannot help wishing that some of the less important details touching the life of Confucius could be exchanged for an authentic personal account, however brief, of his older contemporary. All that we know for certain is that, after having spent most of his life in the State of Chou, he set out at an advanced age towards the West, passed the frontier, and was never heard of again. Thus Lao Tzu's gigantic figure looms but indistinctly through the mist of ages, and to gather some idea of his personality we must be content to fall back on his own rough-hewn sentences. There is one striking passage in which he describes himself, half sarcastically and half in earnest, as a dullard and a clown compared with ordinary men, and this, he seems to indicate, is the result of his adherence to Tao. These words, evidently written in great bitterness of spirit, may have been wrung from him by a sense of his failure to convert the careless generation which would have none of the Tao he venerated as the most precious thing under heaven. In showing himself, the man of Tao, in such a disadvantageous light, his meaning was probably much the same as that of Plato in the allegory of the Cave, where he depicts the blindness and bewilderment of those who descend once more into the darkness of their prison after having contemplated the dazzling brilliance of the sun.

Lao Tzu's despondency would have been greater still, could he have foreseen how his pure and idealistic teaching was destined to be dragged in the mire of degrading superstition, which for centuries has made Taoism a byword of reproach. Though frequently described as one of the "three religions of China," this cult is really little more than an inextricable mass of jugglery and fraud, absorbed from various popular beliefs and other sources, including even the rival creed of Buddhism, and conducted by a body of priests recruited from the very dregs of the Empire. Such a fate, however, is less to be wondered at than deplored, seeing that the great Founder himself took no pains to establish a practicable system. He propounded lofty sentiments, and neglected the homely details without which his ideas could not bear fruit. Moreover, when all is said and done, idealism can never hope to hold its own in human affairs, until indeed the new era dawns of which Plato dreamed long ago, and this world of ours becomes ripe for the dominion of Philosopher-Kings.

1, WILLCOTT ROAD, ACTON,
June 21, 1904.

Footnotes

[1] Lao Tzu, like Plato, recognizes very little distinction between Knowledge and Virtue, the rational and moral sides of man's nature. Virtue with him is simply the knowledge of Tao, just as with Plato it is the knowledge of "the Good."

TAO IN ITS TRANSCENDENTAL ASPECT, AND IN ITS PHYSICAL MANIFESTATION

THE Tao which can be expressed in words is not the eternal Tao; the name which can be uttered is not its eternal name. Without a name, it is the Beginning of Heaven and Earth; with a name, it is the Mother of all things. Only one who is eternally free from earthly passions can apprehend its spiritual essence; he who is ever clogged by passions can see no more than its outer form. These two things, the spiritual and the material, though we call them by different names, in their origin are one and the same. This sameness is a mystery,—the mystery of mysteries. It is the gate of all spirituality.

How unfathomable is Tao! It seems to be the ancestral progenitor of all things. How pure and clear is Tao! It would seem to be everlasting. I know not of whom it is the offspring. It appears to have been anterior to any Sovereign Power. [1]

Tao eludes the sense of sight, and is therefore called colourless. It eludes the sense of hearing, and is therefore called soundless. It eludes the sense of touch, and is therefore called incorporeal. These three qualities cannot be apprehended, and hence they may be blended into unity.

Its upper part is not bright, and its lower part is not obscure. Ceaseless in action, it cannot be named, but returns again to nothingness. We may call it the form of the formless, the image of the imageless, the fleeting and the indeterminable. Would you go before it, you cannot see its face; would you go behind it, you cannot see its back.

The mightiest manifestations of active force flow solely from Tao.

Tao in itself is vague, impalpable,—how impalpable, how vague! Yet within it there is Form. How vague, how impalpable! Yet within it there is Substance. How profound, how obscure! Yet within it there is a Vital Principle. This principle is the Quintessence of Reality, and out of it comes Truth.

From of old until now, its name has never passed away. It watches over the beginning of all things. How do I know this about the beginning of things?

Through Tao.

There is something, chaotic yet complete, which existed before Heaven and Earth. Oh, how still it is, and formless, standing alone without changing, reaching everywhere without suffering harm! It must be regarded as the Mother of the Universe. Its name I know not. To designate it, I call it Tao. Endeavouring to describe it, I call it Great. Being great, it passes on; passing on, it becomes remote; having become remote, it returns.

Therefore Tao is great; Heaven is great; Earth is great; and the Sovereign also is great. In the Universe there are four powers, of which the Sovereign is one. Man takes his law from the Earth; the Earth takes its law from Heaven; Heaven takes its law from Tao; but the law of Tao is its own spontaneity.

Tao in its unchanging aspect has no name. Small though it be in its primordial simplicity, mankind dare not claim its service. Could princes and kings hold and keep it, all creation would spontaneously pay homage. Heaven and Earth would unite in sending down sweet dew, and the people would be righteous unbidden and of their own accord.

As soon as Tao creates order, it becomes nameable. When it once has a name, men will know how to rest in it. Knowing how to rest in it, they will run no risk of harm.

Tao as it exists in the world is like the great rivers and seas which receive the streams from the valleys.

All-pervading is the Great Tao. It can be at once on the right hand and on the left. All things depend on it for life, and it rejects them not. Its task accomplished, it takes no credit. It loves and nourishes all things, but does not act as master. It is ever free from desire. We may call it small. All things return to it, yet it does not act as master. We may call it great.

The whole world will flock to him who holds the mighty form of Tao. They will come and receive no hurt, but find rest, peace, and tranquillity.

With music and dainties we may detain the passing guest. But if we open our mouths to speak of Tao, he finds it tasteless and insipid.

Not visible to the sight, not audible to the ear, in its use it is inexhaustible.

Retrogression is the movement of Tao. Weakness is the character of Tao.

All things under Heaven derive their being from Tao in the form of Existence; Tao in the form of Existence sprang from Tao in the form of Non-Existence.

Tao is a great square with no angles, a great vessel which takes long to complete, a great sound which cannot be heard, a great image with no form.

Tao lies hid and cannot be named, yet it has the power of transmuting and perfecting all things.

Tao produced Unity; Unity produced Duality; Duality produced Trinity; and Trinity produced all existing objects. These myriad objects leave darkness behind them and embrace the light, being harmonised by the breath of Vacancy.

Tao produces all things; its Virtue nourishes them; its Nature gives them form; its Force perfects them.

Hence there is not a single thing but pays homage to Tao and extols its Virtue. This homage paid to Tao, this extolling of its Virtue, is due to no command, but is always spontaneous.

Thus it is that Tao, engendering all things, nourishes them, develops them, and fosters them; perfects them, ripens them, tends them, and protects them.

Production without possession, action without self-assertion, development without domination this is its mysterious operation.

The World has a First Cause, which may be regarded as the Mother of the World. When one has the Mother, one can know the Child. He who knows the Child and still keeps the Mother, though his body perish, shall run no risk of harm.

It is the Way of Heaven not to strive, and yet it knows how to overcome; not to speak, and yet it knows how to obtain a response; it calls not, and things come of themselves; it is slow to move, but excellent in its designs.

Heaven's net is vast; though its meshes are wide, it lets nothing slip through.

The Way of Heaven is like the drawing of a bow: it brings down what is high and raises what is low. It is the Way of Heaven to take from those who have too much, and give to those who have too little. But the way of man is not so. He takes away from those who have too little, to add to his own superabundance. What man is there that can take of his own superabundance and give it to mankind? Only he who possesses Tao.

The Tao of Heaven has no favourites. It gives to all good men without distinction.

Things wax strong and then decay. This is the contrary of Tao. What is contrary to Tao soon perishes.

Footnotes

[1] This sentence is admittedly obscure, and it may be an interpolation. Lao Tzu's system of cosmogony has no place for any Divine Being independent of Tao. On the other hand, to translate ti by "Emperor," as some have done, necessarily involves us in an absurd anti-climax.

TAO AS A MORAL PRINCIPLE, OR "VIRTUE"

THE highest goodness is like water, for water is excellent in benefiting all things, and it does not strive. It occupies the lowest place, which men abhor. And therefore it is near akin to Tao.

When your work is done and fame has been achieved, then retire into the background; for this is the Way of Heaven.

Those who follow the Way desire not excess; and thus without excess they are for ever exempt from change.

All things alike do their work, and then we see them subside. When they have reached their bloom, each returns to its origin. Returning to their origin means rest or fulfilment of destiny. This reversion is an eternal law. To know that law is to be enlightened. Not to know it, is misery and calamity. He who knows the eternal law is liberal-minded. Being liberal-minded, he is just. Being just, he is kingly. Being kingly, he is akin to Heaven. Being akin to Heaven, he possesses Tao. Possessed of Tao, he endures for ever. Though his body perish, yet he suffers no harm.

He who acts in accordance with Tao, becomes one with Tao. He who treads the path of Virtue becomes one with Virtue. He who pursues a course of Vice becomes one with Vice. The man who is one with Tao, Tao is also glad to receive. The man who is one with Virtue, Virtue is also glad to receive. The man who is one with Vice, Vice is also glad to receive.

He who is self-approving does not shine. He who boasts has no merit. He who exalts himself does not rise high. Judged according to Tao, he is like remnants of food or a tumour on the body—an object of universal disgust. Therefore one who has Tao will not consort with such.

Perfect Virtue acquires nothing; therefore it obtains everything. Perfect Virtue does nothing, yet there is nothing which it does not effect. Perfect Charity operates without the need of anything to evoke it. Perfect Duty to one's neighbour operates, but always needs to be evoked. Perfect Ceremony operates, and calls for no outward response; nevertheless it induces respect. [1]

Ceremonies are the outward expression of inward feelings.

If Tao perishes, then Virtue will perish; if Virtue perishes, then Charity will perish; if Charity perishes, then Duty to one's neighbour will perish; if Duty to one's neighbour perishes, then Ceremonies will perish.

Ceremonies are but the veneer of loyalty and good faith, while oft-times the source of disorder. Knowledge of externals is but a showy ornament of Tao, while oft-times the beginning of imbecility.

Therefore the truly great man takes his stand upon what is solid, and not upon what is superficial; upon what is real, and not upon what is ornamental. He rejects the latter in favour of the former.

When the superior scholar hears of Tao, he diligently practises it. When the average scholar hears of Tao, he sometimes retains it, sometimes loses it. When the inferior scholar hears of Tao, he loudly laughs at it. Were it not thus ridiculed, it would not be worthy of the name of Tao.

He who is enlightened by Tao seems wrapped in darkness. He who is advanced in Tao seems to be going back. He who walks smoothly in Tao seems to be on a rugged path.

The man of highest virtue appears lowly. He who is truly pure behaves as though he were sullied. He who has virtue in abundance behaves as though it were not enough. He who is firm in virtue seems like a skulking pretender. He who is simple and true appears unstable as water.

If Tao prevails on earth, horses will be used for purposes of agriculture. If Tao does not prevail, war-horses will be bred on the common.

If we had sufficient knowledge to walk in the Great Way, what we should most fear would be boastful display.

The Great Way is very smooth, but the people love the by-paths.

Where the palaces are very splendid, there the fields will be very waste, and the granaries very empty.

The wearing of gay embroidered robes, the carrying of sharp swords, fastidiousness in food and drink, superabundance of property and wealth:—this I call flaunting robbery; most assuredly it is not Tao.

He who trusts to his abundance of natural virtue is like an infant newly born, whom venomous reptiles will not sting, wild beasts will not seize, birds of prey will not strike. The infant's bones are weak, its sinews are soft, yet its grasp is firm. All day long it will cry without its voice becoming hoarse. This is because the harmony of its bodily system is perfect.

Temper your sharpness, disentangle your ideas, moderate your brilliancy, live in harmony with your age. This is being in conformity with the principle of Tao. Such a man is impervious alike to favour and disgrace, to benefits and injuries, to honour and contempt. And therefore he is esteemed above all mankind.

In governing men and in serving Heaven, there is nothing like moderation. For only by moderation can there be an early return to man's normal state. This early return is the same as a great storage of Virtue. With a great storage of Virtue there is naught which may not be achieved. If there is naught which may not be achieved, then no one will know to what extent this power reaches. And if no one knows to what extent a man's power reaches, that man is fit to be the ruler of a State. Having the secret of rule, his rule shall endure. Setting the tap-root deep, and making the spreading roots firm: this is the way to ensure long life to the tree.

Tao is the sanctuary where all things find refuge, the good man's priceless treasure, the guardian and saviour of him who is not good.

Hence at the enthronement of an Emperor and the appointment of his three ducal ministers, though there be some who bear presents of costly jade and drive chariots with teams of four horses, that is not so good as sitting still and offering the gift of this Tao.

Why was it that the men of old esteemed this Tao so highly? Is it not because it may be daily sought and found, and can remit the sins of the guilty? Hence it is the most precious thing under Heaven.

All the world says that my Tao is great, but unlike other teaching. It is just because it is great that it appears unlike other teaching. If it had this likeness, long ago would its smallness have been known.

The skilful philosophers of the olden time were subtle, spiritual, profound, and penetrating. They were so deep as to be incomprehensible. Because they are hard to comprehend, I will endeavour to describe them.

Shrinking were they, like one fording a stream in winter. Cautious were they, like one who fears an attack from any quarter. Circumspect were they, like a stranger guest; self-effacing, like ice about to melt; simple, like unpolished wood; vacant, like a valley; opaque, like muddy water.

When terms are made after a great quarrel, a certain ill-feeling is bound to be left behind. How can this be made good? Therefore, having entered into an agreement, the Sage adheres to his obligations, [2] but does not exact fulfilment from others. The man who has Virtue attends to the spirit of the compact; the man without Virtue attends only to his claims.

He who tries to govern a kingdom by his sagacity is of that kingdom the despoiler; but he who does not govern by sagacity is the kingdom's blessing. He who understands these two sayings may be regarded as a pattern and a model. To keep this principle constantly before one's eyes is called Profound Virtue. Profound Virtue is unfathomable, far-reaching, paradoxical at first, but afterwards exhibiting thorough conformity with Nature.

Footnotes

[1] Han Fei Tzu explains the passage by pointing out that "Virtue is the achievement of Tao; Charity is the glory of Virtue; Duty is the translation into action of Charity; and Ceremony is the ornamental part of Duty."

[2] Literally, "he holds the left-hand portion of the agreement." In olden times, the terms of a contract were inscribed on a wooden tablet, the debit or obligations being on the left, and the credit or dues on the right; it was then broken in two, and each of the contracting parties kept his own half until fulfilment was demanded, when the validity of the claim was tested by fitting the two halves together.

THE DOCTRINE OF INACTION

THE Sage occupies himself with inaction, and conveys instruction without words. Is it not by neglecting self-interest that one will be able to achieve it?

Purge yourself of your profound intelligence, and you can still be free from blemish. Cherish the people and order the kingdom, and you can still do without meddlesome action.

Who is there that can make muddy water clear? But if allowed to remain still, it will gradually become clear of itself. Who is there that can secure a state of absolute repose? But let time go on, and the state of repose will gradually arise.

Be sparing of speech, and things will come right of themselves.

A violent wind does not outlast the morning; a squall of rain does not outlast the day. Such is the course of Nature. And if Nature herself cannot sustain her efforts long, how much less can man!

Attain complete vacuity, and sedulously preserve a state of repose.

Tao is eternally inactive, and yet it leaves nothing undone. If kings and princes could but hold fast to this principle, all things would work out their own reformation. If, having reformed, they still desired to act, I would have them restrained by the simplicity of the Nameless Tao. The simplicity of the Nameless Tao brings about an absence of desire. The absence of desire gives tranquillity. And thus the Empire will rectify itself.

The softest things in the world override the hardest. That which has no substance enters where there is no crevice. Hence I know the advantage of inaction.

Conveying lessons without words, reaping profit without action,—there are few in the world who can attain to this!

Activity conquers cold, but stillness conquers heat. Purity and stillness are the correct principles for mankind.

Without going out of doors one may know the whole world; without looking out of the window, one may see the Way of Heaven. The further one travels, the less one may know. Thus it is that without moving you shall know; without looking you shall see; without doing you shall achieve.

The pursuit of book-learning brings about daily increase. The practice of Tao brings about daily loss. Repeat this loss again and again, and you arrive at inaction. Practise inaction, and there is nothing which cannot be done.

The Empire has ever been won by letting things take their course. He who must always be doing is unfit to obtain the Empire.

Keep the mouth shut, close the gateways of sense, and as long as you live you will have no trouble. Open your lips and push your affairs, and you will not be safe to the end of your days.

Practise inaction, occupy yourself with doing nothing.

Desire not to desire, and you will not value things difficult to obtain. Learn not to learn, and

you will revert to a condition which mankind in general has lost.

Leave all things to take their natural course, and do not interfere.

LOWLINESS AND HUMILITY

ALL things in Nature work silently. They come into being and possess nothing. They fulfil their functions and make no claim.

When merit has been achieved, do not take it to yourself; for if you do not take it to yourself, it shall never be taken from you.

Follow diligently the Way in your own heart, but make no display of it to the world.

Keep behind, and you shall be put in front; keep out, and you shall be kept in.

Goodness strives not, and therefore it is not rebuked.

He that humbles himself shall be preserved entire. He that bends shall be made straight. He that is empty shall be filled. He that is worn out shall be renewed. He who has little shall succeed. He who has much shall go astray.

Therefore the Sage embraces Unity, and is a model for all under Heaven. He is free from self-display, therefore he shines forth; from self-assertion, therefore he is distinguished; from self-glorification, therefore he has merit; from self-exaltation, therefore he rises superior to all. Inasmuch as he does not strive, there is no one in the world who can strive with him.

He who, conscious of being strong, is content to be weak, he shall be the paragon of mankind. Being the paragon of mankind, Virtue will never desert him. He returns to the state of a little child.

He who, conscious of his own light, is content to be obscure,—he shall be the whole world's model. Being the whole world's model, his Virtue will never fail. He reverts to the Absolute.

He who, conscious of desert, is content to suffer disgrace,—he shall be the cynosure of mankind. Being the cynosure of mankind, his Virtue then is full. He returns to perfect simplicity.

He who is great must make humility his base. He who is high must make lowliness his foundation. Thus, princes and kings in speaking of themselves use the terms "lonely," "friendless," "of small account." Is not this making humility their base?

Thus it is that "Some things are increased by being diminished, others are diminished by being increased." What others have taught, I also teach; verily, I will make it the root of my teaching.

What makes a kingdom great is its being like a down-flowing river,—-the central point towards which all the smaller streams under Heaven converge; or like the female throughout the world, who by quiescence always overcomes the male. And quiescence is a form of humility.

Therefore, if a great kingdom humbles itself before a small kingdom, it shall make that small kingdom its prize. And if a small kingdom humbles itself before a great kingdom, it shall win over that great kingdom. Thus the one humbles itself in order to attain, the other attains because it is humble. If the great kingdom has no further desire than to bring men together and to nourish them, the small kingdom will have no further desire than to enter the service of the other. But in order that both may have their desire, the great one must learn humility.

The reason why rivers and seas are able to be lords over a hundred mountain streams, is that they know how to keep below them. That is why they are able to reign over all the mountain streams.

Therefore the Sage, wishing to be above the people, must by his words put himself below them; wishing to be before the people, he must put himself behind them. In this way, though he has his place above them, the people do not feel his weight; though he has his place before them, they do not feel it as an injury. Therefore all mankind delight to exalt him, and weary of him not.

The Sage expects no recognition for what he does; he achieves merit but does not take it to himself; he does not wish to display his worth.

I have three precious things, which I hold fast and prize. The first is gentleness; the second is frugality; the third is humility, which keeps me from putting myself before others. Be gentle, and you can be bold; be frugal, and you can be liberal; avoid putting yourself before others, and you can become a leader among men.

But in the present day men cast off gentleness, and are all for being bold; they spurn frugality, and retain only extravagance; they discard humility, and aim only at being first. Therefore they shall surely perish.

Gentleness brings victory to him who attacks, and safety to him who defends. Those whom Heaven would save, it fences round with gentleness.

The best soldiers are not warlike; the best fighters do not lose their temper. The greatest conquerors are those who overcome their enemies without strife. The greatest directors of men are those who yield place to others. This is called the Virtue of not striving, the capacity for directing mankind; this is being the compeer of Heaven. It was the highest goal of the ancients.

GOVERNMENT

NOT exalting worth keeps the people from rivalry. Not prizing what is hard to procure keeps the people from theft. Not to show them what they may covet is the way to keep their minds from disorder.

Therefore the Sage, when he governs, empties their minds and fills their bellies, weakens their inclinations and strengthens their bones. His constant object is to keep the people without knowledge and without desire, or to prevent those who have knowledge from daring to act. He practises inaction, and nothing remains ungoverned.

He who respects the State as his own person is fit to govern it. He who loves the State as his own body is fit to be entrusted with it.

In the highest antiquity, the people did not know that they had rulers. In the next age they loved and praised them. In the next, they feared them. In the next, they despised them.

How cautious is the Sage, how sparing of his words! When his task is accomplished and affairs are prosperous, the people all say: "We have come to be as we are, naturally and of ourselves."

If any one desires to take the Empire in hand and govern it, I see that he will not succeed. The Empire is a divine utensil which may not be roughly handled. He who meddles, mars. He who holds it by force, loses it.

Fishes must not be taken from the water: the methods of government must not be exhibited to the people.

Use uprightness in ruling a State; employ stratagems in waging war; practise non-interference in order to win the Empire. Now this is how I know what I lay down:—

As restrictions and prohibitions are multiplied in the Empire, the people grow poorer and poorer. When the people are subjected to overmuch government, the land is thrown into confusion. When the people are skilled in many cunning arts, strange are the objects of luxury that appear.

The greater the number of laws and enactments, the more thieves and robbers there will be. Therefore the Sage says: "So long as I do nothing, the people will work out their own reformation. So long as I love calm, the people will right themselves. If only I keep from meddling, the people will grow rich. If only I am free from desire, the people will come naturally back to simplicity."

If the government is sluggish and tolerant, the people will be honest and free from guile. If the government is prying and meddling, there will be constant infraction of the law. Is the government corrupt? Then uprightness becomes rare, and goodness becomes strange. Verily, mankind have been under delusion for many a day!

Govern a great nation as you would cook a small fish. [1]

If the Empire is governed according to Tao, disembodied spirits will not manifest supernatural powers. It is not that they lack supernatural power, but they will not use it to hurt mankind. Again, it is not that they are unable to hurt mankind, but they see that the Sage also does not hurt mankind. If then neither Sage nor spirits work harm, their virtue converges to one beneficent end.

In ancient times those who knew how to practise Tao did not use it to enlighten the people, but rather to keep them ignorant. The difficulty of governing the people arises from their having too much knowledge.

If the people do not fear the majesty of government, a reign of terror will ensue.

Do not confine them within too narrow bounds; do not make their lives too weary. For if you do not weary them of life, then they will not grow weary of you.

If the people do not fear death, what good is there in using death as a deterrent? But if the people are brought up in fear of death, and we can take and execute any man who has committed a monstrous crime, who will dare to follow his example?

Now, there is always one who presides over the infliction of death. He who would take the place of the magistrate and himself inflict death, is like one who should try to do the work of a master-carpenter. And of those who try the work of a master-carpenter there are few who do not cut their own hands.

The people starve because those in authority over them devour too many taxes; that is why they starve. The people are difficult to govern because those placed over them are meddlesome; that is why they are difficult to govern. The people despise death because of their excessive labour in seeking the means of life; that is why they despise death.

A Sage has said: "He who can take upon himself the nation's shame is fit to be lord of the land. He who can take upon himself the nation's calamities is fit to be ruler over the Empire."

Were I ruler of a little State with a small population, and only ten or a hundred men available as soldiers, I would not use them. I would have the people look on death as a grievous thing, and they should not travel to distant countries. Though they might possess boats and carriages, they should have no occasion to ride in them. Though they might own weapons and armour, they should have no need to use them. I would make the people return to the use of knotted cords. [2] They should find their plain food sweet, their rough garments fine. They should be content with their homes, and happy in their simple ways. If a neighbouring State was within sight of mine—nay, if we were close enough to hear the crowing of each other's cocks and the barking of each other's dogs—the two peoples should grow old and die without there ever having been any mutual intercourse.

Footnotes

[1] Q.d., Don't overdo it.

[2] The old quipo method of recording events, before the invention of writing.

WAR

HE who serves a ruler of men in harmony with Tao will not subdue the Empire by force of arms. Such a course is wont to bring retribution in its train.

Where troops have been quartered, brambles and thorns spring up. In the track of great armies there must follow lean years.

The good man wins a victory and then stops; he will not go on to acts of violence. Winning, he boasteth not; he will not triumph; he shows no arrogance. He wins because he cannot choose; after his victory he will not be overbearing.

Weapons, however beautiful, are instruments of ill omen, hateful to all creatures. Therefore he who has Tao will have nothing to do with them.

Where the princely man abides, the weak left hand is in honour. But he who uses weapons honours the stronger right. Weapons are instruments of ill omen; they are not the instruments of the princely man, who uses them only when he needs must. Peace and tranquillity are what he prizes. When he conquers, he is not elate. To be elate were to rejoice in the slaughter of human beings. And he who rejoices in the slaughter of human beings is not fit to work his will in the Empire.

On happy occasions, the left is favoured; on sad occasions, the right. The second in command has his place on the left, the general in chief on the right. That is to say, they are placed in the order observed at funeral rites. And, indeed, he who has exterminated a great multitude of men should bewail them with tears and lamentation. It is well that those who are victorious in battle should be placed in the order of funeral rites.

A certain military commander used to say: "I dare not act the host; I prefer to play the guest. [1] I dare not advance an inch; I prefer to retreat a foot."

There is no greater calamity than lightly engaging in war. Lightly to engage in war is to risk the loss of our treasure. [2]

When opposing warriors join in battle, he who has pity conquers.

Footnotes

[1] According to Chinese etiquette, it is for the master of the house to make advances, and his guest follows suit. Thus "host" here means the one who takes the initiative and begins the attack; "guest," the one who acts on the defensive. The passage may be merely figurative, illustrating the conduct of those who practise Tao.

[2] I.e., humanity or gentleness, mentioned above as one or "three precious things."

PARADOXES

AMONG mankind, the recognition of beauty as such implies the idea of ugliness, and the recognition of good implies the idea of evil. There is the same mutual relation between existence and non-existence in the matter of creation; between difficulty and ease in the matter of accomplishing; between long and short in the matter of form; between high and low in the matter of elevation; between treble and bass in the matter of musical pitch; between before and after in the matter of priority.

Nature is not benevolent; with ruthless indifference she makes all things serve their purposes, like the straw dogs we use at sacrifices. The Sage is not benevolent: he utilises the people with the like inexorability.

The space between Heaven and Earth,—is it not like a bellows? It is empty, yet inexhaustible; when it is put in motion, more and more comes out.

Heaven and Earth are long-lasting. The reason why Heaven and Earth can last long is that they live not for themselves, and thus they are able to endure.

Thirty spokes unite in one nave; the utility of the cart depends on the hollow centre in which the axle turns. Clay is moulded into a vessel; the utility of the vessel depends on its hollow interior. Doors and windows are cut out in order to make a house; the utility of the house depends on the empty spaces.

Thus, while the existence of things may be good, it is the non-existent in them which makes them serviceable.

When the Great Tao falls into disuse, benevolence and righteousness come into vogue. When shrewdness and sagacity appear, great hypocrisy prevails. It is when the bonds of kinship are out of joint that filial piety and paternal affection begin. It is when the State is in a ferment of revolution that loyal patriots arise.

Cast off your holiness, rid yourself of sagacity, and the people will benefit an hundredfold. Discard benevolence and abolish righteousness, and the people will return to filial piety and paternal love. Renounce your scheming and abandon gain, and thieves and robbers will disappear. These three precepts mean that outward show is insufficient, and therefore they bid us be true to our proper nature;—to show simplicity, to embrace plain dealing, to reduce selfishness, to moderate desire.

A variety of colours makes man's eye blind; a diversity of sounds makes man's ear deaf; a mixture of flavours makes man's palate dull.

He who knows others is clever, but he who knows himself is enlightened. He who overcomes others is strong, but he who overcomes himself is mightier still. He is rich who knows when he has enough. He who acts with energy has strength of purpose. He who moves not from his proper place is long-lasting. He who dies, but perishes not, enjoys true longevity.

If you would contract, you must first expand. If you would weaken, you must first strengthen. If you would overthrow, you must first raise up. If you would take, you must first give. This is called the dawn of intelligence.

He who is most perfect seems to be lacking; yet his resources are never outworn. He who is most full seems vacant; yet his uses are inexhaustible.

Extreme straightness is as bad as crookedness. Extreme cleverness is as bad as folly. Extreme fluency is as bad as stammering.

Those who know do not speak; those who .speak do not know.

Abandon learning, and you will be free from trouble and distress.

Failure is the foundation of success, and the means by which it is achieved. Success is the lurking-place of failure; but who can tell when the turning-point will come?

He who acts, destroys; he who grasps, loses. Therefore the Sage does not act, and so does not destroy; he does not grasp, and so he does not lose.

Only he who does nothing for his life's sake can truly be said to value his life.

Man at his birth is tender and weak; at his death he is rigid and strong. Plants and trees when they come forth are tender and crisp; when dead, they are dry and tough. Thus rigidity and strength are the concomitants of death; softness and weakness are the concomitants of life.

Hence the warrior that is strong does not conquer; the tree that is strong is cut down. Therefore the strong and the big take the lower place; the soft and the weak take the higher place.

There is nothing in the world more soft and weak than water, yet for attacking things that are hard and strong there is nothing that surpasses it, nothing that can take its place.

The soft overcomes the hard; the weak overcomes the strong. There is no one in the world but knows this truth, and no one who can put it into practice.

Those who are wise have no wide range of learning; those who range most widely are not wise.

The Sage does not care to hoard. The more he uses for the benefit of others, the more he possesses himself. The more he gives to his fellow-men, the more he has of his own.

The truest sayings are paradoxical.

MISCELLANEOUS SAYINGS
AND PRECEPTS

BY many words wit is exhausted; it is better to preserve a mean. The excellence of a dwelling is its site; the excellence of a mind is its profundity; the excellence of giving is charitableness; the excellence of speech is truthfulness; the excellence of government is order; the excellence of action is ability; the excellence of movement is timeliness.

He who grasps more than he can hold, would be better without any. If a house is crammed with treasures of gold and jade, it will be impossible to guard them all.

He who prides himself upon wealth and honour hastens his own downfall. He who strikes with a sharp point will not himself be safe for long.

He who embraces unity of soul by subordinating animal instincts to reason will be able to escape dissolution. He who strives his utmost after tenderness can become even as a little child.

If a man is clear-headed and intelligent, can he be without knowledge?

The Sage attends to the inner and not to the outer; he puts away the objective and holds to the subjective.

Between yes and yea, how small the difference! Between good and evil, how great the difference!

What the world reverences may not be treated with disrespect.

He who has not faith in others shall find no faith in them.

To see oneself is to be clear of sight. Mighty is he who conquers himself.

He who raises himself on tiptoe cannot stand firm; he who stretches his legs wide apart cannot walk.

Racing and hunting excite man's heart to madness.

The struggle for rare possessions drives a man to actions injurious to himself.

The heavy is the foundation of the light; repose is the ruler of unrest.

The wise prince in his daily course never departs from gravity and repose. Though he possess a gorgeous palace, he will dwell therein with calm indifference. How should the lord of a myriad chariots conduct himself with levity in the Empire? Levity loses men's hearts; unrest loses the throne.

The skillful traveller leaves no tracks; the skillful speaker makes no blunders; the skillful reckoner uses no tallies. He who knows how to shut uses no bolts—yet you cannot open. He who knows how to bind uses no cords—yet you cannot undo.

Among men, reject none; among things, reject nothing. This is called comprehensive intelligence.

The good man is the bad man's teacher; the bad man is the material upon which the good man works. If the one does not value his teacher, if the other does not love his material, then despite their sagacity they must go far astray. This is a mystery of great import.

As unwrought material is divided up and made into serviceable vessels, so the Sage turns his simplicity [1] to account, and thereby becomes the ruler of rulers.

The course of things is such that what was in front is now behind; what was hot is now cold; what was strong is now weak; what was complete is now in ruin. Therefore the Sage avoids excess, extravagance, and grandeur.

Which is nearer to you, fame or life? Which is more to you, life or wealth? Which is the greater malady, gain or loss?

Excessive ambitions necessarily entail great sacrifice. Much hoarding must be followed by heavy loss. He who knows when he has enough will not be put to shame. He who knows when to stop will not come to harm. Such a man can look forward to long life.

There is no sin greater than ambition; no calamity greater than discontent; no vice more sickening than covetousness. He who is content always has enough.

Do not wish to be rare like jade, or common like stone.

The Sage has no hard and fast ideas, but he shares the ideas of the people and makes them his own. Living in the world, he is apprehensive lest his heart be sullied by contact with the world. The people all fix their eyes and ears upon him. The Sage looks upon all as his children.

I have heard that he who possesses the secret of life, when travelling abroad, will not flee from rhinoceros or tiger; when entering a hostile camp, he will not equip himself with sword or buckler. The rhinoceros finds in him no place to insert its horn; the tiger has nowhere to fasten its claw; the soldier has nowhere to thrust his blade. And why? Because he has no spot where death can enter.

To see small beginnings is clearness of sight. To rest in weakness is strength.

He who knows how to plant, shall not have his plant uprooted; he who knows how to hold a thing, shall not have it taken away. Sons and grandsons will worship at his shrine, which shall endure from generation to generation.

Knowledge in harmony is called constant. Constant knowledge is called wisdom. [2] Increase of life is called felicity. The mind directing the body is called strength.

Be square without being angular. Be honest without being mean. Be upright without being punctilious. Be brilliant without being showy.

Good words shall gain you honour in the market-place, but good deeds shall gain you friends among men.

To the good I would be good; to the not-good I would also be good, in order to make them good.

With the faithful I would keep faith; with the unfaithful I would also keep faith, in order that they may become faithful.

Even if a man is bad, how can it be right to cast him off?

Requite injury with kindness.

The difficult things of this world must once have been easy; the great things of this world must once have been small. Set about difficult things while they are still easy; do great things while they are still small. The Sage never affects to do anything great, and therefore he is able to achieve his great results.

He who always thinks things easy is sure to find them difficult. Therefore the Sage ever anticipates difficulties, and thus it is he never encounters them.

While times are quiet, it is easy to take action; ere coming troubles have cast their shadows, it is easy to lay plans.

That which is brittle is easily broken; that which is minute is easily dissipated. Take precautions before the evil appears; regulate things before disorder has begun.

The tree which needs two arms to span its girth sprang from the tiniest shoot. Yon tower, nine storeys high, rose from a little mound of earth. A journey of a thousand miles began with a single step.

A great principle cannot be divided; therefore it is that many containers cannot contain it. [3]

The Sage knows what is in him, but makes no display; he respects himself, but seeks not honour for himself.

To know, but to be as though not knowing, is the height of wisdom. Not to know, and yet to affect knowledge, is a vice. If we regard this vice as such, we shall escape it. The Sage has not this vice. It is because he regards it as a vice that he escapes it.

Use the light that is in you to revert to your natural clearness of sight. Then the loss of the body is unattended by calamity. This is called doubly enduring.

In the management of affairs, people constantly break down just when they are nearing a successful issue. If they took as much care at the end as at the beginning, they would not fail in their enterprises.

He who lightly promises is sure to keep but little faith.

He whose boldness leads him to venture, will be slain; he who is brave enough not to venture, will live. Of these two, one has the benefit, the other has the hurt. But who is it that knows the real cause of Heaven's hatred? This is why the Sage hesitates and finds it difficult to act.

The violent and stiff-necked die not by a natural death.

True words are not fine; fine words are not true.

The good are not contentious; the contentious are not good.

This is the Way of Heaven, which benefits, and injures not. This is the Way of the Sage, in whose actions there is no element of strife.

Footnotes

[1] There is a play on the word p'u, simplicity, the original meaning of which is "unwronght material."

[2] There must always be a due harmony between mind and body, neither of them being allowed to outstrip the other. Under such circumstances, the mental powers will be constant, invariable, always equally ready for use when called upon. And such a mental condition is what Lao Tzu here calls "wisdom"

[3] That is, a principle which applies to the whole applies also to a part. Because you may divide the containing whole, you are not at liberty to divide the principle.

LAO TZU ON HIMSELF

ALAS! the barrenness of the age has not yet reached its limit. All men are radiant with happiness, as if enjoying a great feast, as if mounted on a tower in spring. I alone am still, and give as yet no sign of joy. I am like an infant which has not yet smiled, forlorn as one who has nowhere to lay his head. Other men have plenty, while I alone seem to have lost all. I am a man foolish in heart, dull and confused. Other men are full of light; I alone seem to be in darkness. Other men are alert; I alone am listless. I am unsettled as the ocean, drifting as though I had no stopping-place. All men have their usefulness; I alone am stupid and clownish. Lonely though I am and unlike other men, yet I revere the Foster-Mother, Tao.

My words are very easy to understand, very easy to put into practice; yet the world can neither understand nor practise them.

My words have a clue, my actions have an underlying principle. It is because men do not know the clue that they understand me not.

Those who know me are but few, and on that account my honour is the greater.

Thus the Sage wears coarse garments, but carries a jewel in his bosom.

Hindu Mysticism
by S.N. Dasgupta

Table of Contents

PREFACE

BOTH on the continent and in America, Hindus are associated with mysticism, but, so far as I know, the subject of Hindu mysticism has as yet received no systematic treatment, either in the way of general introduction, or in the way of a comprehensive account. The man in the street cannot, as a rule, distinguish between the lower and the higher forms of mysticism. He looks upon mysticism in general with some kind of superstitious awe or reverence, and he thinks of it as an obscure and supernatural method by which, in some unaccountable manner, miraculous feats may be performed or physical advantages reaped—departed spirits made visible, fortunes told, muscles developed, riches earned without effort, dangerous and incurable diseases cured by simple amulets or blessings, infallible prophesies made, and the like. I shall not say anything as to whether or not such phenomena are possible, for my present interest concerns not facts but beliefs. But whether or not the phenomena actually occur, they imply beliefs that there are short cuts to the attainment of advantages through mysterious, supernatural or miraculous powers undiscoverable by reason. I refer to this as inferior mysticism, because the purposes relate solely to the attainment of inferior mundane benefits. Distinguishable therefrom is the belief that the highest reality or the ultimate realisation and fulfilment (whatever may be their nature) cannot be attained by reason alone, but that there are other avenues to them, namely, the firm and steady control of will, the development of right emotions, or both combined, or by them both along with the highest functioning of reason. This is superior and true mysticism because it is directed to the liberation of the spirit and the attainment of the highest bliss.

Mysticism in Europe has a definite history. In spite of the variety of its types, it may roughly be described to refer to the belief that God is realised through ecstatic communion with Him. With the Islamic mystics, the Christian mystics, and the devotional mystics or bhaktas of India, the vision of God and His grace is attained through devotional communion or devotional rapture of various kinds. But in all these mystics, we find a keen sense of the necessity of purity of mind, contentment, ever alert striving for moral goodness, self-abnegation, and one-pointedness to God. There can be no true mysticism without real moral greatness. This mysticism should therefore be distinguished from a mere delusory faith that God often grants us a vision of Him or appears to us in dreams, or from a faith in the infallibility of the scriptures and so forth, for the latter are often but manifestations of credulity or of a tendency to believe in suggestions, and may often be associated with an inadequate alertness of critical and synthetic intellect.

I have defined mysticism as a belief or a view, but in reality it means much more than that. In the life of the true mystics, beliefs exert a great formative influence. They are no mere intellectual registrations of opinions or temporary experiences, but represent the dynamic, the dominant tone of their personality as it develops and perfects itself. Mysticism is not an intellectual theory; it is fundamentally an active, formative, creative, elevating and ennobling principle of life. I have not here taken note of poems or thoughts involving merely mystical beliefs but have touched only upon those which are the outward expressions of a real inner flowering of life in the persons of those who have tried to live a saintly life of mysticism.

Mysticism means a spiritual grasp of the aims and problems of life in a much more real and ultimate manner than is possible to mere reason. A developing life of mysticism means a gradual ascent in the scale of spiritual values, experience, and spiritual ideals. As such, it is many-sided in its development, and as rich and complete as life itself. Regarded from this point of view, mysticism is the basis of all religions—particularly of religion as it appears in the lives of truly religious men.

An acquaintance with Indian religious experience shows that there are types of religious and mystical experience other than that of an intimate communion with God. I have therefore made my definition of mysticism wider, so that it may include not only the Islamic, Christian, and the Bhakti forms of Indian mysticism but other types of Indian mysticism as well. I could not hope to give an exhaustive analysis or even a fairly comprehensive treatment of the chief features of the different types of Indian mysticism within the limits of these six lectures. I have therefore attempted only a brief general outline of some of the most important types, indicating their mutual relations, sometimes genetically and sometimes logically. I have omitted all reference to the connected metaphysical issues, as a comprehensive treatment of these philosophical problems may be found in my "A History of Indian Philosophy" (Cambridge University Press), the first volume of which has already been published and the other volumes are in the course of publication.

I have first described the sacrificial type of mysticism. This cannot in all its particulars be regarded as a mysticism of a superior order, but it develops many features of the higher types and marks the starting-point of the evolution of Indian mysticism. I have then discussed the four chief types of mysticism: the Upanishad, the Yogic, the Buddhistic and the Bhakti, though there are many branches of these particular types upon which I could not enter. I have mentioned some other minor types of mysticism. In addition there are some which are of a syncretistic nature, exhibiting elements of belief and duties of two or three distinct types of mysticism in combination. I could not present them all. The five main types that I have here described, however, may be regarded as fundamental;

and, though very much more could have been said in the way of elaboration and illustration, all their striking characteristics have been briefly touched upon and materials have largely been drawn directly from the original sources. I hope that I may in the future have an opportunity to take up the subject again and to deal with it more elaborately.

Perhaps I should have entitled the present volume "The Development of Indian Mysticism." But the word "Indian" might be misunderstood in America. I have therefore selected "Hindu Mysticism," "Hindu" standing for Indian. I have dropped the word "Development" to avoid any initial impression of forbidding technicality. For similar reasons diacritical marks have been omitted.

I now have the very pleasant duty of thanking the Harris Foundation Lecture Committee which did me the honour of asking me to deliver these lectures and President Walter Dill Scott, Professor Edward L. Schaub and Professor T. W. Koch, the Secretary of the committee. Considering the high reputation of my predecessors, who were outstanding scholars in their respective branches of learning, I feel extremely diffident about my own humble performance. I have received so much hospitality and kindness in America that I shall always think of this great country with appreciative enthusiasm and admiration. But I can never express adequately my gratefulness and thanks to Professor Edward L. Schaub, who was chiefly responsible for my invitations to the American Universities and who helped me so generously in seeing these lectures through the press, as well as in suggesting many changes of style and expression—to say nothing of his personal courtesies and cordiality which will always endear his name to me.

S. N. Dasgupta.

LECTURE I: SACRIFICIAL MYSTICISM

THE Hindus possess a body of sacred compositions called the Vedas. Of these there are four collections. Two of them comprise original hymns. The contents of the others consist largely of poems derived from the former two. The collections of original hymns, known as the Rig Veda and the Atharva Veda, include, respectively, 1028 original hymns of about 10600 stanzas and 731 hymns of about 6000 stanzas. All of these were kept in memory and transmitted by recitation and close memorizing on the part of teachers and pupils in an unbroken chain of early traditions from a time when writing was probably not known. The opinions of scholars vary greatly regarding the antiquity of this literature; some think that the hymns were composed about 6000 B. C. or at a still earlier date, while others think that they were composed about 1200 B. C. or 1000 B. C. The Vedic hymns are probably the earliest important religious documents of the human race.

The hymns of the Atharva Veda contain among other things descriptions of charms for curing diseases, prayers for long life and health, imprecations against demons, sorcerers and enemies, charms pertaining to women—to secure their love or arouse jealousy, and the like—charms for securing harmony and influence in an assembly, charms for securing the prosperity of household, fields, cattle, business, gambling, etc., charms in expiation of sins and defilement. The hymns of the Rig Veda, on the other hand, are often praises of various deities, who are frequently mere personifications of the different powers of nature, such as the rain-god, the wind-god, the fire-god, and the like. The prayers in these hymns are praises of the greatness and power, the mysterious nature, and the exploits of these deities, as well as prayers for various favors. Often the favors sought are of the nature of material blessings, such as long life, vigorous offspring, cattle and horses, gold, etc. Prayers for the advancement of the inner spiritual achievements of man, for righteousness or moral greatness, prayers expressing a passionate longing for the divine or a humble submission of the mind to the divine will are not so frequent. Most of these prayers were recited in the performance of certain prescribed rituals. Though from the praises of the gods one might infer that it was the gods who were supposed to bestow the benefits, it was in fact the complete set of ritualistic performances that was considered to be the cause of the showering of the benefits. It was supposed that these ritualistic performances when carried out in all their details, precisely and accurately, could by their joint and mysterious effect produce a mysterious something whereby the prayers were fulfilled.

I shall omit from my discussion the hymns of the Atharva Veda which deal only with spells, witchcraft and incantations. But while I take for examination those hymns of the Rig Veda which express beautiful ideas about the nature-deities and which voice personal requests for material comforts or for advantages, it should be understood that they also were chanted in connection with the performance of rituals and sacrifices. It is difficult to determine whether in the earliest period definite theories had been formulated regarding the intimate and indispensable connection between the chanting of these hymns of personal appeal and the performance of the rituals. But if we judge by the Vedic literature of the Brahmanas (probably composed shortly after the hymns, and later appended to them) which indicate authoritatively the place of these hymns in the ritualistic observances and specify what hymns were to be uttered under what ritualistic conditions and in what order or manner, it seems almost certain that the prevailing form of what is commonly called the Vedic religion may in strictness not be considered as a religion in the ordinarily accepted meaning of this term. Many of the ritualistic observances, or yajna, required the help of a large number of priests, and large quantities of butter, rice, milk, animals, etc. They had to be performed with the most elaborate details from day to day, for months together and sometimes even for ten or twelve years; and it was enjoined that all the observances should be performed in exact accordance with the prescriptions laid down in the Brahmana literature. Even the slightest inaccuracy or the most trifling inexactness would be sufficient to spoil the entire effect of the sacrifice. But if the sacrifices were performed with the strictest accuracy, then the material advantages for which they were performed were bound to come regardless of the good will or the ill will of the gods to whom the prayers were offered. Tvashtar had performed a sacrifice for the birth of a son who might kill Indra, but owing to a slight error in pronunciation the meaning of the prayer was changed and the sacrifice produced a son who was not a killer of Indra but of whom Indra was the killer.

This idea of sacrifice is entirely different from anything found in other races. For with the Vedic people, the sacrifices were more powerful than the gods. The gods could be pleased or displeased; if the sacrifices were duly performed the prayers were bound to be fulfilled. The utterance or chanting of the stanzas of the Vedic hymns with specially prescribed accents and modulations, the pouring of the melted butter in the prescribed manner into the sacrificial fire, the husking of rice in a particular way, the making and exact placing of cakes, all the thousand details of rituals—often performed continuously for days, months and years with rigorous exactness—was called a yajna (frequently translated into English, "sacrifice"). All the good things that the people wanted, be it the birth of a son, a shower of rain, or a place of enjoyment in heaven, were believed to be secured through the performance of these sacrifices. It is possible that when these hymns were originally composed, they were but simple prayers to the deified powers of nature, or that they were only associated with some simple rituals. But the evidence that is presented to us in the later Vedic and non-Vedic records containing descriptions of these sacrifices and discussions respecting their value, convinces us beyond doubt that it was the performance of these sacrifices, perfect in every detail in accordance with the dictates of the sacrificial manuals, the Brahmanas, that was believed to be capable of producing everything that a man could desire. A direct consequence of this apparently unmeaning necessity of strictest accuracy of ritualistic performances is a theory that came to be formulated and accepted in later periods, namely, that the sacrificial rites revealed such supernatural wisdom that they could not have been made by any one but were self-existent. It came to be held that the hymns of the Vedas, as well as the sacrificial manuals, were without authorship; that they existed eternally, prescribing certain courses of ritualistic procedure for the attainment of particular advantages and prohibiting certain undesirable courses of action. Consistently with the sacrificial theory it was also believed that the meanings of the hymns, so far as they described events or facts of nature or the exploits and the conduct of the gods were of a legendary character, that their true value consisted in the enjoining of particular courses of action or of dissuading people from other courses of action.

Religion in its ordinarily accepted sense means a personal relationship with some divine or transcendent person to whom we submit and to whom we pray for material advantages or for spiritual or moral enlightenment. But here was a belief in the divinity or the uncreatedness of a literature—the Vedas—which was believed to contain within itself the secret laws of the universe. Here there was a conception of commands, categorical in nature and external in character, without the least suggestion of any commander. Though these commands were supposed not to have emanated from any person, they may nevertheless in some sense be described as transcendent, for they were regarded as far above human wisdom. No reason could be given why a particular sacrificial performance should produce any particular kind of material advantage. There stand the commands—commands which had revealed themselves to the minds of the various sages, which had no beginning in time, which do not imply any commander, and which are absolutely faultless and unerring in their directions.

The sacrifices, thus, were supposed to possess a mysterious power capable of regulating and modifying the workings of the universe for the advantage of individuals; and the Vedic commands were thought to embody omniscience respecting the ways of the world. Though the repository of omniscience, the Vedas were not conceived as divulging to us their secrets but merely as providing a body of directions which, if followed, would give whatever advantages one craved in this life or the next. The sacrifices (yajna) or their mysterious powers, are called dharma, a term which in Indian vernaculars is often used wrongly to translate the English word "religion." The Vedic hymns, the priests, and the sacrifices are also called "the great" by the application of the term brahman, which in later Indian philosophy and religion had such a momentous history.

What we have described is no ordinary magic of spells and incantations, but a repository of the cosmic secrets and cosmic forces. These impersonal commands unite in them the concepts of an unalterable law and perfect omniscience; they imply therefore the possibility of reaping all the comforts of this life and of the after-life by submission to them and compliance with them. But they involve no law-giver, no divine person, no author of the universe or of the destinies of human beings who must be pacified, obeyed or loved, and by whose grace we receive the blessings of life. We can control our own destinies, and have whatever we may want, if we only follow the commands. There is no other mystery of life save this great mystery of the Vedic commands, and these are absolutely inscrutable. These commands do not teach ordinary laws of social life or of behavior toward our fellow-beings, or anything that we could discover by our own intelligence and wisdom. Neither do they teach us anything that we could learn by experience or reason. They give direction for the attainment of the good things of this life or of the after-life only in so far as the means thereto are absolutely undiscoverable by us. They are not a body of facts, but a body of commands and prohibitions. Yet they do not represent commands of the inner conscience or of the spirit within us; they do not give us any food for the spirit. They represent an objective and unalterable law realistically conceived, and they relate to desires for material comforts in this life or the life in heaven. This concept gives us all the principal elements of religion except that of a divine person. The acceptance of the blessings of this life as gifts from God, and a sense of our duty to please Him by submission and prayer are, therefore, not implied in this system of Vedic sacrifices. What is implied is some great impersonal force which harmonises ourselves and our destinies with the happenings and events of the world of nature. Instead of God we find here a body of commands which demand our obedience and reverence; but the source of their power and the secret of their omniscient character and uncreatedness cannot be determined by us through reason or experience. But this ritualistic mysticism—if we may be permitted thus to call it—must be distinguished from the simple feelings and ideas that are found in the hymns themselves. In all probability the latter did not originally imply the complicated ritualistic hypotheses of the later period.

The forces of nature with their wonderful manifestations of inexplicable marvels appeared to the early sages like great beings endowed with life and personality. They were treated at times as friendly, but again as hostile. Sometimes the mystery of the natural phenomena seemed stupifying in its psychological effect. The laws of nature were at that time unknown, and there was no obstacle to the free flight of the imagination. When the Vedic sage saw the sun proceeding in his upward and downward course through the sky he cried out in his wonder:

"Undropped beneath, not fastened firm, how comes it
That downward turned he falls not downward?
The guide of his ascending path,—who saw it?"

The sage is full of wonder that "the sparkling waters of all rivers flow into one ocean without ever filling it." He perceives the unalterable course of the sun from day to day, and the succession of day and night, and he exclaims with delight: "Every day, in unceasing interchange with night and her dark wonders, comes the dawn with her beautiful ones to reanimate the worlds, never failing in her place, never in her time." Again, he is puzzled when thinking whither the shining ones of the sky disappear, and he cries forth in amazement:

"Who is it knows, and who can tell us surely
Where lies the path that leads to the Eternals?
Their deepest dwellings only we discover,
And hidden these in distant secret regions."

In how many hymns does the singer express his wonder that the rough red cow gives soft white milk. To the god Indra he cries:

"Grant me, O God, the highest, best of treasures,
A judging mind, prosperity abiding,
Riches abundant, lasting health of body,
The grace of eloquence, and days propitious."

To the God of the destroying storm he prays:

"Let me through thy best medicines, O Rudra,
My life on earth prolong a hundred winters.
From us dispel all hatred and oppression,
On every side calamity drive from us.

Where then, O Rudra, is thy hand of mercy,
The hand that healing brings and softens sorrow,
That takes away the ills which the gods send?
Let me, O mighty one, feel thy forgiveness.

The hero gladdened me amid tumult
With greater might when I his aid entreated;
Like some cool shade from the Sun's heat protected

May I attain to Rudra's grace and refuge."

Again when he is penitent he would ask forgiveness of the god Varuna, the personification of the all-embracing heaven, and say:

"If we to any dear and loved companion
Have evil done, to brother or to neighbour,
To our own countryman or to a stranger,
That sin do thou O Varuna forgive us."

 Or,

"Forgive the wrongs, committed by our fathers,
What we ourselves have sinned in mercy pardon;
My own misdeeds do thou O God take from me,
And for another's sin let me not suffer."

Or, again,

"If ever we deceived like cheating players,
If consciously we have erred or all unconscious
According to our sin do not thou punish;
Be thou the singer's guardian in thy wisdom."

But besides these prayers, we sometimes find poems composed by the Vedic people, descriptive of their varied experiences of ordinary life. Thus a gambler gives his experience as follows:

"My wife has never angered me nor striven,
Was ever kind to me and my companions;
Though she was faithful to me, I have spurned her,
For love of dice, the only thing I value.

The gambler's wife deserted mourns; his mother
Laments her son, she knows not where he wanders
And he in debt and trouble, seeking money,
Remains at night beneath the roof of strangers.

And when I say that I will play no longer,
My friends abandon me and all desert me;
Yet then again I hear the brown dice rattling
I hasten, like a wanton to her lover."

Again we read:

"The gambler hurries to the gaming table,
'Today I'll win,' he thinks in his excitement.
The dice inflame his greed, his hopes mount higher;
He leaves his winnings all with his opponent."

When we read these hymns we see in them the simple prayers of a simple primitive people impressed with the inexplicable and varied phenomena of a tropical climate. They turn to the forces behind the latter as personified deities, describing the phenomena and offering their simple prayers. We find in these prayers experiences of simple wonder, of sufferings and of simple enjoyments. But when we come to the sacrificial stage of development we find a religious outlook in which the independent simple meanings of the hymns possess importance only for their sacrificial utterance in particular contexts. During the particular ritual observances the different verses were often torn out of their contexts and were combined with others which apparently had little or no relation with them and no conceivable bearing on the performances during which they were chanted or uttered. They were simply the means for the performance of the sacrifices. Their simple meanings as descriptions of things or events or phenomena or ideas were dropped from consideration. The value attached to them centered about their being uttered or chanted in particular Vedic sacrifices in accordance with certain sacrificial canons of interpretation. The entire significance of these hymns consisted either in their use as directions for the performance of certain sacrificial duties or in their utterance in these sacrifices under prescribed conditions as found in the sacrificial manuals, the Brahmanas, which were considered as part of the Vedas. Thought and feeling were driven from their places of importance in human nature, and the whole emphasis was laid on the interpretation of the Vedic literature as a system of duties involving commands and prohibitions, and nothing else. Some of these duties were compulsory, while others were voluntary in the sense that they had to be performed only when one wanted to secure some desired end unattainable by any means discoverable by his reason or experience.

The authority which this system of Vedic injunctions and prohibitions was supposed to possess was so high as to demand the entire submission of one's will and thought. Their claims did not stand in need of any justification by reason or logic, for they were supposed to be guides in a sphere where reason and experience were utterly helpless. The only fruitful way in which reason could be employed with regard to these Vedic commands was by accepting their authority and then trying to explain them in such a way that their mysterious nature might be reconciled to us. These Vedic commands cannot be described as "revelations" in the ordinary Christian sense of the term; for the latter presupposes the existence of a living God able and willing to bestow the body of truths that man requires, whereas the Vedic commands are devoid of any notion of a law-giver. This sacrificial mysticism, if it may be so called, does not recognize any God or supreme being from whom these commands emanate or who reveals them to man. The commands are taken as eternal truths, beginningless and immortal, revealing themselves to man and demanding man's submission to them. Nevertheless they are not spiritual or inner truths revealed from within man himself; they are external and impersonal commands which contain within themselves the inscrutable secrets of nature and of the happiness of man.

The fact that the Vedas were regarded as revelations of eternal truths, truths which no human reason could ever challenge, naturally divested reason of confidence in its ability to unravel the mysteries of man and of the world. Even in the somewhat later days of the evolution of Vedic culture, when there grew up a school of thinkers who disbelieved the claim that the whole of the Vedas were nothing but a body of commands and prohibitions and who held that there were at least some particular portions of the Vedas which dealt with the eternal truths of spiritual facts and experiences of reality, the belief remained unshaken that what the Vedas gave one as truths were unshakeable and unchallengeable by reason or by experience. This means a definite lowering or degradation of reason in its capacity as truth-finder. Reason calls for counter-reason and leads through an endless regressus without ever being able to lead to truth. The Vedas, then, are the only repository of the highest truths, and the function of reason is only to attempt to reconcile these truths with our experience and sense-observation. It is surprising that reason has continued to remain in this subordinate position throughout the development of Indian religious and philosophical thought almost to our own days. No change, no new idea could be considered to be right or could be believed by the people, unless it could also be shown that it had the sanction of the Vedas. Reason was never trusted as the only true and safe guide.

The word "mysticism" is a European word with a definite history. Most European writers have used it to denote an intuitive or ecstatic union with the deity, through contemplation, communion, or other mental experiences, or to denote the relationship and potential union of the human soul with ultimate reality. But I should for my present purposes like to give it a wider meaning which would include this and the other different types of mysticism that I may be discussing in the course of this series of lectures. I should like to define mysticism as a theory, doctrine, or view that considers reason to be incapable of discovering or of realising the nature of ultimate truth, whatever be the nature of this ultimate truth, but at the same time believes in the certitude of some other means of arriving at it. If this definition be accepted, then this ritualistic philosophy of the Vedas is the earliest form of mysticism that is known to India or to the world. This Vedic mysticism prepared the way for the rise of the other forms of mysticism that sprang up in India. Subsequent lectures will deal with these later forms, in some of which at least it will be easy to notice their similarity to Western types of mysticism with which Western readers are more or less familiar.

The main elements of the sacrificial mysticism of the Vedas may be summarised as follows: First, a belief that the sacrifices when performed with perfect accuracy, possess a secret, mysterious power to bring about or produce as their effect whatever we may desire either in this life or in the hereafter. Second, the conception of an unalterable law—involved in such invariable and unfailing occurrences of effects consequent upon the performance of these sacrifices. Third, an acceptance of the impersonal nature of the Vedic literature, as having existed by itself from beginningless time and as not created or composed by any person, human or divine. Fourth, the view that the Vedic literature embodies nothing but a system of duties involving commands and prohibitions. Fifth, a recognition of the supreme authority of the Vedas as the only source of the knowledge of ultimate truths which are far beyond the powers of human reason. Sixth, the view that truth or reality, whether it be of the nature of commands or of facts (as was maintained by the later Vedic schools of thought, the Upanishads), could be found once for all in the words of the Vedas. Seventh, the belief that the Vedic system of duties demands unfailing obedience and submission. Two definite characteristics emerge from these: first, the transcendent, mysterious, and secret power of the sacrifices, replacing the natural forces personified as gods; second, the ultimate superiority of the Vedas as the source of all truths, and as the unchallengeable dictators of our duties, leading to our material well-being and happiness. The assumption of the mysterious omnipotence of sacrifices, performed by following the authoritative injunctions of the Vedas independently of reason or logical and discursive thought, forms the chief trait of the mysticism of the Vedic type. There is nothing here of feeling or even of intellect, but a blind submission, not to a person but to an impersonal authority which holds within it an unalterable and inscrutable law, the secret of all powers which we may want to wield in our favor.

The next step in the development of this type of mysticism consists in the growth of a school of thought which sought to intellectualise the material sacrifices. It encouraged the belief that it was quite unnecessary actually to perform the sacrifices requiring the expenditure of enormous sums of money for the collection of materials and for labor. The same results might be as well obtained through certain kinds of meditation or reflection. Thus, instead of the actual performance of a horse sacrifice, in which the immolation of a horse is accompanied by other rituals engaging the services of large numbers of men and the expenditure of funds such as kings alone could provide, one might as well think of the dawn as the head of a horse, the sun as its eye, the wind as its life, the heaven as its back, the intervening space as its belly, the sky as its flesh and the stars as its bones. Such a meditation, or rather concentrated imagining of the universe as a cosmic horse, would, it was maintained, produce all the beneficial results that could be expected from the performance of an actual horse sacrifice. Thus, these attempts to intellectualise sacrifices took the form of replacing by meditation the actual sacrifices, and this substitution was believed to produce results which were equally beneficial. This meditation by substitution gradually took various forms: certain letters of the alphabet had, for example, to be thought of, or meditated upon, as Brahman or some other deity, or as vital functions of the body, or as some personified nature deity. This meditation was supposed to produce beneficial results. It should not be supposed that the sacrificial forms were entirely supplanted by these new forms of substitution-meditations. Rather did they spring up side by side with them. These forms of meditation did not mean prolonged contemplation, or any logical process of thinking, but merely the simple practice of continually thinking of one entity, process, or letter as another entity or process.

Even in modern India there are still many men who believe that the repetition of mystical formulas (apparently meaningless combinations of letters, or the names of some deities) is capable of producing beneficial results. Even the worship of a round or an oval stone as the god Vishnu or Siva, or again the worship of a waterjug or an image as a particular god or goddess, is nothing but a modified form of substitution-meditation, one thing being considered and meditated upon as another. These practices are to be distinguished from the ordinary spells and incantations commonly believed in by uneducated people. These substitution-meditations are often believed to be productive of virtue. They form the normal modes of worship of the ordinary Hindu and have now taken the place of the old sacrifices. Nevertheless the old Vedic sacrifices are also to a certain extent performed on occasions of marriages and other domestic ceremonies, as an indispensable part of those ceremonies which still claim to belong entirely to the Vedic order.

But, refraining from further references to modern India, let us pick up our thread of discussion and note the next stage in the development of the substitution-meditations. Although the latter were in their conception doubtless as mystical and magical as the old sacrifices, they represent an advance. For in them the mystical powers are supposed to reside not in external performances, but in specific forms of meditation or thinking. This represents an approach toward a consciousness of self and toward a recognition of the mystical powers of thought and meditation of a peculiar type. But it was only after an almost endless and fruitless search that the highest idea of self and the highest idea of world mystery and its solution dawned in the minds of the Vedic thinkers. What we find at this stage is merely that the Vedic thinkers had become conscious of the activity of thought and of imagination, and had begun to realise that the activity involved in thinking ought to be considered to be as potent a power as the activity involved in the actual performances of material sacrifices. Man's inner thought and his performance of sacrificial duties in the world outside are both regarded as capable of producing mysterious changes and transformations in nature which would benefit man. Passages are to be found in the literature where the vital and other inner processes of the self are compared with a sacrifice. The three periods of human life are considered as being the same as the three bruisings of the sacrificial plant soma; and the functions of hungering, eating and begetting are considered to be the same as the different ceremonies of the soma sacrifice. Logical thinking in Vedic times seems to have taken the form of crude generalisation. The fundamental operation of logical thinking is generalisation based on a scrutiny of facts of experience, noting differences and avoiding false identifications. But in the early stages of Vedic thinking, generalisations were very crude and based on insufficient data, slurring points of difference and making bold identifications. Thus from the fact that we perspire through heat, there arose the cosmological belief that out of fire there came water.

From observation of three principal colors, red, white and black (the colors of fire, water and earth) sprang the idea that the universe is made up of the three elements, viz., fire, water and earth. It was thought that wherever there was red, it was due to the existence of fire, wherever there was white it was due to the existence of water, and wherever there was black, it was due to the existence of earth.

By a similar loose process of generalisation the word Brahman came to denote the Vedic verses, truth, sacrifices, and knowledge. Etymologically the word means "The Great." Probably it signified vaguely and obscurely the mysterious power underlying these sacrifices and the substitution-meditations. Both the ideas involved in the conception of Brahman as the highest power and the highest knowledge were derived from the notion of the sacrifices. Thus we read in the celebrated man-hymn of the Rig Veda that the gods offered the supreme man as a sacrifice and that from this great oblation all living creatures, as well as the atmosphere, sky, earth and the four quarters, came into being. Three parts of this supreme man transcend the world while one part of him is the whole world about us; and yet, he is himself both the sacrifice and the object of the sacrifice.

But while I have just emphasised the importance of the mysticism of sacrifice in the development of the mystical conception of Brahman as the supreme being, it would be wrong to hold that the mysticism of the sacrifices is alone responsible for the evolution of the great concept of Brahman. Side by side with the concept found in the Rig Veda of the many gods as personifications of the forces of nature, there was also growing a tendency toward the conception of one supreme being, and this tendency gradually gained in force. Thus, in Rig Veda X. 114.5 we find a verse in which it is said that the deity is one, though he is called by various names. One of the hymns (R. V. X. 129), again, runs as follows:

"Then there was neither Aught nor Naught, no air nor sky beyond.
What covered all? Where rested all? In watery gulf profound?
Nor death was then, nor deathlessness, nor change of night and day.
That one breathed calmly, self-sustained; naught else beyond it lay.
Gloom hid in gloom existed first—one sea eluding view.
The one a void in chaos wrapt, by inward fervor grew.
Within it first arose desire, the primal germ of mind,
Which nothing with existence links, as ages searching find.
The kindling ray that shot across the dark and drear abyss,—
Was it beneath or high aloft? What bard can answer this?
There fecundating powers were found and mighty forces strove,
A self-supporting mass beneath, and energy above.
Who knows and who ever told, from whence this vast creation rose?
No gods had then been born. Who then can e'er the truth disclose
Whence sprang this world, whether framed by hand divine or no,
Its lord in heaven alone can tell, if he can show."

Again, in the Atharva Veda (X, 7.) we find a hymn dedicated to Skambha where the different parts of this deity are identified not only with the different parts of the material world but also with a number of moral qualities such as faith, austere fervor, truthfulness, etc. All the thirty-three gods of the Vedas are contained within him and bow down to him. He is also called Brahman, "The Great." In the next hymn of the Atharva Veda (X. 8) Brahman is adored and spoken of as presiding over the past and the future, and he is said to be residing within our hearts and to be the self which never decays but is self-existent and self-satisfied. This appears to be very much like the idea of the Upanishads of which I shall speak in my next lecture. In the Shatapatha Brahmana, also, we hear of Brahman as having created the gods; and in the Taittiriya Brahmana, Brahman is said to have created the gods and the entire world.

Thus we find that the conception of one great being who created the world and the gods, and who is also the power presiding over our lives and spirits, was gradually dawning in the minds of a few people. And though the sacrificial theory tended to lead away from the ordinary meanings of these Vedic hymns, the development of the sacrificial theory itself also made for the conception of some mysterious force which reconciled the destinies of the world and nature with those of men and their desires. This mysterious power, it was held, is resident not only in things external but also in activities of the inner life; it manifests itself in the power of thought, as is exemplified by the mysterious efficacy of the substitution-meditations. What was the nature of this mysterious power? It is difficult to answer this question. We have seen that its conception varied in significance according to the mode of its development and the sources from which it evolved. But when once the conception was formed, all these constituent notions were mixed together. People regarded Brahman as the highest, but they did not know how Brahman was to be known. Those who started with the sacrificial bias, thought substitution-meditations to be the way to a knowledge of Brahman. And so we find various instructions regarding meditation upon objects, such as the wind, life, fire, etc.,—even upon unmeaning letters.

But parallel with this tendency went another, viz., an intellectual search after Brahman, the highest, which displayed a contempt for sacrifices. We find Brahmins going out of their own sphere to warrior castes and kings for secret instruction about the nature of Brahman. There are narratives in which we find that kings belonging to the warrior caste fill proud Brahmins with a sense of discomfiture by exposing the ignorance of the latter concerning the secret nature of Brahman. Thus Balaki Gargya approached King Ajatashatru with the request to be allowed to explain to him the nature of Brahman. He then tried twelve times in succession to define Brahman as the presiding person in the sun, moon, lightning, ether, wind, fire, water, etc.; and in each case King Ajatashatru refuted him by showing the lower position that such presiding persons occupy in the whole of the universe, whereas] Brahman should be that which is the highest. Again, we find another narrative in which five Brahmins meet and discuss the question, "What is our Atman and what is Brahman?" They proceed to Uddalaka Aruni with the question. When Uddalaka mistrusts his ability to answer the question, all six go to King Ashvapati Kaikeya for instruction. King Ashvapati first asks them what it is that they worship as Atman or Brahman, anticipating their error that they still regard Atman or Brahman as a new kind of external divinity. The six Brahmins explain Atman in succession as the heaven, the sun, the wind, space, water, and the earth, and in so doing assume it to be an objective and an external deity more or less like the old Vedic deities. This shows us a stage of thought in which people somehow understood Brahman to be the highest principle, but yet found it difficult to shake off their old conceptions of external deities or personifications of nature. Again we find Sanatkumara instructing Narada regarding the nature of Brahman. In so doing Sanatkumara starts from "Name," by which he probably understands all conceptual knowledge. With his peculiar logic, which is difficult for us to follow, he observes that speech is greater than name, that mind is greater than speech, that imagination is greater than mind, and so on. Passing in succession through a number of such concepts, from lower to higher, he ultimately stops at that which is absolutely great, the unlimited, beyond which there is nothing and within which is comprehended all that is to be found in the outer and the inner world.

The most important point to be noted in the development of this stage of thought is that worship or prayer is possible only as directed toward a deity conceived with limited powers and as occupying a subordinate position in the universe. But with reference to that which is conceived as the highest truth and the highest power, there is no longer the possibility of external forms of worship. We shall find in the next lecture not only that it is not possible to worship Brahman but that it is not possible to reach Brahman by logical thought or any kind of conceptual apprehension. Thus in a Upanishadic story, referred to by Shankara, we are told of a person who approached a sage Bahva and sought from him instructions regarding the nature of Brahman. Bahva did not speak. He was asked a second time; still he did not speak. Yet again he was asked, but still he did not speak. When the inquirer became annoyed by this, Bahva told him that he was, from the first, by his silence telling him how Brahman was to be described: Brahman is silence and so cannot be represented in speech. There are, however, unmistakable indications that there were still some who believed that even the highest could be worshipped and adored and that men could still submit themselves to Him as to the highest personal God who comprehends us all and controls us all. But the idea that was gradually gaining ground with some of the most important sages, and which will be expounded in the next lecture, was that Brahman, as the highest, is no ordinary personal God who can be induced by worship to favor us or who can be approached by the pure intellect or even by feeling. Brahman still retains its mysterious character as the highest power, truth, being and bliss which can neither be worshipped nor known by ordinary means of knowledge. But its nature can be realised, and realised so perfectly that the realisation will be like the bursting of a shell of light, a revelation which will submerge the whole of one's life together with all that it contains. The next lecture will describe this type of mysticism of the Upanishads, which represents one of the highest and best, and undoubtedly one of the most distinctive, types of mysticism that India has produced.

The Upanishads form the concluding portions of the Vedic literature, both chronologically from the point of view of the development of ideas. They were composed later than the priestly manuals, the Brahmanas, and the manuals of substitution-meditations in the Aranyaka literature, and they form the most authoritative background of all later Hindu philosophical thought. They possess the high authority of the Vedas and are the source of the highest wisdom and truth. The word "Upanishad" has been interpreted etymologically by Shankara to mean "that which destroys all ignorance and leads us to Brahman." It has also been interpreted to mean a secret or mystical doctrine, or a secret instruction, or a secret and confidential sitting. I have elsewhere, in my History of Indian Philosophy, shown how all the different systems of orthodox Indian philosophy look to the Upanishads for light and guidance, differently interpreting the Upanishad texts to suit their own specific systems of thought. Eleven of these, Isha, Kena, Katha, Prashna, Mundaka, Mandukya, Taittiriya, Aitareya, Chandogya, Brihadaranyaka, and Svetashvatara, are probably the oldest. They vary greatly in length: while the Isha Upanishad would occupy but a single printed page, Brihadaranyaka would occupy at least fifty pages. Since the longer ones probably contain compositions of different periods and of different authorship they represent various stages of evolution and exhibit different intentions. Being the concluding portions of the Vedas, they are called the Vedanta. Their interpretations by different later writers gave rise to different systems of Vedanta philosophy. (One of these well-known forms of Vedanta philosophy was made known to the western world for the first time by a gifted Hindu, Svami Vivekananda.) The Upanishads themselves, however, do not seem to have been written in a systematic, well-connected and logical form. They are mystical experiences of the soul gushing forth from within us; they sparkle with the beams of a new light; they quench our thirst, born at their very sight. It was of these that the German philosopher Schopenhauer said: "How does every line display its firm and definite and throughout harmonious meaning. From every sentence deep, original, and sublime thoughts arise and the whole is pervaded by a high and holy and earnest spirit. . . . In the whole world there is no study, except that of the originals, so beneficial and so elevating as that of the Upanishads. It has been the solace of my life, it will be the solace of my death." Cases are known in which even Christian

missionaries, sent out to India to teach church doctrines to clergymen or to preach Christianity among the Indians, became so fascinated by the high and lofty teachings of the Upanishads that they introduced the teaching of the Upanishads in the Church and as a consequence were compelled to resign their posts. To Hindus of all denominations there is nothing higher and holier than the inspired sayings of the Upanishads. To them we shall address our attention in the next lecture.

LECTURE II: THE MYSTICISM OF THE UPANISHADS

IN the last lecture reference was made to a few of the monotheistic hymns of the Rig Veda and the Atharva Veda. Others might be cited; for instance, the adoration hymn to Hiranyagarbha (R. V. X. 121) who is therein described as the lord of the universe.

"In the beginning rose Hiranyagarbha,
Born as the only lord of all existence.
This earth he settled firm and heaven established:
What god shall we adore with our oblations?
Who gives us breath, who gives us strength, whose bidding
All creatures must obey, the bright gods even;
Whose shade is death, whose shadow life immortal:
What god shall we adore with our oblations?
Who by his might alone became the monarch
Of all that breathes, of all that wakes or slumbers,
Of all, both man and beast, the lord eternal:
What god shall we adore with our oblations?
Whose might and majesty these snowy mountains,
The ocean and the distant stream exhibit;
Whose arms extended are these spreading regions:
What god shall we adore with our oblations?
Who made the heavens bright, the earth enduring,
Who fixed the firmament, the heaven of heavens;
Who measured out the air's extended spaces:
What god shall we adore with our oblations?"

Or one may point to such hymns as the following:

"Who is our father, our creator, maker,
Who every place doth know and every creature,
By whom alone to gods their names were given,
To him all other creatures go to ask him."

But such hymns are not numerous and probably belong to the last epoch of the composition of the Vedic hymns. Most of the Vedic hymns exhibit a conspicuous tendency toward the polytheistic personification of nature. From most of them the monotheistic tendency is well-nigh absent.

So, also, the literature of the sacrificial manuals, the Brahmanas, emphasizes the doctrine of the sacrifice. The adoration hymns of the different gods have lost their independent value and are esteemed only on account of the fact that these verses, sometimes mutilated and torn out of their context, are uttered or chanted in connection with various sacrificial rituals. This literature also contains some passages of a monotheistic or pantheistic character; but the emphasis is almost entirely on the performance of the sacrifices. In the Aranyaka literature, which contains the substitution-meditations, the value and power of thought is realized for the first time. But it is only in the Upanishads that one finds the earliest instances of a sincere and earnest quest after Brahman, the highest and the greatest.

The most important characteristic which distinguishes the science of Brahman from the science of the sacrifices consists in the fact that the former springs entirely from inner, spiritual longings, while the latter is based almost wholly on mundane desires. The science of sacrifice aimed at the acquirement of merit, which could confer all the blessings of life in consequence of due obedience to the Vedic and ritualistic injunctions and prohibitions. The science of Brahman, however, did not seek any ordinary blessings of life. It proceeded from the spiritual needs of our soul which could be satisfied only by attaining the highest aim. All that is mortal, all that is transient and evanescent, all that gives men the ordinary joys of life, such as wealth or fame confer, are but brute pleasures and brute satisfactions, which please only so long as men allow themselves to be swayed by the demands of their senses. In the hurry and bustle of our modern life, of rapid movements over land, sea and air, in this age of prolific scientific inventions and appliances which add to our material comforts and luxury, in this age of national jealousies and hatreds, which in the name of patriotism and freedom often try to enslave others or monopolize the necessities and luxuries of life for the use of the people of a particular country, it is easy to forget that we have any needs other than the purely material ones. With all the boasted culture of our modern age, with all our advancement of science and progress, do we ever stop to think just what we mean by progress? We have no doubt discovered many new facts of nature, and brought many natural forces under our control. But like vultures soaring high in the air, with greedy eyes fixed on the bones and flesh of the carrion in the field below, are we not, in all our scientific soarings, often turning our greedy eyes to sense gratifications and trying to bind science to the attainment of new comforts and luxuries? The new comforts and luxuries soon become absolute necessities, and we eagerly press forward to the invention of some other new modes of sense gratification and luxury. Science debased to the end of spreading death and of enslaving humanity, or to the end of procuring newer and newer sensations, a life spent in the whirlpool of fleeting pleasures, varied, subtle, and new, and in the worship of the almighty dollar is what most of us tend to call progress. We live more for the body than for the soul. Our body is our soul; our body is our highest Brahman. The story is told in the Chandogya Upanishads that Virochana and Indra went to Prajapati to receive instructions regarding the nature of the self, or of Brahman the highest. Prajapati gave a course of false instructions, apparently to test the powers of discrimination of his two pupils Virochana and Indra. He asked them to get themselves well-dressed and appear at their best, and then to look into a mirror. When they did so and saw the image of their own bodies in the mirror, Prajapati told them that it was their well-dressed bodies reflected in the mirror that was the true self and the highest Brahman; and they went away satisfied with the answer. Indra, indeed, later returned to Prajapati dissatisfied with the answer; but Virochana (probably an old ancestor of ours) was satisfied with the answer that there is nothing higher than what appears to our senses, our earthly body, and our earthly joys.

But what a different answer do we get from Maitreyi, the wife of Yajnavalkya in the Brihadaranyaka Upanishad II. 4. Yajnavalkya, wishing to become a hermit, explained to his two wives Maitreyi and Katyayani that he wished to divide his wealth between them so that they might live independently while he was away seeking his higher spiritual destiny. But Maitreyi replied: "Well, sir, if you could give me all the wealth of the world, could I become immortal by that?" "No," said Yajnavalkya, "you will only live in pleasure as the rich men do, but I can promise you no hope of immortality through wealth." Maitreyi replied, "Well, sir, what shall I do with that with which I cannot be immortal? Tell me if you know anything by which I may be immortal."

It is this spiritual craving for immortality that distinguishes the mental outlook of the sages of the Upanishads from our own. Yet this desire for immortality is no mere desire for personal survival continuing the enjoyment of pleasures under newer and happier conditions of life, whether in this world or in heaven. This quest for immortality, as it is found in the Upanishads, is in no sense a yearning for personal immortality, the decayless, diseaseless, deathless existence of the individual with his body in full vigor of youth. Neither is it the desire for a bodiless existence of a self fond of sensual joys and sense gratifications and fettered by all the needs and necessities of mundane relations and mundane gratifications. This quest for immortality is identical with the quest of the highest self, the highest truth and reality, the highest Brahman. It is the perception and realization of the inner spring of our life and the inmost spirituality of man as he is within himself, beyond the range of sense and of discursive thought. If it were a sense-feeling—color, taste, touch, or sound—it might easily be pointed out as this or that sense-datum. It is an ineffable, non-conceptual, inner experience, lying in its own unfathomable depth. When a lump of salt is thrown into the sea, it is entirely dissolved in it; by no means can any part of the lump be recovered in its original form, but every part of the water tastes saline. Similarly, when this stage of supra-consciousness (prajnana) is reached, all ordinary experiences are submerged and dissolved in this. great, infinite, limitless, homogeneous experience. Like the calm and changeless consciousness of deep, dreamless sleep, is this stage where all duality has vanished: there is no person who knows, nor anything that he is aware of. Ordinary knowledge presupposes a difference between ourselves, our knowledge, and that of which we are aware. When I see a color, there is the "I" which sees, there is the knowledge of the color and also the color itself. When I smell, there is the "I" that smells and the smell; when I think, there is the "I" that thinks and that which is thought; when I speak there is the "I" that speaks and that which is spoken. No one would for a moment think of identifying these. But at this stage of the non-conceptual intuition of the self—an unspeakable, ineffable experience—there is no trace of any duality, and we have one whole of blissful experience wherein is distinguished no one that knows and nothing that he is aware of. All ordinary states of knowledge imply a duality of knower and that which is known; but this is an experience where all duality has vanished.

Nevertheless this experience is not something which is wholly beyond, or wholly out of all relation with, our conscious states of dual experience. For it is the basis, or background, as it were, of all our ordinary knowledge involving the knower and the known. In music, the different notes and tones cannot be grasped separately from and independently of the music itself, and when we are busy in apprehending separately the different notes we miss the music or the harmony which is in itself a whole of experience that cannot be taken in parts, in the multiplicity of the varied notes. So it is with this ineffable experience, which in reality underlies all our ordinary experiences and states of knowledge as the basis or ground of them all; when we are lost in the discursive multiplicity of our ordinary experience, we miss this underlying reality. But when once again we are in touch with it, our so-called personality is as it were dissolved in it, and there ensues that infinitude of blissful experience in which all distinctions are lost. Whatever is dear to me, as e.g., father, mother, wife, money, fame, etc., is so because I love my own self so dearly. It is because I can find the needs of my self best realized through these that I love these. None of these can be ends in themselves; it is only the self that can be an end unto itself, irrespective of any other ulterior end or motive. None of the many-sided interests, desires, and activities of the self represent the self in its entirety or in its essence. It is only this supra-conscious experience, which actually underlies them all, that can be called the real self and that for which everything else exists. Everything else is dear to me because my self is dear to me; but this supra-conscious experience underlies the so-called personality, or self, as its very essence, truth and final reality.

It is indeed difficult for us, with the traditions and associations of our modern world, to believe in the reality of this intuitional experience, unless we attempt to realize it ourselves—unless, by turning our minds entirely away from sense-objects and sense-enjoyments, we deliberately, with faith and firmness, plunge into the depths of this new kind of experience. It cannot be expressed in words or understood by conceptual thought; it reveals itself only to supra-conscious experience. The language of the sages of the Upanishads seems strange to us; but we cannot hope to understand a thing of which we have had no experience. Talk to a child of ten about the romantic raptures of love felt by a pair of lovers, or of the maddening intoxication of sense cravings; what would he understand of it? Talk to a Greenlander about the abominable heat of an African desert; will he be able to imagine it? When an experience is to be realized, the powers of mere logical thinking or of abstraction or of constructive imagination are not sufficient for the purpose. Only another realization of the same experience can testify to its truth. We are here concerned with an experience which is non-conceptual, intuitive, and ultimate. But, what is more, subtle, fine and formless as it is, it is said to be the source, basis, and ground of everything else. According to a story told in the Chandogya Upanishad VI, when Shvetaketu returned after a stay of twelve years at the house of his preceptor, where he studied all the Vedas, he became arrogant, considered himself to be a wise man, and hardly ever talked with others. His father said to him: "Well, Shvetaketu, what have you learned that you seem to think yourself so wise? Do you know that which when once known everything else becomes known? When you once know what iron is, you know all that can be made out of iron, for these are in essence nothing but iron; we can distinguish the iron vessels from iron only by their specific forms and names. But whatever may be their names and forms, the true essence in them all, whether they be needles, pans or handles, is nothing but iron. It is only that you find therein so many forms and names. What are these names and forms worth without the essence? It is the essence, the iron, that manifests itself in so many forms and names; when this iron is known, all that is made of iron is also known. It is the ineffable reality, the ultimate being which is the essence of everything else. As rivers which flow into the sea lose all their individuality in it and cannot be distinguished, so all divergent things lose their individuality and distinctness when they are merged in this highest being, the ultimate reality from which they have all sprung forth. Fine and subtle though this experience be, yet it is in reality the entire universe of our knowledge. A small seed of an oak tree when split open reveals nothing that we can call worth noting, yet it is this fine kernel of the seed that holds within it the big oak tree."

The chief features of this Upanishad mysticism are the earnest and sincere quest for this spiritual illumination, the rapturous delight and force that characterize the utterances of the sages when they speak of the realization of this ineffable experience, the ultimate and the absolute truth and reality, and the immortality of all mortal things. Yet this quest is not the quest of the God of the theists. This highest reality is no individual person separate from us, or one whom we try to please, or whose laws and commands we obey, or to whose will we submit with reverence and devotion. It is, rather, a totality of partless, simple and undifferentiated experience which is the root of all our ordinary knowledge and experience and which is at once the ultimate essence of our self and the highest principle of the universe, the Brahman or the Atman. There is, indeed, another current of thought, evident in several passages of different Upanishads, in which Brahman is conceived and described as the theistic God. This will be dealt with separately later on. The special characteristic of the line of thought that has now been described is a belief in a superior principle which enlivens our life, thoughts, actions, desires and feelings, which is the inmost heart of the self of man, the immortal and undying reality unaffected by disease and death, and which is also the ultimate and absolute reality of the universe.

A story is told in the Katha Upanishad according to which King Vajashravasa made a sacrifice involving a gift of all the valuables that he possessed. When everything of the sort had been given away, he made a supplementary gift of his cows which were all old and useless. His son Naciketas, finding that these gifts would be more embarassing than useful to the recipient, disapproved of his father's action. He thought that his father had not finished giving his "all" until he, his son, was also given away. So he asked his father, "To whom are you going to give me?" He was dear to his father; so his father did not like this question and remained silent. But when the question was again and again repeated, the father lost his temper and said, "I give you over to death." Then Naciketas went to the place of Yama, the king of death, where he remained fasting for three days and nights. Yama, willing to appease him, requested him to take any boons that pleased him. Naciketas replied that men do not know what happens to people when they have passed from earthly life, whether they still continue to exist or whether they cease to exist; and he requested Yama to answer this question on which there were so many divergent opinions. Yama in answer said that this was a very difficult question and that even the gods did not know what becomes of man after he passes away from his earthly life; that, therefore, he would rather give Naciketas long life, big estates, gold in abundance, horses, elephants, and whatever else in the way of earthly enjoyment might seem to him desirable. But the philosophical quest was dearer to Naciketas than all the earthly goods that the king of death could bestow upon him. Money, he thought, can not satisfy man; money is of use only so long as a man lives, and he can live only so long as death does not take him away. This quest of the ultimate destiny of man, of his immortal essence, is itself the best and the highest end that our hearts may pursue. So Naciketas preferred to solve this mystery and riddle of life rather than to obtain all the riches of the world and all the comforts that they could purchase.

The king of death appreciated the wisdom of Naciketas' choice. He explained that there are two paths, the path of the good and the path of the pleasant, and that they are different paths, leading to two entirely different goals. The mad hankering after riches can only justify itself by binding us with ties of attachment to sense-pleasures which are short-lived and transitory. It is only the spiritual longing of man after the realization of his highest, inmost, truest, and most immortal essence that is good in itself, though it does not appeal to greedy people who are always hankering after money. Desire for money blinds our eyes, and we fail to see that there is anything higher than the desire for riches, or that there is anything intrinsically superior to our ordinary mundane life of sense-pleasures and sense-enjoyments. The nature of the higher sphere of life and of the higher spiritual experiences cannot be grasped by minds which are always revolving in the whirlpool of mad desires for riches and sense-enjoyments. As the sage, in his serene enjoyment of spiritual experiences, may well think sense-pleasures dull, insipid, and valueless, so the multitude who live a worldly life of ordinary pleasures and enjoyments, fail to perceive the existence of this superior plane of life and the demands of the spirit for the realization of its immortal essence. They think that nothing exists higher and greater than this mundane life of ordinary logical thought and sense-enjoyments. Most men live on this ordinary level of life; they see, hear, taste, touch and smell. They think and they argue. They have a mind which thinks, feels, and wills, and they have senses which seek their own gratification. They employ the former in the service of the latter and every day discover newer and subtler ways of sense-gratification; they also employ the latter to serve the former by furnishing sense data to guide and check the course of logical thought and the development of science. The more men, upon comparing opinions, find themselves agreeing that they possess nothing of a more lofty character, the more they cease to believe in the validity and truth of the existence of anything undying in man. They fail to notice that the life they are living has had the effect of chilling and freezing the clear flowing stream of spiritual experiences and of stifling the spiritual instincts and longings of the soul. Generations of lives spent without once turning the eyes to the spiritual light within have served to build up traditions, beliefs, and tendencies of such an order that faith in the existence of the higher spirituality of man is lost. Discourse about the spirituality of man in its highest sense appears to most men to be no more than a myth of by-gone days or the result of the undue nervous excitation or heated imagination of a religious intoxication. The net result of our modern education, civilization, and culture has been the disappearance of the belief that there is anything higher than the gratification of man's primitive instincts under such checks as society requires, the pursuit of the physical sciences, and the successful employment of the art of reasoning for the satisfaction of all the diverse interests of human beings. So Yama, the king of death, says to Naciketas that the majority of the people do not believe that there is anything higher than the ordinary mundane life, being content with the common concerns and interests of life; that it is only the few who feel this higher call and are happy to respond to it and to pursue a course of life far above the reach of the common man.

But what is this undying spiritual essence, or existence? Cannot our powers of reasoning, as they are employed in philosophical discussion or logical arguments, discover it? If they can, then at its best it can be nothing loftier than thought and can not be considered as the highest principle by which even thought itself and all conscious processes, as well as the functioning of all sense-operations, are enlivened and vitalized. So Yama tells Naciketas that this highest spiritual essence in us cannot be known by discursive reason. Only persons who have realized this truth can point this out to us as an experience which is at once self-illuminating and blissful and which is entirely different from all else that is known to us. Once it is thus exhibited, those who have the highest moral elevation and disinclination to worldly enjoyments can grasp it by an inner intuitive contact with the reality itself (adhyatmayoga). This truth is indeed the culmination of all the teaching of the Vedas.

To Naciketas' question as to what becomes of men when they leave this earthly life, Yama's answer is that no one is ever born and no one ever dies. Birth and death pertain only to our physical bodies, but our essence is never born and never dies. The birth and death of the physical body may well be explained by reference to physical causes, and there is not much of a mystery therein. But man cannot be identified with his body, nor can he be identified simply with the life which he has in common with all other animals, and even with plants. Life, in a large measure, seems to be nothing but a harmonious functioning of the inner organs of the body; but no one would say that these movements of the organs can be called "man." There is a superior principle which vitalises and quickens the process of life, enlivens the activity of thought, moves the senses to their normal and regular operations, which is realized, or intuited, as the very essence of our inner illumination, and which is also the highest and ultimate principle underlying all things.

We are here face to face with the real mysticism of the Upanishads. This highest essence of man, the self, the Brahman, is difficult of perception; it is hidden, as in a deep cavern, in that deathless being who exists from the beginning of all time and beyond all time. It is the subtlest, the smallest of the small and yet the greatest of the great. It exists changeless and just the same one when everything else that it has vitalized has ceased to exist. This, our inmost self, cannot be known by much learning or scholarship, nor by sharp intelligence, nor by strong memory. It can only be known, or intuited, by the person to whom it reveals its own nature. In one place we are told that it can be intuited only by an inner, direct, and immediate touch. In another place it is said that it can only be perceived by those who have practised the perceiving of fine truths by a superfine intelligence of the highest order (Katha I. 3.12). The path to this superior intuition is like the edge of a sharp razor, dangerous and difficult. It is beyond all sense-knowledge; and he who intuits this secret truth of the beginningless, endless, unchangeable and eternal overcomes all death. For, once one realizes oneself to be identical with this highest principle, death and the fear of it sink into insignificant, illusory nothingness.

There is, however, another line of thought running through the different Upanishads in which Brahman appears as the supreme Lord from whom everything has proceeded and who is the source of all energy. Thus in the Kena Upanishad we find the query: "By whose will and directed by whom does the mind work, and directed by whom did life first begin? By whose will does the organ of speech work, and led by whom do the eye and the ear perform their respective functions?" Then comes the answer: "It is from Him that the organ of speech, the ear, the eye, the mind and life have all derived their powers; He is the thought of thought, the mind of mind, and the life of life. So neither mind nor eye, neither ear nor speech, can tell us anything about Him, because neither the eye nor the ear nor the mind can reach Him, but He alone is the agent operative through all these organs and making the eye perceiver, the ear hearer, the mind a thinker and the life a living force. But He, in his own nature, cannot be grasped by any one of these."

A story is told to illustrate the greatness of Brahman as the supreme and all-powerful Lord. All the gods were at one time congratulating themselves on their own greatness, though all the while it was Brahman alone who was great. Brahman saw the false conceit of the gods and appeared before them as the all-powerful Lord. The gods sent the god of fire to him to enquire who this great Lord was. Agni, the god of fire, approached him and this great Lord asked Agni who he was and what he could do? Agni replied that he was the god of fire and could burn the whole world. Brahman then put before him a straw and asked him if he could burn it. Agni tried with all his might to burn it, but failed. Thereupon Agni returned to the gods saying that he could not learn who this great lord was. Vayu, the wind-god, approached Brahman and said that he was the wind-god and could blow away the whole world. Again Brahman placed a straw before him, asking him to blow it away if he could. Vayu also failed and came back to the other gods. Then Indra came forward to inquire who this great Lord was, but Brahman had already disappeared from the scene. Thereupon a bright glorious goddess appeared in the sky and told him that this supreme Lord was Brahman, that He alone was great, and that all the powers of the gods of fire, wind, etc., were derived from him.

It is said in the Katha VI. 1-3 that all the worlds are maintained in him. He is like a big tree which has its roots far below and its branches above, forming the visible universe around us. He is the great Life from which everything else has come into being. Nothing dare ignore, disobey, or outstrip Him. He is like a great thunder of fear over us all. It is by His fear that the fire and the sun give heat, that the wind blows, and that Death runs about. He is elsewhere described (Brrh. IV. IV. 22) as the controller, Lord and master of all. He is the

Lord of all that has been and all that will be. He is the creator of the universe and the world belongs to Him and He to the world (Brrh. IV. IV. 13). Yet He is the inmost self of all living beings (sarvabhutantaratma) and the immortal inner controller of them all (antaryamin). But, though He is the controller and creator of all, yet it is He who has become this visible universe of diverse names and forms. Just as the wind and the fire appear in different forms, so He also appears in all the varied forms that present themselves to us in this world. Being one in Himself, He has become the visible many of the universe. But yet He is absolutely untouched by faults and defects of this mortal world. As the Sun which by its light illumines all colors and forms for the eye and is yet unaffected by the defects of our eyes, so the Brahman, who by his light has brought all things into existence and continues as their inmost essence, is yet wholly unaffected by their defects, their mortal and transitory forms.

Whether the teaching of the Upanishads is to be called pantheism or not will depend on the definition of pantheism. Certainly there are some passages such as those just considered which describe Brahman as having spread Himself in diverse forms in all the objects that we see around us. This might readily be taken as indication of some form of materialistic pantheism. But this is merely one phase or aspect of the matter. It seems to be contradicted by the idea of Brahman as the creator, ruler, and controller, by whose will everything moves and the order of events is kept in its right place undisturbed. Neither life nor death nor any of the powers of nature can transgress his orders; He is a thundering fear over us all, and yet He is also the bridge by which all the diverse things of the world are connected with one another and with man, their spiritual master. This latter conception, which is present in many passages of the Upanishads, is apparently dualistic and implies a personal God. The Shvetashvatara Upanishad abounds in passages of an avowedly dualistic character. There it is said that He alone is the Lord of all bipeds and quadrupeds, the protector and master of the universe, and yet is hidden in all beings. The duality between the individual soul and God is also definitely expressed in at least two of the earlier Upanishads, Mundaka 3. 1. 1 and Shvetashvatara 4. 6,

where, with reference to Brahman and the individual, it is said that two birds which are alike in nature and friendly to each other reside in the same tree, but that one of them (the individual) eats sweet fruits (i.e. of his own deeds) while the other is happy in itself without eating any fruit whatsoever. In the same Shvetashvatara Upanishad, the sage is described as saying: "I know this great person who resides beyond all darkness (of sin and ignorance), as bright as the sun. He who knows Him escapes death and there is no other way of escape. There is nothing superior to Him, and there is nothing which is greater than Him, and there is nothing smaller than Him. He stands alone by Himself in the Heavens unmoved like a tree, and yet the world is filled by this person." But this also is a passing phase. In a passage immediately preceding that in the

Mundaka Upanishad just referred to, it is said that Brahman is right before us in the front; Brahman is behind us in the back; Brahman is on the right and on the left. Again it is said in the Katha Upanishad: "He who perceives diversity in this world suffers the death of all deaths." "He is the controller and the self of all beings; He makes the one form many, being one He satisfies the desires of the many."

The most important emphasis of the Upanishads seems to be on that ineffable experience which lies hidden in the background of all our experiences and at the same time enlivens them all. Yet the experiencer himself is lost, and dissolved as it were, in this superior experience, where there is neither experiencer nor that which is experienced. This experience, or state, cannot be intellectually grasped; it can only be pointed out as different from all that is known, or from all that can be described as "this" or "that." One can only assert that "It is not this," "It is not this." It is like the state of a deep dreamless sleep, like the feeling of intense bliss where neither the knower nor the known can be distinctly felt but where there is only the infinitude of blissful experience.

The various commentators upon the Upanishads belonging to different schools of thought and yet each interested to secure for himself the support of the Upanishads, have been fighting with one another for the last twelve hundred years or more to prove that the Upanishads are exclusively in favor of one party as against the others. Thus some contend that the Upanishads teach that Brahman alone exists and all the rest that appears is false and illusory. Others hold that the Upanishads favor the doctrine of modified duality of man in God and of God in man. Still others maintain that the Upanishads give us exclusively a doctrine of uncompromising duality. And so forth. Passages have often been twisted and perverted, and many new connections and contexts have been introduced or imposed upon the texts, to suit the fancy or the creed of the individual commentator. I think all these interpretations are biassed and onesided, and therefore inexact. The Upanishads reveal to us different phases of thought and experience, not a consistent dogmatic philosophy. The apparent inconsistency of the different phases of thought is removed if we take a psychological point of view and consider them as different stages of development in the experience of minds seeking to grasp a sublime, ultimate but inexpressible truth. This truth has a logic of its own, different from the logic of discursive thought wherein distinctions are firm and rigid, where concepts are like pieces of brick mortared together by the logical movement of thought. Its logic is that of experience in which the apparently contradictory ideas or thoughts lose their contradictoriness and become parts of one solid whole. The different phases of experience are lived through and enjoyed as inalienable parts of one great experience. When attempts are made to describe any particular phase of this experience it will naturally seem to conflict with the other phases in the eyes of those who have not the capacity of realising the concrete whole experience and who can only look at the phases from an external and a purely intellectual point of view where distinctions cannot be obliterated. When a lover embraces his beloved in his first kiss, he may feel her as the holiest angel, as his own dear life or as the embodiment of all his happiness, as, Shelley says, his "Spouse, Sister Angel, Pilot of the Fate,"

"Of unentangled intermixture, made

By love, of light and motion; one intense

Diffusion, one serene Omnipresence." But these epithets when applied to a woman can hardly be justified, according to intellectual standards, as properly applied, though the lover may have felt an indescribable sweetness of love in which all these diverse sentiments melted together to form its taste and flavor. The different phases of experience and belief which we find in the Upanishads need not therefore be taken out and pitted against one another. They may all be regarded as stages of experience between which the minds of the sages oscillated in attempting the realisation of a truth which was beyond speech, beyond thought and beyond all sense-perception. It was sometimes felt as the great over-lord, the controller, creator, ordainer, and master of all, sometimes as the blissful spiritual experience, and sometimes as the simple unity in which all duality has vanished.

This truth, person, or absolute—whatever it may be called—was felt as the highest embodiment of moral perfection. It is complete self-illumination, bodiless, faultless, sinless and pure. It is, as it were, covered by a cup of gold in such wise that we, looking at the shiny cup, miss the real treasure that lies concealed beneath. Its illumination reveals itself only when our minds have turned away from all the external lights of the outside world; for where this light is shining, all the other lights of the sun, the moon, and the stars have ceased to give light. The Upanishads tell us again and again that it cannot be perceived by any of our senses and that it cannot be comprehended by reasoning, or by logical and discursive thought, or by discussions, scholarship and much learning, or even by the reading of the scriptures. Only those who have ceased from all sinful actions and have controlled all their sense desires, who are unruffled by passions of all kinds and are at peace with themselves, can have the realization of this great truth by the higher intuitive knowledge (prajnana, as distinguished from jnana, or cognition). In Mundaka III. 1, it is said that we can attain this self by truth, control, spiritual fervor and absolute extinction of all sex desires. Only the sages who have purged themselves of all moral defects and faults are capable of perceiving this holy spiritual light within themselves. The Upanishads never tire of repeating that the revelation of this truth is possible only through the most perfect moral purity which results in a natural illumination of intuitive perception when one seeks to attain this partless essence through meditation. Not only can this truth not be perceived by the eye or described in speech; but it cannot even be gained as a boon, or gift, by pleasing the gods or by ascetic practices or by sacrificial performances. It can only be attained by an intuition (para) which is superior in kind to the Vedic knowledge of sacrifices, called the lower knowledge (apara). By supreme moral elevation and untiring and patient search one can come in touch with Brahman and can enter into Him, but one must abandon all his mundane desires by which he is bound to earthly things. And when through this high moral elevation, control of desires, meditation and the like, one comes face to face with this highest reality, or Brahman, he is lost in it like rivers in the sea; nothing remains of him which he can feel as a separate individual, but he becomes one with Brahman. This is known by the seer through his heart when his senses have ceased to move and when his thought and intellect have come to a dead halt. No one can describe what that existence is; one can only say that it is "being," nothing more. Here all the knots of the heart are untied, all doubts are dispelled, and there is one spiritual light of unity that shines forth in its serene oneness.

LECTURE III: YOGA MYSTICISM

THE last lecture dealt with the ineffable intuitive experience which the sages of the Upanishads regarded as absolute and ultimate in nature. The Upanishads, however, indicate no definite method for arriving at the perception of this truth. It is made clear that the pathway consists not in erudition or scholarship, and that it is not traversed by any sharpness of intelligence. The truth is such that it cannot be conceived by the human mind or described by language. One of the fundamental conditions of attaining it is the complete elevation of the moral life, including the absolute control of all passions and desires, the abandonment of worldly ambitions and hopes, and the attainment of an unruffled peace of mind. But the dawning of the supra-consciousness which can reveal this truth does not, even so, depend entirely on our own efforts; there is something like divine mercy that must be awaited. This self can only be realized by those to whom it reveals itself. The perfecting of our moral life is a prerequisite; but no method deliberately and consciously pursued is sufficient to bring us all the way into the full realization of the highest truth. In at least one or two of the Upanishads indications of a different line of thought and method of realization are to be found. Thus in Katha III, our senses are compared with horses which are always running after their respective sense-objects. He who is not wise but is without control over his own mind cannot control his senses, just as a bad driver cannot control his horses. If anyone wishes to make his way to his highest goal, he should have wisdom for his driver and his mind as the reins of the horses of the senses. In Katha VI, it is said that there is a state in which the five senses, thought, intellect, and mind all cease to operate, and this highest stage of absolute sense-restraint is called "Yoga," or spiritual union.

There are ample literary evidences that from very early times—from at least 700 or 800 B. C.—people were in the habit of concentrating their minds on particular objects and thereby stopping the movement of the mind and the senses and achieving wonderful, miraculous powers. It is difficult to say how the ancient Indians discovered this mode of mental control. But it seems very probable that as at first practised it did not form a part of any metaphysical system of thought but was simply the practise of mental concentration and breath control for the sake of the resulting peace and quietness of mind, as well as of the miraculous powers which could be achieved thereby. The powers of hypnotism, or mesmerism, seem to have been very well known in ancient India and were also included among the powers that could be derived from the yoga practices.

A story is told in the Mahabharata (13.40) that Devasharma, a sage, had a very beautiful wife, named Ruci, whom he carefully guarded from the seductive influences of Indra who desired to possess her. Once he had to go away to perform sacrifices at a distant place, and he left his wife under the protection of his pupil Vipula. The pupil knew that Indra could resort to many clever disguises and that it would be difficult to protect Ruci from him by guarding her by any external means. So he decided to enter into her mind by his powers of yoga and to control her behavior and speech from within. Accordingly, he sat in front of his teacher's wife and remained staring at her eyes, inhibiting all movements of his own body. In this way he entered into her body and remained there awaiting his teacher's return. Nov Indra, thinking that the lady was alone in the house, came there in his fine and radiant form. He saw there the inanimate body of Vipula, the pupil, with its eyes absolutely motionless as if they were painted on canvas. He also saw the lady sitting there in all her resplendent beauty. On beholding Indra, she wished to rise and greet him; but being controlled from within by her husband's pupil, she could not succeed in doing as she desired. Indra spoke to her in his own charming manner, telling her that he had come there for her and that he was Indra. Perceiving that the lady was showing signs of becoming fascinated, Vipula controlled all her senses and limbs from within in such a way that, though she desired very much by rising from her seat to receive Indra, she could not do so. When Indra found her silent and unresponsive, he again spoke to her and asked her to rise and receive him. Again, though she wanted to welcome him, Vipula controlled her speech so that she told Indra that he had no business to come to her, and she was ashamed that she so spoke against her will. Indra then understood the whole affair and was much afraid. Vipula then returned to his own body and took Indra to task for his misbehavior.

Many other stories, illustrating the various kinds of miraculous powers of yoga, might be repeated. But let us turn to a consideration of the principal use of the yoga practices for the spiritual enlightenment, the ultimate and absolute freedom of man, as described by Patanjali, the great yoga writer of about 150 B. C. Patanjali not only describes the principal yoga practices, but he gives a philosophical basis to the whole system and indicates, for the first time, how yoga may be utilized for the emancipation of man from the bondage of his mind and senses. It was explained in the last lecture that the sages of the Upanishads believed in a supra-conscious experience of pure self-illumination as the ultimate principle, superior to and higher than any of our mental states of cognition, willing, or feeling. The nature of this principle is itself extremely mystical; many persons, no doubt, are unable to grasp its character. It has been shown that, even in the days of the Upanishads, it was recognized to be obscure, and that the sages were never tired of saying that it could neither be perceived by the eye nor conceived in thought; but that, nevertheless, the sages believed in its existence as the ultimate being and not as an experience of ecstatic feeling or any other kind of transient psychological state. It was regarded as the real self and the ultimate reality. It is this view of self that is the root, as it were, of Indian mysticism.

If we ask ourselves what we understand by "I," we shall all find that, though it is in the most constant use, it is also the obscurest word in all our dictionaries. About the meaning of the word, in one sense we can never doubt; for there is no person who can ever doubt whether he is himself or another person. But when we try to understand what it definitely and actually means, it appears to be one of the most elusive of words. It certainly cannot designate merely our bodies; nor does it mean any particular idea or feeling of a temporary character. So we have to admit that while we all understand what it means we cannot define it. This is not the place to enter into all the recondite philosophical discussions to which the problem of the nature of the self has given rise. But some attempt must be made to explain what the Indians understood by the immortal and unchangeable self. Some believed this self to be the same in all persons, while others believed it to be many; but the conception of its nature was more or less the same in most of the systems of Indian thought. It was pure, contentless consciousness, altogether different from what we understand by idea, knowledge, or thought. Our thoughts and feelings are changeful; but this mysterious light of pure consciousness was changeless. The ultimate aim of the yoga processes (as of most of the Indian systems of thought) is to dissociate ourselves from our sensations, thoughts, ideas, feelings, etc., to learn that these are extraneous associations, foreign to the nature of self but adhering to it almost so inseparably that the true self cannot be easily discovered as a separate and independent entity.

But with the Indian sages this doctrine of a transcendent self was not merely a matter of speculative philosophy. For philosophy came to them much later than the actual practice of the liberation of this true self from the bondage of the association with all our so-called psychical states, ideas, feelings, emotions, images and concepts. It is very difficult for a Western mind of today to understand, or appreciate, the minds of the Indian seers. They felt a call from within the deep caverns of their selves—a call which must have started from a foretaste of their own true essence—which made all earthly pleasures or hopes of heavenly pleasures absolutely distasteful to them. They could feel satisfied only if they could attain this true freedom, their true self. To appreciate their experience at all one must, in imagination, take a long jump backward of about twenty-five centuries and across the waters of the Atlantic and the Indian oceans, and picture to oneself the valley of the lofty snow-capped peaks of the Himalayas looking high up to the infinite of the heavens and, far beyond, the peaceful groves and cottages where the innocence and forbearance of man had

endeared him to trees and beasts alike, where no other sounds disturbed the
serene forest-dwellers than the breezy rustling of the lofty Sal trees and the
grovy palms. The necessities of the men who dwelt there were few. They often
wore clothes made from birch bark, and ate fruits and vegetables that grew wild
in the hermitage and rice which grew without much trouble of cultivation. The
cows of the hermitage supplied them with milk and butter. They did not take
any animal life for food; the birds ate from their hands, the soft-eyed gazelles
roamed about their huts, made of straw or leaves of trees, and the peacocks
danced in the shady groves of their forest walks. The clear, transparent waters
of the holy river Ganges and other rivers watered their hermitages, and the cool
breezes delightfully refreshed their bodies and minds when the wearisome
tropical heat had relaxed their nerves and muscles into inaction. These men
had no riches, and they did not seek them. Their natural needs were few, and
it never occurred to them that these could be augmented or multiplied. They
thought, rather, that what needs they had were in themselves too numerous
and could be indefinitely curtailed. Even in rather recent times a story is told
to the effect that a scholar in Bengal, called Ramnath, was visited by Raja
Krishnachandra of Bengal who wanted to bestow riches on him and asked him
if he had any wants. The scholar replied that he had plenty of rice in his house
and that he could make his soup out of the sour leaves of the tamarind tree
which grew in his yard; the only difficulty that he had was with regard to some
intellectual problems which he was still not able to solve. For men who live in
a world of sky-scrapers, motor cars and comforts of all sorts, with its varied
scientific, political and social ambitions, with its desire for wealth and its highly
developed system of trade and commerce, it is inevitably difficult to appreciate,
or rightly understand, the minds of those who felt disinclined to all worldly
things and were uneasy until they could touch their own inmost self. Theirs,
however, was no ordinary pessimism, as is too often supposed by unsympathetic
and shallow-minded scholars, who lack the imagination and the will to
understand the Indian thought and culture of the past. They felt dissatisfied
with the world not because the world had no pleasures or joys to offer, but
because their desire for attaining their highest good, their true selves, was so
great that it could tolerate no compromise with any other kind of desire. The
sole ambition of the yogins, or the seers who practised the yoga discipline, was
to become absolutely free from all kinds of bonds and from all kinds of
extraneous determination.

The problem of how to become free naturally raised the question as to who
is to become free and from what. The logic of the yogins is irresistible. It is the
self which has to become free; in fact it is always free. The self is the ultimate
principle of pure consciousness, distinct from all mental functions, faculties,
powers, or products. By a strange, almost inexplicable, confusion we seem to
lose touch with the former so that we consider it as non-existent and
characterize the latter with its qualities. It is this confusion which is at the root

of all our psychological processes. All mental operations involve this confusion by which they usurp the place of the principle of pure consciousness so that it is only the mind and the mental operations of thought, feeling, willing, which seem to be existing, while the ultimate principle of consciousness is lost sight of. If we call this ultimate principle of consciousness, this true self, "spirit" and designate all our functions of knowing, feeling, and willing collectively as "mind," then we may say that it is only by a strange confusion of mind with spirit that the mind comes to the forefront and by its activities seems to obscure the true light of the spirit. Our senses run after their objects and the mind establishes relations between the sense-data, or sensations, and deals with the concepts formed therefrom as it carries on the processes of logical thought with the aid of memory. The external objects which draw minds to them are not in themselves directly and immediately responsible for obscuring the spirit or in binding it to them. It is, rather, the mind and its activities by which the true nature of the spirit seems to be obscured so that the mind usurps the rightful place of the spirit. What is necessary, therefore, is to control the activities of the mind and to stop all mental processes. If we can in this way kill the mind, all logical thought and all sense processes will be killed with it. The light of the spirit will then shine alone by itself unshadowed by the darkening influence of thought. The spirit, the ultimate principle of consciousness, and the self are one and the same thing, the three terms expressing the threefold aspect of its nature. But this entity, by whichever name it is called, is to be distinguished from mind, whose activities are thoughts, feelings, etc. We may here employ a simile. We may say that the spirit is like a pure white light covered by the colored dome of the mind. This colored dome hides the pure white light, and, without changing the nature of the white light by its own color, makes the latter appear as colored and wrongfully appears itself to be a source of colored light, though it has no light whatsoever of itself. We fail to recognize the white light within and take it for granted that the colored dome is itself a colored light. The only way to restore the purity of the white light is by smashing the colored dome. Similarly, the only way in which the spirit may be made to realize, in its own non-conceptual way, its own lonely light is by breaking the mind to pieces.

The mind lives by its activities of sensing, perceiving and conceiving. It creates illusions and hallucinations, revives past experiences in memory, and sometimes passes into a state of sleep in which it creates dreams. If the movement of the mind could be entirely stopped, its disintegration would be effected. The process of yoga consists in so controlling the activity of the mind that it ceases to pass through its different states. The cessation of all mental states is yoga. These mental states as they rise and pass away are not altogether lost. They continue in the subconscious mind as impressions which are revived by proper excitations. As they are thus revived and repeated, and return to the subconscious, the impressions become strengthened, growing more and more powerful and more likely to occur as conscious states. Thus, for example, when we once devote ourselves to making money and to enjoying the comforts it can procure, we become more and more deeply absorbed in earning money and enjoying its comforts. Similarly, the scholar through days and nights of study in his library grows ever more attached to his occupation of study. It is in this way that the tendencies of the mind become strengthened; repeating themselves almost mechanically they keep alive the continual flow of the mind from one state to another. Yoga consists in stopping the conscious and subconscious mental flow entirely and absolutely.

It is easy to see that no one will think of destroying his mind unless his desire for the absolute freedom of the spirit becomes so great that all the activities of the mind, all his sense-enjoyments, all his thoughts and feelings, lose all interest for him and appear to him to be entirely valueless. This disinclination to all worldly things, called vairagya, is the first thing which leads the yogin to seek the way of yoga to deliver himself forever from all mundane experiences. The seer is as sensitive as the pupil of the eye. Just as a speck of dust, which passes altogether unnoticed on any other part of the body, causes great pain when it gets into the eye, so the suffering, which is absolutely unnoticed by the ordinary person, is felt keenly by the seer. All ordinary pleasures appear to be distasteful to him. There is nothing in anything worldly that can give him any satisfaction. He is in that mood in which he is dissatisfied with them all and wishes to shun them.

Such a state of mind cannot be produced unless the mind has risen to the highest plane of moral elevation. Unless the mind is made absolutely pure there cannot be any steady disinclination toward worldly things. A seer must abstain from all injury to living beings. His tenderness should extend not only to all human individuals but to all living beings. He would not willfully take the life of, or injure, any living being. He would not steal the property of any other person. He would be absolutely truthful in thought, word and deed. Veracity consists in the agreement of words and thoughts with facts. But it must always be employed for the good of others and not for their injury. If it proves injurious to living beings, with whatever intention it be uttered it is not truth. Though outwardly such a truthful course may be considered virtuous yet since by his truth he has caused injury to another he has in reality violated the ideal of absolute non-injury. The seer must have a complete control of the sex tendencies. He must not desire anything more than the bare necessities. For the acquisition of things always entails attachment and greed, and injury to others in acquiring and preserving them. If in performing the great duty of universal non-injury, and in cultivating the other virtues auxiliary to it, a man be troubled by thoughts of sin, he should try to substitute for the sinful ideas those which are contrary to them. Thus, if the old habit of sin tends to drive him along the wrong path, he should, in order to banish it, entertain ideas such as the following:—"Being burnt up as I am in the fires of the world, I have taken refuge in the practice of yoga, which gives protection to all. Were I to resume the sins which I have abandoned, I should certainly be behaving like a dog which eats its own vomit—I should be acting as if I were to take up again that which I had once put aside." Thus one should habituate himself to meditation upon the harmful effects of the tendencies which are leading him along the wrong path. The habituation to this contrary tendency consists in continually thinking that these immoral tendencies cause an infinity of pain and error. Pain and error are the unending fruits of these immoral tendencies and in the recognition of this lies the power of righting the trend of our thoughts.

Other moral qualities of a positive character are considered indispensable to a seer toiling on the path of yoga. These are: purity, contentment, indifference to physical difficulties of heat, cold, etc., study and self-surrender to God. Purity here means both physical and mental cleanliness. Contentment means that self-satisfied condition of the mind in which we are at peace with ourselves, having ceased to run after new wants. Indifference to physical difficulties is also a virtue to be acquired by the yogin, who should be able to bear calmly the bodily wants of hunger and thirst, heat and cold. He should also be able to stop his physical movements for a considerable length of time, and be able, as well, to stop his desire to talk with others and to remain absolutely dumb.

In the last lecture, on the Upanishadic mysticism, it was shown that when such a high standard of moral elevation is reached and we seek to know the inmost essence of self, the self often reveals its own true nature through a direct intuition which is beyond the grasp of the mind and the senses. The yogins, however,not only emphasized the necessity of the highest moral perfection but they also required a particular course of physical and mental discipline as indispensable to the realization of yoga's high ideal. The yogins emphasized not only the negative aspect of morality, such as abstinence from injury, falsehood and the like, but also such positive moral virtues as purity and contentment. The four cardinal virtues which a yogin was required to possess were universal friendship (maitri), compassion for all who suffer (karuna), happiness in the happiness of others (mudita), and a sympathetic consideration for the failings of others (upeksha). But even these were not deemed sufficient; they were only preliminary acquirements which the yogin must possess before starting with his yoga practices. The acquisition of these moral virtues went, indeed, a long way in restraining the mind from running after sense-objects and from being disturbed by greed, passions and antipathies; for the yogin was self-controlled, contented, pure in mind and body, and peaceable and charitable toward all living beings. But still he must be able to control his bodily movements. He must therefore habituate himself to sitting in one posture for a long time, not only for hours and days but often for months and years together. This implied the attainment of a power to bear calmly hunger and thirst, heat and cold, and all physical hardships.

In order that the movement in the body may be reduced to a minimum, it is necessary to acquire a control over breathing. To practice the science of breath-control, the yogin seats himself firmly, fixes his eyes on an object beyond him, or rather on the tip of his own nose or on the point between his two eye-brows, and slowly inhales a full breath. At first the breath that is taken in is kept perhaps for a minute and then slowly exhaled. The practice is continued for days and months, the period of the retention of the breath taken in being gradually increased. With the growth of breath-control, one may keep his breath suspended, without exhalation or inhalation, for hours, days, months and even years together. With the suspension of the respiratory process the body remains in a state of suspended animation, without any external signs of life. The heart ceases to beat, there is neither taking in of food nor evacuation of any sort, there is no movement of the body. There is a complete cessation of the respiratory process as, with his mouth shut and his tongue turned backwards behind the tonsils stopping the passage of air firmly like a lid, the yogin sits in his fixed posture in an apparently lifeless condition. Even in modern times there are many well-attested cases of yogis who can remain in this apparently lifeless condition for more than a month. I have myself seen a case where the yogin stayed in this condition for nine days. The case of Saint Haridas is well-known. He remained buried underneath the ground for forty days under strict vigilance of guards. When, after forty days of breathless and foodless condition of suspended animation, he was brought out of the earth, there was apparently no life in him, no movement of breath, no heart-beats. But after his body had been rubbed and much water had been poured on him he again came back to life and began to breathe normally.

Various methods of purifying the body were gradually discovered by which the yogin could so temper the body as to make it immune to diseases. In earlier times, before the elaborate bodily disciplines had been discovered, the yogin prayed to God and depended on His grace for the immunity from disease which was so necessary to the proper performance of his yoga duties. But later on, the yogin tried to be more or less independent of God's grace and discovered a whole system of bodily exercises, breathing exercises, and automatic internal washings by which his body became so tempered that no diseases could easily attack him. These consisted, first, in habituating the body to keeping fixed postures which required various muscular movements. By this means the yogin could make his body flexible, reduce its unnecessary fat, and attain full control over his voluntary muscles. For these postures required the exercise of all the voluntary muscles. Second, through the breathing exercises which could be performed in different forms and in different degrees of intensity, combined with the different postures, the yogin obtained control over the various involuntary muscles which regulate the operation of the viscera, including the bladder and the excretory organs, the heart, the stomach, etc. Added to these was, third, the thorough washing away of the impurities which, being secreted by some of the internal organs, obstruct their normal activity and lower their power of resistance. These washings can be easily performed by the control that the yogin acquires over his inner involuntary muscles. Thus, for example, the yogin can take water into the intestines by expelling air from these cavities and thus forcing in water by the downward path from a tub in which he may be sitting at the time. He can expel air from these cavities by means of the control that he has over the muscles of those organs which to a normal person are quite involuntary. Thus, at any time that he likes he can thoroughly wash his stomach, his bladder, urethra, etc. He has thus a thorough access to all the important cavities of the body where impurities may be produced and deposited. In short, by the combined operation of postures, breath-control, breathing exercises, and the voluntary washings of the impurities from all the important cavities of the body, he can so increase his power of physical resistance as to remain practically immune to all diseases.

But these are all merely external preparations to fit the body for the yoga practices. The real yoga practice of the mind can be properly begun only when these preliminaries have been to a large extent acquired so that the chances of external bodily disturbances and internal disturbances due to passions, antipathies, attachments, etc., have been minimized. The yogin begins this superior mental yoga by concentrating at first on any gross physical object. This concentration is not the ordinary concentration of thought as exemplified in any scientific or literary work. For this latter type of concentration consists in the limiting of the mind's activity to matters associated with the object of attention. Thus, if we concentrate on the writing of a poem or the description of scenery, what we do is to restrain the mind from flying off to other objects in which we are not interested at the time and to focus it upon the relations between various associated images and thoughts. The mind is in such cases in a lively state of movement within a limited sphere, always seeking to discover new relations or to intensify the comprehension of relations and facts already known. But yoga concentration aims not to discover any new relations or facts or to intensify any impression; it aims solely to stop the movement of mind and to prevent its natural tendency towards comparison, classification, association, assimilation and the like. The fixing of the mind on an object is done I with the specific purpose of pinning it to that object and of preventing its transition to any other object. By this process the mind becomes one with the object, and so long as it is pinned to that object its movement is stopped. At the first stage of this union, there is knowledge of the name and the physical form of the object to which the mind has been pinned. But at the next stage nothing is known of the object in its ordinary relations of name and form, but the mind becomes one with the object, steady and absolutely motionless. This state is called a state of samadhi, or absorptive concentration. This stage arises when the mind by its steadiness becomes one with its object, divested of all associations of name and concept, so that it is in direct touch with the reality of the thing uncontaminated by associations. In this state, the object does not appear as an object of my consciousness but my consciousness, becoming divested of all "I" or "mine," becomes one with the object itself. There is no awareness here that "I know this," but, the mind having become one with the thing, the duality of subject and object disappears, and the result is the transformation of the mind into the object of its concentration. Our ordinary knowledge of things is full of false and illusory associations which do not communicate to us the real nature of the object; but when such an absorptive union of object and mind takes place, a new kind of intuition is produced, called prajna, similar to the Upanishadic intuition, called prajnana, and thereby the real nature of the thing is brought home to us. This prajna knowledge, which is a new kind of intuition produced by stopping the movement of the mind, is entirely different from the ordinary logical type of cognition of thoughts, images, etc. This intuition is a direct acquaintance, more or less similar to direct perceptual vision but free from the ordinary errors of all sense-perception. Such a steadiness can however be achieved only after continual practice. A yogin must be always watchful, particularly in the first stages, to keep his mind steadily on the object of his concentration. He must have, therefore, an inexhaustible fund of active energy (virya).

On the negative side we have, therefore, disinclination to worldly things; on the positive side, firm faith in the efficacy of the yoga process and vigorous energy exercised in steadying the mind in contemplation. Gradually, as the yogin becomes more proficient, he selects subtler and finer objects for his concentration; and at each stage in this refinement, new forms of intuitional prajna, or yoga knowledge, dawn. With' this advancement, the yogin develops many miraculous powers over natural objects and over the minds of men. Truths wholly unknown to others become known to him. Though all these powers confirm his faith in the yoga process, he does not allow himself to be led away by their acquisition, but steadily proceeds toward that ultimate stage in which his mind will be disintegrated and his self will shine forth in its own light and he himself will be absolutely free in bondless, companionless loneliness of self-illumination.

This prajna, or yoga intuitional knowledge, may be considered as a new dimension of knowledge wholly different from any other kind of knowledge derived by the movement of the mind. The most fundamental characteristic of yoga mysticism consists, on its negative side, not only in a disbelief in the ability of sense-perception and logical thought to comprehend the ultimate truth about the absolute purity and unattached character of our true self; but also in a disbelief in the possibility of the realisation of this highest truth so long as the mind itself is not destroyed. On its positive side, it implies that intuitional wisdom is able to effect a clear realisation of truth by gradually destroying the so-called intellect. The destruction of mind, of course, also involves the ultimate destruction of this intuition itself. So neither the intuition nor our ordinary logical thought is able to lead us ultimately to self-realisation. There are thus three stages of knowledge. First, our ordinary sense-knowledge and logical thought which always deal with the world and worldly objects and which appear valueless to us when we are in spiritual exaltation and are anxious to attain the highest truth. Second, the intuitional yoga wisdom, which can only be attained when, as a result of the highest moral elevation and the yoga practices, the mind can be firmly steadied on an object so that it becomes one with that object and all its movements completely cease. This yoga wisdom gives us a direct non-conceptual vision of, or acquaintance with, the ultimate truths concerning all objects on which our minds may be concentrated; and gradually, as the yogin begins to concentrate on subtler and finer objects, such as mind, self, etc., higher and nobler truths concerning these become known to him. Though we are free to concentrate on any object whatsoever, it is desirable for the quicker attainment of our goal that we should concentrate on God—surrender ourselves to Him. In the most advanced state of this yoga intuition, all the truths regarding the nature of the true self, of the mind and of the material world and its connection with mind, become clear, and as a result of this and also as a result of the gradual weakening of the constitution of the mind, the latter ceases to live and work and is dissociated forever from the spirit or the self. It is then that the spirit shines forth in its own lonely splendor, free from the bondage of the mind which had so long by its activities led it towards false worldly attachments and to a false non-appearance of its own pure nature in all the varied products of ordinary knowledge, feeling and willing which make up our worldly life. The highest and ultimate revelation of truth is therefore not only non-conceptual and non-rational, but also non-intuitional and non-feeling. It is a self-shining which is unique.

LECTURE IV: BUDDHISTIC MYSTICISM

THE process of yoga described in the last lecture consists of a threefold course, viz., high moral elevation, physical training of the body for yoga practice, and steady mental concentration associated with the revelation of yoga wisdom, which leads to a knowledge of reality as it is. This system of thought and practice, though not without unique and distinctive features, was largely an adoption from very early times. Thus the heretical school of the Jains, which, like the Buddhistic school, holds to a monastic religion, but which was founded earlier than 500 B. C., the date of the Buddha, also considered yoga as the means of liberation of the soul. For the Jains, the liberated state of the soul is not one of pure, feelingless, non-conceptual, non-intuitional self-illumination, but is a state of supreme happiness in which the liberated self possesses a full perfection of all kinds of knowledge: perceptual, logical, alogical, intuitional and trance cognition. This liberation is attained, they believe, by the performance of yoga. Yoga with them consists mainly of a high elevation of character and complete cessation from the doing of evil, like the yoga of Patanjali described in the last lecture. They lay great emphasis on the principle of non-injury, but they also urge the necessity of the other virtues demanded by the yoga of Patanjali. Here, then, we have a system of thought according to which high moral elevation, by the cessation from all evil-doing and the acquirement of all the positive virtues is supposed to reveal a knowledge of reality as it is, and ultimately to liberate us from the bondage of our deeds and bring us to a state of perfect happiness, perfect knowledge and perfect power. The Jains, like the yogins, also believe that without the control of the mind no one can proceed in the true path. All our acts become controlled when our minds become controlled. It is by attachment and antipathy that man loses his independence. It is thus necessary for the yogin that he should be free from both attachment and antipathy and become independent in the real sense of the term. When a man learns to look upon all beings with an equal eye, he can effect such freedom, in a manner impossible even by the practice of the strictest asceticism through millions of years.

The Buddha himself, as the legendary account of his life tells us, once went out with his friends for a ride on horseback through the fields outside his capital. There he saw that, as the fields were being ploughed by the peasants, many insects were being mutilated and killed with each drive of the plough; and he saw also the sufferings of the poor beasts that were employed in the field. Extremely affected by these sufferings, he dismounted from his horse and sat on the grassy ground to reflect on the ultimate destiny of all beings. He realized that sufferings, diseases, old age and death are evils to which we are all subject. At that moment he saw a monk who said that, being afraid of births and deaths, he had renounced the world for his eternal salvation. The suggestion affected him very deeply. He therefore decided to renounce the world and seek to discover the way to the extinction of all sorrows, sufferings, diseases, old age and death. After testing many ways followed by other people, the Buddha himself adopted the path of yoga for the attainment of the truth that he ultimately discovered. As he sat with fixed determination he was tempted in various ways by Mara, the Buddhist Satan, but all these temptations failed and the Buddha remained firm in his purpose.

In the teachings and instructions found in Pali works ascribed to the Buddha, it is said that we are bound, without and within, by the entanglements of desire and that the only way of loosening these is by the practice of right discipline, concentration and wisdom. Right discipline or sila means the desisting from the commission of all sinful deeds. This is the first prerequisite. Thereby one refrains from all actions prompted by bad desires. Concentration or samadhi is a more advanced effort. By it all the roots of the old vicious tendencies and desires are destroyed, and one is led to the more advanced state of a saint. It leads directly to prajna or true wisdom; and by this wisdom one achieves his final emancipation. Here also, as in the yoga of Patanjali, the individual must habituate himself to meditating on the fourfold virtues of universal friendship, universal compassion, happiness in the happiness of all, and indifference to any kind of preferment, whether of himself, his friend, his enemy or a neutral party. By thus rooting out all misery he will eventually become happy; he will avoid thoughts of death and live cheerfully, and will then pass over to the idea that other beings would also fare similarly. He may in this way habituate himself to thinking that his friends, his enemies and all those with whom he is not connected might all become happy. He may fix himself in this meditation to such an extent that he obliterates all differences between the happiness of himself and that of others. He remembers that if he allows himself to be affected by anger he would weaken the self-restraint which he has been carefully practising. If some one has done a vile action by inflicting an injury, that cannot be a reason why he should himself do the same by being angry with others. If he were finding fault with others for being angry, could he himself indulge in anger? A saint who has thus made his sila or right discipline firm enters into a state of concentration which has four stages of gradual advancement. In the fourth or the last stage both happiness and misery vanish and all the roots of attachment and antipathies are destroyed. With the mastery of this stage of concentration there comes the final state of absolute extinction of the mind and of total cessation of all sorrows and sufferings—Nirvana.

It is easy to see that this system of yoga is very much akin to Patanjali's yoga; and it is not improbable that both Patanjali and Buddha but followed a practice which had been in existence from much earlier times, so that neither of them may be credited with its discovery. But there is one point in which there is at least a good deal of theoretical difference between Buddha's system and that of Patanjali. The ultimate goal of all concentration and its highest perfection with the Buddha is absolute extinction, while with Patanjali it is liberation of the spirit as self-illumination.

It is indeed very difficult to describe satisfactorily the ultimate mystical stage of Buddhistic Nirvana. For in one sense it is absolutely contentless. It is the state of deliverance from all sorrow and from all happiness. Yet, as the ultimate ideal of all our highest strivings and the goal of all our moral perfection and concentration, it was an ideal which was in the highest degree attractive to the Buddhists. Had it been conceived as pure and simple extinction or annihilation, it could not have had the attraction for the Buddhists that it did. In many passages it is actually described as blissful. In other passages it is held to be like the extinction of a flame. Some European scholars have considered the descriptions of Nirvana by the Buddhists to be incoherent or inconsistent. It is not surprising that European scholars, who are temperamentally often very different from the Buddhists of India, should fall into error in trying to comprehend the mystical state of Nirvana. Whether we read the teachings of the Upanishads or of the yoga of Patanjali, the ultimate state representing the goal of all the spiritual quest and spiritual strivings of the sages is set forth as absolutely contentless and non-conceptual. It is the self no doubt, but this self is entirely different from the self with which we are familiar in all our ordinary worldly concerns. It is the extinction of all our sorrows and pleasures and all our worldly experiences as much as is Nirvana. It is a state of absolute dissolution of all world-process. Though a blissful state, there is no distinction here between the bliss and the enjoyer of the bliss. But still it is just such a non-logical ultimate state that could stimulate the highest strivings of the best men of India. To call it blissful is not to understand bliss in an ordinary way. For this mystical bliss is incomprehensible by the intellect.

Nirvana was conceived as a state similar to that just described. If it was compared to the extinction of a flame, this was quite proper. For is it not a state in which all worldly experiences entirely and absolutely cease to exist? Yet it is blissful in the sense that it can stimulate our spiritual cravings and spiritual strivings to the highest degree. The Hindus thought that at this state there is only the self-luminous self. The Buddhists, however, could not say what exists at this state for they denied the existence of the self. But the teaching of the Hindus is scarcely more comprehensible, except for the fact that at least from the grammatical and literary point of view we have in "the self-luminous self" a positive expression. But this self is as indescribable as is the state of Nirvana, except by the negative method of "not this," "not that." But still this state was rightfully called immortal and blissful because it was looked upon by the Buddhists as the end of all their sufferings, the goal of all their spiritual strivings, and the culmination of spiritual perfection. What is especially emphasized, from the negative point of view, is that it is absolutely non-logical in its nature. It has no describable essence. The mysticism of the Buddhist consists in a belief in this essenceless state of Nirvana 1 as the state of ultimate perfection and ultimate extinction, to be realized by the complete extinction of desires and the supra-intellectual wisdom of the yoga practice.

So, though, for academic and philosophical discussions, the essenceless state of the vacuity of Nirvana is absolutely different from the pure self of yoga liberation, yet from the point of view of mystical experience both are too deep and unfathomable for ordinary comprehension. Both are transcendent, unworldly, and contentless in their nature; and the methods of their realization are also largely similar.

In digressing, I shall now turn your attention to other forms of mysticism inviting a belief in non-logical methods of achieving one's highest goal of power, happiness, wisdom or emancipation, and shall speak of Indian asceticism. The Taittiriya Brahmana, which was composed probably as early as 700 B. C. (if not even earlier) speaks of Brahmacharya in the sense of studying the Vedas with due self-control. We find there the story of Bharadvaja who practised Brahmacharya for one whole life which was as long as three lives. Indra approached him and, finding him decayed and old, said, "Bharadvaja, if I were to give you a fourth life, what would you do with it?" He answered, "I would use it in practising Brahmacharya." The word tapas etymologically means heat, and in the Atharva Veda (XVII. 1. 24) is actually used in the sense of the heat of the sun. But by an extension of meaning the word was used to denote also the exertion of mental energy for the performance of an action and for the endurance of privations of all kinds, of heat, cold, and the like. It was regarded as a great force which could achieve extraordinary results. Thus it is said in the Taittiriya Upanishad that the Great Being performed tapas and having done so created all the world. In Rig Veda (X. 167. 1) Indra is said to have gained Heaven by tapas. Tapas was thus probably understood from very early times as some kind of austere discipline, the exact nature of which, however, was rather vague, changeable and undefined.

In Ashvaghosha's Buddhacharita, which was written probably during the first century of the Christian era, we find that the Buddha was told by an ascetic in the forest how different ascetics lived like birds, by picking up grains left in the fields; others ate grass like animals; some lived with snakes; some sat still, like ant-hills, with nests of birds in the tangles of their long hair and snakes playing on their bodies; some lived in water, with tortoises eating parts of their bodies, thinking that misery itself is virtue and that the highest happiness in Heaven can be achieved by under-going sufferings of all kinds. Even in recent times Indian ascetics have inflicted on themselves various kinds of self-mortifications for the merits that are supposed to be derived from them. Thus a Brahmin ascetic at Benares is known to have lived for thirty-five years on a flat board studded with iron nails or spikes on which he sits and lies down at full length and which he never leaves night or day. Another common form of self-torture is to raise one or both arms above the head, and to hold them there until they become stiff and atrophied. Some ascetics are known to live with four fires burning very near them on their four sides and with the sun shining over their heads. Others undertake prolonged fastings and take vows of silence for years.

We read in the Puranas that self-mortification by itself was believed to generate a force. By virtue of the force, power or energy of these self-mortifications, an ascetic who performed them could exact from the god he worshipped, any boon that he wanted and the god could not refuse to grant him the boon even though he knew that the effect of granting it would be seriously mischievous. In the Ramayana, the greatest epic of India, the story is told of Ravana, the great demon who carried away Sita, the wife of Rama. Ravana had won the boon from Prajapati that he could not be killed by gods or demons, and it was by virtue of this boon that he could conquer all the gods, though he was ultimately killed by Rama, a man. A story is told of a demon who had a boon from the god Shiva that the person on whose head he would put his hands would he reduced to ashes. When the boon was granted, the demon wanted to test its truth by putting his hands on the head of the god Shiva himself. Shiva was very much afraid and started to fly away with the demon pursuing him in hot haste. But the god Shiva had no power of taking away the favor that he had granted, for it was earned by the force of the tapas of the demon. Vishnu, who came to rescue the god Shiva, played a trick upon the demon. The latter was asked to test the truth of the boon about which he was sceptical on his own head and thus he was reduced to ashes. This tapas is often described as a fire. Unless the boon is granted and the ascetic desists from his tapas, it is believed that the fire of his tapas might even burn the whole world as it were. The force of these stories is that there was a belief that self-mortification is itself a source of great power and that by it one could gain any desire, be it an immortal life in Heaven, the conquest of all the worlds, or any other fanciful desire—even the liberation from all bondage. We thus find that, just as in the Vedic school sacrifice was conceived as a power which could produce any beneficial results that the sacrificer wanted, so in this Puranic school there was the belief that tapas as self-mortification could give an individual anything he craved. It was a power by itself. These tapas performances were apparently carried out to please certain gods, just as oblations were offered to the Vedic gods in sacrifices; yet the god with reference to whom the tapas was performed had no power to refuse the boon. The boons were exacted from the gods by the power of tapas, whether or not the gods willed to grant them of their own free volition, just as the effects of sacrifice did not in any way depend on the good will of the gods to whom offerings were made at those sacrifices.

We know that tapas as the power of endurance of physical privations and troubles was an indispensable accessory of both the Buddhist yoga and Patanjali's yoga. The gradual abandonment of desires until their ultimate extinction could be effected, was essential both to yoga and to Buddhism. It is true that the Upanishads do not speak of the extinction of desires, but they certainly praise self-control as an indispensable desideratum. There is indeed the law of karma which requires that every person reap the fruits of his actions, whether good or bad, and that if the life of the present birth is not sufficient for the experience of the sufferings or the joys which are put to his account in accordance with the measure of his vice or virtue, he will enjoy or suffer the fruits of his deeds in another birth. So, in an endless chain of births and rebirths, moves on the cyclic destiny of man. All his rebirths are due to the fact that he is filled with desires, and for their fulfillment he performs actions out of attachments, passions, antipathies, etc. By the law of karma (which acts automatically according to some, and is controlled by the will of God according to others) he enjoys or suffers the fruits of his actions in this or in subsequent births. So if the successive chain of births is to be terminated, the accretion of the fruits of karma must be stopped, and if the accretion of karma is to be stopped, desire must be rooted out. I shall not enter into the subtle question as to whether the place of superior importance belongs to karma or to the extinction of desires in the Hindu, Buddhist and Jaina schemes of life. Whichever of the two may be considered the more important in each particular Hindu or Buddhist system of thought, they are nevertheless indissolubly connected. For out of desires come the actions and their fruits, and out of actions and the enjoyment or suffering of their fruits of pleasures or sorrows come further desires, and so on. However, if one looks at the matter psychologically, the extinction of desires may be considered the more important, since it is for Indian philosophy the indispensable ethical desideratum for all spiritual achievement. If the ultimate freedom of the spirit and the cessation of the cycle of births and rebirths be the ultimate ethical and spiritual goal, this can only be attained by the extinction of desires and the termination of the accretion of the fruits of our deeds. The development of the ideal of tapas is a direct result of this ideal of the extinction of desires. It was probably thought in some circles that control of desires implies on its positive side the idea of self-mortification. Logically it certainly does not. But the mistaken transition is easy. So there grew up a system of practice in which people thought that self-mortifications are of the highest merit and are capable of giving anything that might be desired. Soon degeneration set in. Self-mortifications were probably introduced as supplementary to the control of desires. They then came to be practiced for the indulgence of desires for attaining heaven or superior power, and thus began to perform functions similar to those that were ascribed to sacrifices in Vedic circles.

The Buddha himself, as the legendary account of Ashvaghosha's Buddhacharita relates, directs the same criticisms as the above against the practice of self-mortification. He deplores the fact that, after leaving all worldly comforts, relatives and friends, men should with all these self-mortifications called tapas, desire only the satisfaction of desires. People are afraid of death, but when they seek the satisfaction of desires this leads to births, and thus they again face death of which they are afraid. If self-mortification is by itself productive of virtue, then the enjoyment of pleasures must be vicious. But if it is believed that virtue produces pleasures or happiness, and if pleasures are vices, then virtue produces vice, which is self-contradictory. It is strange, however, that the Buddha himself, when he wanted to attain to the highest wisdom or philosophy, undertook for six years the most rigorous asceticism and with all his limbs emaciated was almost on the point of death. He did not, of course, aim at the fruition of any ordinary desires, but at the discovery of the wisdom by which birth and death and all the sufferings associated with them could be stopped. All the same, he at first followed the custom then prevalent among ascetics and underwent the most austere discipline. But at the end of six years he realized that the performance of asceticism was unnecessary and without value for the attainment of the higher wisdom. He then bethought himself as to how he might regain his former strength and physique.

He thought that by hunger, thirst and fatigue the mind loses its ease, and that if the mind is not at ease one cannot by its use attain the highest wisdom. It is by the due satisfaction of the senses that the mind comes to its ease, and it is the easy, peaceful, and healthy mind in a healthy body that can attain the wisdom of yoga concentration. So the Buddha gave up his old forms of hard ascetic practice and tried to regain his health by proper food, bathing, etc. His associates, however, who probably knew only the old forms of practice, and were therefore shocked over his abandonment of them, left him. It was only after he had thus recovered his health that he could resist all the temptations of Mara, the Buddhistic Satan, and attain by concentration, highest wisdom. The wisdom that the Buddha attained seems to have been more of the nature of logical thought, but the goal that was to be attained by such wisdom was the mystical, inexpressible, essenceless Nirvana; and the direct means by which this could be attained was not logical thought or reasoning or scriptural or other kinds of learning, but the extinction of all desires (trishna-kshaya).

The principal virtues of universal friendship, universal compassion, etc., to which reference has already been made, were appreciated early in Buddhism and also in the yoga of Patanjali. But it may well be argued that there was scarcely any place for the active manifestation of universal friendship or universal compassion in a scheme of life which was decidedly individualistic. No one who sought the absolute freedom of his own self, or the extinction of his whole personality like the extinguishing of a flame, and who sought the cessation of his own rebirths and sorrow as the only goal and the only ambition to be realized, could have much scope for any active manifestation of universal friendship. The altruistic ideal can therefore at best be merely a disposition, and can manifest itself merely in a negative way, e.g., in non-injury to any being. But a person who holds such an individualistic notion of salvation cannot, in his scheme of life, have any leisure or opportunity for the doing of active good to others.

In the Hindu Puranas or religio-mythological works, written in poetry, we sometimes come across tales of wonderful self-sacrifice for the good of the gods or even for the good of animals who sought protection. But tales of self-sacrifice from the motive of universal friendship are very rare, and they do not seem to fit in with the Hindu ideal of personal and individual liberation. A story is told that when the gods were in great trouble in their war with Vritra, a demon, they approached the sage Dadhichi. For it was decreed by fate that the demon could be killed with a weapon made of Dadhichi's bones but with nothing else. Dadhichi, in response to the request of the gods, willingly gave up his life, in order that the gods, with a weapon made of his bones, might destroy the demon. A story is also told of King Shibi, who was tested by the gods Indra and Agni. Agni took the form of a pigeon, and Indra that of a pursuing hawk. The pigeon took shelter with King Shibi. The latter would not give it over to the hawk because the pigeon had taken shelter with him and under these circumstances he would rather give up his own life than allow the pigeon to be killed. At last the hawk said that he would be satisfied if King Shibi would give from his own body flesh of the same weight as that of the pigeon, and the king cut the flesh of his thigh with his own sword. This, however, is a case of the kshatriya's virtue of giving shelter to those who seek it, even at the sacrifice of one's own life. It does not exemplify self-sacrifice for the good of beings in general, out of pure motives of universal friendship. The tale is a Brahmanic adaptation of a Buddhist story called Shibijataka, in which King Shibi is said to have torn out his eyes and made a gift of them out of motives of pure charity alone. In another story in the Mahabharata, Shibi is said to have cut up his own son as food for a Brahmin who desired the son's flesh for dinner; and to please the Brahmin Shibi was prepared to join in eating the dinner consisting of his own son's flesh. The motive here was the supreme duty of pleasing the Brahmins and giving them whatever they wanted.

But though the ideal of universal friendship and compassion does not seem to have been an active creed among the Hindus or among the followers of the Hinayana school of early Buddhism, it assumed a rôle of paramount importance in the Mahayana school of Buddhism. Here universal altruism and universal compassion, and happiness and sorrow in the happiness and sorrow of others, form the dominant principle. The philosophy of the Mahayana Buddhism was peculiarly idealistic. It taught that matter as such has no existence in any form, and that all things perceived are but creations of the mind, and more like a magic show than reality. Everything, according to it, is essenceless and indescribable, mere phantom creation of the mind. Indeed, mind itself is not ultimately real in any sense, but is as illusory a creation as all other things created by it. It is the realization of this that was called bodhi or perfect knowledge. Those who perceive this truth attain perfect knowledge and, like a flame extinguished, reach Nirvana or the final deliverance from all sorrows and rebirths.

There is a lower order of saints called arhats, or pratyekabuddhas. These pratyekabuddha saints are said to be of a lower order because they live alone by themselves like the rhinoceros. By their spiritual endeavors, they obtain a logical understanding of the way in which all worldly things originate and pass away; and by meditation on the essencelessness of all things, they attain perfect knowledge and Nirvana. They are not instructed by any one, nor do they teach others to attain the knowledge that they gain. They are accustomed from the beginning to lead a lonely life like the Hindu yogis, and the instruction of others does not interest them. They are therefore regarded as being only Buddhas or enlightened ones of a lower order.

The higher Buddhas are those who aim not only at the vision of truth for destroying their inner notion of self or ego and all desires of existence and non-existence,but also at doing good to all living beings and constantly practicing the great virtues. Their enlightenment includes not only the possession of the truth indispensable to salvation, but also omniscience, universal knowledge of all details of things, and omnipotence. The perfect Buddha attains these powers not only through his prolonged meditations, by which he gets insight into the principles of all things, but also through his infinite merits of constantly performing the great virtues of charity, patience, etc. The man who aims at the attainment of this superior Buddhahood is called a Bodhisattva (one who is on the way to the attainment of perfect knowledge). His superior aim consists in this that, at the cost of personal sufferings, he wishes the temporal happiness of others. He continually desires for others supreme and temporal happiness, and for himself the Buddhahood as a means of realizing this service to others. Even after the saint attains true enlightenment and knows that there is no essence in anything and that nothing exists, he continues to practice the virtues of charity, morality and patience, and to mature the qualities of his supreme enlightenment.

We sometimes hear very remarkable stories of Buddhist saints, even of actual historical saints, who showed supreme self-control and compassion for others. Thus it is said of Aryadeva, a great Buddhist teacher of the second century, that he once defeated in argument a teacher of non-Buddhistic doctrines. A young disciple of this defeated teacher, greatly enraged over his teacher's defeat, determined to murder Aryadeva and awaited a suitable opportunity. One day Aryadeva was preaching the doctrine of the essencelessness of all things, and was refuting heretical views before his pupils in a solitary forest. After this instruction, while he was taking a walk alone, the enemy stabbed him from ambush, saying, "You conquered my teacher with your knowledge, but I now conquer you with my sword." Aryadeva, holding fast with his hands his stabbed belly, bade the would-be assassin take his three clothes and bowl and escape over the mountains in monk's garb so that others might not capture and punish him. He further told him that he was very sorry for him because of the seeds of sinful deeds that he was sowing. The murderer was deeply moved by the saint's compassion and sympathy, and asked Aryadeva to teach him the doctrine. Even in his wounded condition Aryadeva began to teach him the Buddhist doctrine of the essencelessness of all things. After giving him some instructions Aryadeva fell in a swoon and his assailant escaped. Soon afterwards Aryadeva's pupils came and enquired about the murderer. To them the teacher replied that there was no one who was killed or who killed, no friend and no enemy, no murderer, that everything was a delusion due to ignorance.

He who is kind and good and has a great propensity for doing good to others, and who, though incapable of committing a sinful action for himself, may yet be so moved by love for his fellow beings as to commit a wrong action for them, is fit to take the vow of a Bodhisattva who would spend all his future career for the good of others. His enthusiasm is not for the egoistical calm of the saint who is anxious for his own deliverance; he is moved by the most altruistic of all motives, viz., compassion for all creatures. It is such a person who takes the vow of Bodhisattva or one who aspires to the goal of a future Buddha.

But even then it is one thing to take a vow and another thing to fulfil it. Ordinarily one's unconstrained love is given to himself and it is only by reflection that the Bodhisattva learns to care wholly for the welfare of others. At the lower stages, his nature leaves him at the mercy of his inclination; his knowledge of truth is but slight, and the direct penetrating sight of the yoga meditations is entirely lacking to him. But by a continual repetition of his high aspirations, and by a more and more studious practice of the good works which they involve, he gradually comes to the higher stages of progress. As he enters these, wishing to bear the burden of the sins of all human beings in the hells and elsewhere, he becomes free from all fears of evil reputation, rebirth, death, etc. Becoming more and more perfect, he gradually masters the virtues of faith, compassion, affection for all, disinterestedness, reverence for self and for others. All his actions are for the good of others, and his only thought is that he may be serviceable to all beings.

The person who intends to enter upon the higher career of a Bodhisattva and ultimately to become the perfect Buddha, places himself under the guidance of a religious preceptor, performs the moral or pious works, and undertakes the vow of bodhi. He thinks that it is only by a desire to become a perfect Buddha for the salvation of men, and by dedicating himself to the good of all beings, that the sins of his past lives can he wholly removed. He confesses his own guilt and imperfections and deplores them. He wishes to dedicate all the fruits of his virtuous deeds, merit and piety to the good of all creatures and for the attainment of their Bodhi. He wishes to be the bread for those who are hungry, and the drink for those who are thirsty. He devotes himself by his love to all beings; and in his compassion for their sufferings, he gives all that he is, to all creatures. It is by such determinations that he produces in himself the proper state of mind with which one may start in the high career of a Bodhisattva. He has then to keep a strict vigilance over his thoughts and over the resolutions that he has taken, and keep a continued watchfulness over mind and body. He must also perform the great virtues called paramitas, for thinking, though good in itself, is not enough by itself; it must be continually supplemented by the exercise of the great virtues. He should restrain himself from all evil by continued watchfulness over his mind and body, and by self-control attained in this way. But he must also continually perform the great virtues in order to strengthen his life in progressive good.

One of the most important of these virtues is that of giving due scope to compassion (karuna). The aspirant thinks that his neighbor suffers pain as he suffers his. Why should he be anxious about himself and not about his neighbor? Such a man may even commit a sin if he knows that this will be beneficial to one of his fellow-beings. For the sake of doing good to others he should always be prepared to abandon even his meditations or even his chastity. It is through this universal compassion that he can reconcile all beings to himself—by almsgiving, amiability, obligingness, and sharing the joy and sorrow of others. But he ought also to take care that his tendency to charity do not become so excessive as to stand in the way of his spiritual advancement. For it is only on a high stage of spirituality that he can make himself most genuinely serviceable to others. To give even one's flesh and blood for the good of others is good, but the giving of spiritual food is certainly better. It is not good to sacrifice one's body to satisfy the appetite of a tiger when that body in a sound condition can be utilized for giving spiritual instruction to others.

Careful adherence to morality, consisting of purity of intention, reformation after transgression, and regard for the law of right conduct, is another of the important conditions which a Bodhisattva should strictly meet. Without going into any details, the main principle of morality consists in abstaining from all actions hurtful to others, or the maxim, "Do not do to others what you would not like others to do unto you." But apart from this negative virtue of abstention, he should also acquire the positive virtues of devotion to study, reflection and meditation, reverence to the teacher, nursing the sick, confession of guilt, association with people in their good and useful undertakings and in their difficulties and sicknesses, giving them right teaching, etc.,—in short, doing good to all people in all possible ways.

Another important virtue is patience or control of anger, for anger is the greatest of all sins. He should also practice the virtue of energetically conquering all incapacity of body and mind, all attachment to pleasures and want of firm determination. This he can do by thinking of the evil effects of these traits and by recalling that, unless he can firmly keep himself to the strict path of virtue, he will never be able to cross the ocean of suffering, and that, however low may be his present state, he may by continued exertion raise himself to the highest stage of perfection of the Buddhas. He should also derive additional strength by thinking: first, of his great desire to rid himself and all other beings from all their sins: second, of his great pride over undertaking to bear the burdens of all creatures; third, of his joy in undertaking new tasks as soon as the old ones are finished—his happiness is in action itself, and he seeks in action no other fruit than the pleasure of the action done; fourth, of his self-mastery of attention, and of keeping his mind and body always completely alert. If he for any reason fails once, he must discover the cause and see that he may not fail again.

Two further virtues are contemplation or concentration and the true wisdom which realizes the nothingness of all things. It is surprising how a metaphysics of extreme idealism, of the nothingness and essencelessness of all things, or of nihilism, could set for the achievement of the highest spiritual perfection a program of life and endeavor which is altruistic in the most extreme degree imaginable. What is required is a state of perfection in which the individual esteems the ultimate state of mystical deliverance—Nirvana or extinction—to be of little consequence, and is prepared to undergo all troubles, and refuse to enter Nirvana, unless and until all beings become good and happy and come to the path of deliverance. Out of the doctrines of self-control and the ideal of the extinction of desires, there has thus come a scheme of life in which desirelessness is attained by magnifying the scope of desires from the individual to the universal, by rejecting personal good for the sake of the good of others. This good is not sought with a view to any selfish aims, for the seer knows that nothing exists and that all forms and names are empty and essenceless. But he takes it upon himself to do this because of his supreme compassion and of his determination to devote himself to the service of his fellow-beings and to bring to them the light of perfection. The milk of human kindness flows through him, and it is this flow of kindness in him which leads him to his highest perfection. With him, as Shantideva (a great authority) says, even contemplation occupies only a lower place. For he attains to his highest only by persisting in the path of compassion.

The two cardinal features of his conduct are a firm conviction of the equality of his self with that of his neighbor and the substitution of his neighbor's self for his self. Each of these features involves a clear insight into the nature of things. If with great strength one can duly exemplify them, he attains all the merits of a Bodhisattva. He understands that our only enemy is our selfish "ego." Thus, he speaks to his own self, "Renounce, O my thought, the foolish hope that I have still a special interest in you. I have given you to my neighbor, thinking nothing of your sufferings. For if I were so foolish as not to give you over to the creatures, there is no doubt that you would deliver me to the demons, the guardians of hell. How often, indeed, have you not handed me over to those wretches, and for what long tortures! I remember your long enmity, and I crush you, O self, the slave of your own interests. If I really love myself, I must not love myself. If I wish to preserve myself, I must not preserve myself."

LECTURE V: CLASSICAL FORMS OF DEVOTIONAL MYSTICISM

WE have described the ideal of supreme self-control and of the extinction of all desires as an indispensable requirement for the attainment of high perfection. This end is believed to be reached by replacing egoism with unlimited universalism, the individual learning to desire his own good by desiring the good of others. But such an unlimited universalism could hardly be practiced within the limited sphere of the duties and activities of a householder. The ideal yogin who renounced the world and spent a life of supreme self-control and suppression of all desires, and who practiced his yoga courses in which all movements of his body are inhibited, could not live in society and follow the ordinary vocations of life. Cut off from society, he pursued a goal of individualistic perfection.

But the general Hindu system of life was not monistic, individualistic, or separatistic. Hindu society was divided into four castes. We find (1) Brahmins, who followed the scholarly and the priestly line of work, studied the Vedas, gave spiritual instruction and performed the sacrifices; (2) Kshatriyas, the warrior caste who protected the weak from the attacks of the strong, governed kingdoms as kings, and gave to the Brahmins all protection and encouragement in their scholarly and priestly works; (3) Vaishyas, or the trading and pastoral caste, who increased the wealth of the country by trading and farming; and (4) Shudras, or the servant caste, recruited from the non-Aryans who found a home in the Aryan societies and served as menials to the Brahmins, Kshatriyas and Vaishyas.

The Brahmin went to live with his teacher from the age of eight and remained with him until he had completed the study of the Vedas. He then returned from the house of his teacher and was bound according to the injunction of the scriptures to get married, to perform regularly the sacrifices, to be united with his wife and procreate sons, to teach students, and to make gifts or charities to proper persons at auspicious times and at holy places. Upon reaching the age of fifty he had to retire to forest life with his wife, and give himself up to holy thoughts and the leading of a holy life. In the last stage of his life, it was necessary for him to renounce even his forest life of retirement. He had to sever himself from all his attachments, lead the life of a hermit and get his food by begging. Of these four stages of life, called Brahmacharya, Grihastha, Vanaprastha, and Yati, the householder's life was regarded as the best. For this stage (ashrama) provided an opportunity for the doing of good to the people of all the other stages of life, by gifts, by the performance of sacrifices, by instruction to teachers,and by the procreation of good sons who might become the future supporters of society. Performance of sacrifices, teaching, and the procreation of sons were regarded as debts with which every Brahmin was born, and no Brahmin had any right to seek the individualistic goal of a hermit's life unless and until he had discharged these duties for the major portion of his life.

Similarly, it was regarded as the duty of a Kshatriya to protect the weak and to fight in a good cause, and of a Vaisya to carry on trading and farming. The performance of the class of duties belonging to each caste at its specific stage of life is the imperative duty (dharma); transgression of it was held to be transgression of duty and hence vicious (adharma). What was expected of every man was that he follow the specific duties allotted to his caste, satisfy his desires of life, and enjoy the pleasures of life. It was a balance in which equal attention was paid to the performance of the allotted duties and to the satisfaction of personal needs and desires that was regarded as the true ideal of life for all normal persons. Only in exceptional cases did the Hindu scheme of life admit the renouncement of this life (trivarga) of threefold duties in a search for the attainment of the goal of liberation (apavarga). The yearning after a higher life was an actual and soul-stirring experience among spiritually-minded persons. They were allowed the privilege of renouncing the life of ordinary pleasures, and of seeking to kill all other desires and to attain true knowledge, by intuition, moral elevation, yoga or even by asceticism. In their case alone, however, was this exception made. But even then the exception was not very readily admitted in orthodox Hindu circles. We remember the great effort that Shankara, the great Vedanta teacher, had to make, especially in his commentary on the Gita, to establish this point. He taught that those who attained higher knowledge (jnana) were exempt from the allotted duties of ordinary persons. These duties were obligatory only for those who did not attain the higher knowledge. But Shankara's interpretation of the Gita was objected to by other authorities.

The Gita is a work of great sanctity and popularity among the Hindus. It consists of seven hundred simple verses, of which the first chapter of forty-six verses forms the introduction. It is written in the form of a dialogue between Lord Krishna and Arjuna, the great warrior who, on the battlefield of the terrible Indian civil war described in the classic heroic poem Mahabharata, is appalled at the prospect of the fearful impending destruction and refuses to fight. Lord Krishna tries to persuade him, in the Gita, that as a Kshatriya, (a man of the military caste) it is his duty to fight. To add strength to his persuasion he makes use of many moral and religious arguments. Traditionally this theme forms a part of the fifth canto of the Mahabharata. Though its date is uncertain, it may well be believed to have been written about the . second or the third century B. C. It discards self-mortification and believes in three kinds of tapas: first, bodily discipline—respect to gods, Brahmins and the wise, purity, sincerity, chastity and non-injury; second, speech discipline—sweet and truthful speech, and study; and third, mental discipline—contentment, self-control, amiability, purity of mind, and meditation.

But the great solution of the Gita is the compromise it advances between the worldly life of allotted duties and the hermit life of absolute renouncement, and between a life of lawful and proper enjoyment and the absolute extinction of desires. The program that it proposes is, on the one hand, that we purify our minds, purging them of all attachments and passions by dedicating all the fruits of our actions to God; and yet, on the other hand, that we continue to perform all the duties belonging to our particular caste or stage of life. It is not the actions but our own inclinations and passions that really bind us. But if we can augment our faith in and our affection for God to such an extent that in our love for Him we free ourselves from all other attachments while yet we continue to perform the allotted and normal duties, the actions can in no wise bind us to a lower goal. A life dedicated to God, and lived for and in love of Him, is a life which is inevitably ennobled to the highest degree. A seer who has been able to liberate himself from the tendency to self-seeking and from attachment is never over-pleased at any good fortune nor over-sorry at any misfortune. His is a calm and unruffled life. He takes the pleasures and sorrows of life without the least perturbation; he has no fear and no anger; he is firm in himself, unshakeable and unmoved. Yet he follows the daily routine of social and other duties.

The Gita seems to reject the doctrine that the body and mind may be made entirely motionless or inactive. Simple physical conditions could make the body move; and it urges that it is only a false show of morality when the body is controlled and yet one continues to think of doing bad things or to harbor thoughts of attachment. The mysticism of the Gita consists in the belief that the performance of actions without personal attachment or self-seeking motive, and with a dedication of their fruits to God, leads a man to his highest realization or liberation. Knowledge is praised, but only because true knowledge is conducive to the acceptance of such a life of desireless self-surrender to God. A man who has no personal motive in an action really does not perform the action though to all appearances he may seem to be so doing. It is only such a person who my truly be called a yogin. His is a mind that is constantly fixed on God, and he performs all his duties for the sake of duty, out of reverence to the law, and with complete self-surrender to God.

Self-surrender to God, or self-abnegation, however, does not in the Gita involve a personal relationship of communion and love so much as it does the moral qualities of compassion, universal friendship, humility, contentment, want of attachment, self-control and purity. The expectation is emphasized that a person possessed of these moral qualities will be equally unruffled in sorrow and in happiness and that he will be the friend of all. Mind and intellect are to be concentrated on God, and all actions are to be surrendered to Him. This does not necessarily mean a superabundance of love. It may be an offshoot of the old yoga ideal of Patanjali. Here it is enjoined that the mind and intellect be concentrated on God, for, if this is done, God, being satisfied by this attachment, will help the yogin, and by His divine grace the yogin may achieve his goal much more easily than would otherwise be possible. The idea of the surrender of all actions to God is also to be found in the yoga of Patanjali. Though the writer of the Gita admits breath-control as a discipline, yet his whole emphasis is laid on self-abnegation and self-surrender to God. Breath-control seems to be given only a subordinate value, that of a means of purifying the mind. We have, therefore, in the Gita a new solution of how a man may attain his highest liberation. He may remain a member of society and perform his allotted duties provided he has the right sort of moral elevation, has fixed his mind on God, has dissociated himself from all attachment, and, by self-surrender and self-abnegation, has devoted himself to God. It is faith in the special grace of God to those who have surrendered themselves to Him that forms the essence of the Gita.

Though the idea of love for God does not show itself in any prominent way in early Sanskrit literature, except in the Pancaratra literature, it is very improbable that the idea was not known from very early times. For some of the monotheistic Vedic hymns reveal an intimate personal relation with the deity, implying affection; and in the Buddhist literature we find frequent references to love for the Buddha.

In the Vishnu Purana we are given the story of Prahlada. Because of his devotion to Hari, his father tormented him in various ways and sought to put him to death by throwing him into fire or into the sea, by administering poison, and by various other methods. But he was saved from all these perils by the grace of Hari, and as a true devotee of the great Lord he was not in the least angry with his father. In all the adoration to Hari, whether on the part of Prahlada or as otherwise reported in the Vishnu Purana and in many of the other early Puranas, the great Lord is adored and praised metaphysically or philosophically as the great Being from whom everything has come forth and to whom everything will return, as the great controller of the universe and the great lord who is residing within us and is controlling us, and as the prime mover of the material cosmic world which is only a manifestation of his power. The subtle and primal cosmic matter is a concrete expression of the energy of the Lord. By His will it is set in active operation and transforms itself into the visible universe. The universe, therefore, though in a sense different from Him, is ultimately sustained and supported by Him; created by Him, it will ultimately return to Him. Many are the hymns in the Puranas which praise God in this philosophical manner and extol His great powers. There are also numberless instances in which God is said to be pleased by philosophic meditation, and in consequence appears to the devotee, to speak with him, and to grant him the boon he seeks.

The earlier literature does not always emphasize the feeling element in devotion. In the Vishnu Purana, however, we find that when God came face to face with Prahlada and asked him if he had a boon to crave, he besought the same attachment for the Lord that ordinary people have for sense enjoyments. The devotion that Prahlada had previously shown was a concentration on God and a serene contemplation in which he became one, as it were, with the Lord. Ramanuja, the great Vedanta commentator of the 11th century, also defines devotion (bhakti) as a contemplation of God unbroken as the smooth and ceaseless flow of oil. But that such a contemplation necessarily implies love of God as its inner motive cannot be denied, and Ramanuja also describes this ceaseless contemplation as having its main source in love for God, who was so dear to the devotee. But all that I wish to point out in this connection is that, in this aspect of devotion, contemplation and communion are more prominent than any exuberance of feeling. Prahlada was attached to God by his love of Him; God was the dearest of all dear things to him. It was this inmost and most deep-seated love for God that stirred him to withdraw his mind from all other things and to enter into such a contemplation of God that he became absorbed in Him, his whole personality lost in an ecstatic trance unity with God. But this did not satisfy Prahlada. He desired such a devotion to God that the very thought of Him would bring the same sort of satisfaction that persons ordinarily have in thinking of sense-objects. He desired not only contemplative union but longed also to taste God's love as one tastes the pleasures of the senses.

It is the contemplative union with God that we find in the Gita, and the transition to it from the state of yoga concentration is not difficult to understand. Self-surrender to God, the higher moral elevation, and concentration on God are all present in Patanjali's yoga. But here the objective was the destruction of the mind through psychical exercises accompanied by the complete inhibition of bodily and mental activity. Later the devotee seeks to attain liberation through the special grace of the Lord, which he can hope to acquire by such contemplative union.

In later Indian thought the method of yoga on the one hand receded in favor of that of bhakti or devotion; on the other hand, its pure form became greatly complicated by the development of many mysterious doctrines and rites which became associated with it, sought its support, and claimed to be forms of it. But my time is limited and I cannot enter into these latter forms of mysticism. Nor can I describe those mystical religious movements which, arising as a reaction against the dominant religious ideal of extreme sense-control and the practice of desirelessness, tried to formulate certain principles and methods by which one could attain his highest goal not by sense-control but by sense-enjoyments. In these schemes, sense-indulgence under certain specified conditions was considered not only harmless but an indispensable desideratum. They probably started among some of the Buddhist schools and they soon became very common among certain sects of the Hindus. But the elucidation of these ideas would require a special course of lectures. I shall, therefore, leave them and pass directly to the development of the mysticism of love to God, as it is presented in the Bhagavata Purana and other relevant later literature.

It is in the Bhagavata Purana, whose date is probably the eleventh century A. D., that we first meet with the idea of devotion as the supreme source of a bliss or spiritual enjoyment that is itself the highest goal and so completely usurps the place of wisdom or philosophical knowledge. Even in the Gita true wisdom was regarded as a fire which reduces to ashes, as it were, all the past deeds whose fruits were not yet on the point of being enjoyed. But in the Bhagavata we read (11.14) that it is bhakti which destroys all the past sins. The old principle of self-surrender to God and a life spent in God-intoxication is the happiest of all lives. A man of such self-surrender has nothing else but God as his possession: he is supremely self-controlled, and the enjoyment that he has from his constant association with God keeps him absolutely happy and content with all things. Such a man does not aspire to any heavenly happiness or even to liberation. Devotion is regarded as having also a protective virtue. Even an ordinary devotee who is often led away by his sense attachments is so purified by this devotion that he is no longer overcome by external attachments or passions. The Lord can be realized by bhakti and by nothing else. Neither the performance of the allotted duties nor knowledge combined with the austere discipline of tapas can purify a man who is devoid of all bhakti. This bhakti, however, is no longer the old contemplative meditation of God, stirred by a deep-seated love. It is the ebullition of feelings and emotions of attachment to God. It manifests itself in the soft melting of the heart and expresses itself in tears, inarticulate utterances of speech, laughter, songs and dances, such as can only be possible through a mad intoxication of love. This kind of bhakti is entirely different from the calm contemplative life of complete self-abnegation and self-surrender to God and a mind wholly immersed in God and the thought of God.

The Bhagavata Purana is aware of the three methods of approach by knowledge, work and devotion, and also of the approach through yoga. Moreover, while emphasizing the superiority of devotion, it does not deny the efficacy of the other methods of approach. The latter are also described in the Gita; indeed, the Gita also emphasizes the bhakti method. Both the Gita and Bhagavata criticize the older course of the Vedic sacrifices, but neither of them has the boldness to pass an unconditional condemnation. The Gita says that one should perform these sacrifices, which are obligatory, with a pure and desireless mind. The fault of those who devote themselves to sacrifices is that they are filled with ordinary desires for pleasures and are not acquainted with any higher goal of life. To one who is infused with the higher ideal of life and can emancipate himself from desires by self-surrender to God, the performance of sacrifices, as of any other kinds of action, can do no harm. Indeed, it is good that under these circumstances one should not forsake his allotted duties.

The Bhagavata holds that the only efficacy of the Vedic restrictions and prohibitions is to be found in the fact that they offer a check on the natural inclinations of man and ultimately help him to desist from sense-activities and sense-propensities. The promise of heavenly rewards as the result of the performance of sacrifices is only a trick to incline people to accommodate themselves to modes of life offering only a restricted scope of sense-gratification. Its appeal is therefore only to those of the lowest plane. Those who are of the next higher order and have been able to accommodate themselves to a life of desirelessness would perform the obligatory duties without in the least looking forward to their fruits. In the next higher stage, a man may follow the path of yoga, or the path of wisdom respecting the supreme unity of Brahman, or any other line of devotion.

The path of devotion, however, is most fitted for those who are neither too much attached to sense-desires nor too much detached from them. Such men may adopt the line of bhakti and thereby purify their minds and, by self-surrender to God and the taste of supreme human happiness in their love, become averse to all other desires and enjoyments. Thus they learn to live a life of supreme devotion. They come to experience such intense happiness that all their limbs and senses become saturated therewith and their minds swim, as it were, in a lake of such supreme bliss that even the bliss of ultimate liberation loses its charm. Such an individual desires to live on, enjoying the love of God with heart, soul and body. When he acquires such a bhakti, it purifies his mind from all passions and impurities, and destroys all the bonds of his deeds and their fruits. For such a person is so attached to God that there is nothing else for which he cares; without any effort on his part, other attachments and inclinations lose their hold over him. So great is his passion for God that it consumes all his earthly passions. It is so great that it is its own satisfaction; it seeks nothing beyond itself. It stands by itself. As a great spring of happiness, it is ultimate and self-complete.

The bhakta who is filled with such a passion does not experience it merely as an undercurrent of joy which waters the depths of his heart in his own privacy, but as a torrent that overflows the caverns of his heart into all his senses. Through all his senses he realizes it as if it were a sensuous delight; with his heart and soul he feels it as a spiritual intoxication of joy. Such a person is beside himself with this love of God. He sings, laughs, dances and weeps. He is no longer a person of this world. The germ of this love is already found in the Vishnu Purana, where Prahlada seeks as a boon that bhakti which is an attachment for God no less strong than the attraction to sense-objects felt by ordinary sensual persons.

Vallabha, a later writer, defines bhakti as a great, firm feeling of love, associated with a sense of God's superiority and greatness. It places the bhakta or the devotee in a subordinate position. The latter is described as approaching God as one approaches his master, desiring mercy and protection and soliciting His special grace. But this idea of seeking protection and special grace, with a sense of God's supreme superiority, and finding oneself happy in thinking of the greatness of the superior Being, is by no means restricted to Hindu circles. There are numerous evidences of Buddhists praising the Buddha and seeking his protection, and finding great joy in extolling his great qualities and powers. Bhaktishataka of Ramachandra Bharati of the 13th century may be referred to as a typical instance.

This kind of bhakti is also associated with the doctrine of prapatti, or taking refuge in God, and is to be found among many classes of Vaishnavas, including the followers of Ramanuja. Prapatti consists in taking refuge in God with great faith and with the strong conviction that it is God and God alone who can help one to attain one's end. Like the fabled bird Chataka that would rather die of thirst than drink any water other than that falling from the clouds, the devotee looks to God for succor, and would seek no other help. Believing that God alone is the saviour, the devotee depends entirely on Him, and refuses to take any other course than that of remaining in entire dependence upon Him. God, for him, is the great master of whom he is the humble servant; God is the controller alike of his mind and his body.

This is only a detailed method of the self-surrender already referred to in the Gita. Naturally the latter also is based on a belief in the great mercy of God, who is sure to free the devotee who with complete reliance has taken refuge in Him as his master and Lord. But in this case the prapatti or taking refuge in God is always with a purpose. It is for the realization of an end that the devotee relies on the mercy, goodness or grace of God. He believes that he can by this means alone attain what he wants. But the bhakti praised in the Bhagavata is of a sort superior to this. It is a devotion without motive of any kind. It is the love of God proceeding directly from the heart and not prompted by any reason. The true bhakta does not love God because he seeks something from Him, but he loves Him freely and spontaneously. He sacrifices everything for this love. It is his only passion in life and he is filled with God. God is attracted by such love and always abides with such a bhakta and encourages his great love for him. All distinctions of caste, creed or social status vanish for those who are filled with this true and sincere devotion to God. It is a great leveller. To the eye of a true bhakta all beings are but manifestations of God's power, and they are all equal. Impelled by this idea of universal equality and by the idea of God being in all things and all things in God, he is filled with such a sweetness of temper that howsoever he may be tyrannized over by any one he cannot think of inflicting any injury in return. Nor can he remain unaffected when he sees the sufferings of his fellow-beings, however lowly or depraved they may be.

The question is sometimes asked whether such devotional systems of mysticism are pantheistic. To this no satisfactory reply can be given without a proper definition of pantheism. Without entering into any discussion regarding the meaning of this term or the distinctive metaphysical features of the different systems of Vaishnavism, I can here say only that all these systems in a manner agree as to the duality of God and man. They consider man as a manifestation of the power of God. Though ultimately sustained and always controlled by God, man is for all empirical purposes different from Him. This psychological, logical and ontological difference between God and man is the basis of devotion and worship. In the development of devotion there may, however, come a stage in the mind of the devotee when he becomes one with the Lord in the exuberance of his feelings. But at the next instant the experience may again be differentiated into a feeling of duality and of distinction between him and God. The devotee may then come to regard himself as a servant of God or His son, or friend, or spouse. It cannot be said, in this inner dialectic of feeling, which of the phases is the truer and has a greater claim to our acceptance. For we have here an alternation of feeling which sometimes expresses itself as an experience of communion or contemplative unity with God and then by its own inner movement passes for its own realization into the various other modes of relationships through which ordinary human love expresses itself. It is a circular movement. At one stage within it, man becomes God, but, at the other, God slowly becomes man and participates with him in diverse human relationships of love and its joys.

Love of God is not a thing which we produce in ourselves by excessive brooding or by self-hypnotism or by any other method. It is a permanent flame, slowly burning in the caverns of all our hearts. Only, however, when it gains strength through study, and through association with other devotees at an opportune moment, do we come to know of it. The basis of all religions is this love of God. For if this love of God were not vital to us, all that the great prophets have been trying to preach would have been unreal and futile. If it were not a real experience which in some sense is shared by us all, an experience which ennobles us and raises us far above the selfish pettinesses of life, no prophet and no religious deed would be able to appeal to our higher natures and establish the claims of religion. Religion is by nature an other-worldly attitude of life—one which we have along with our worldly attitude. "Man does not live by bread alone," is a very elastic proposition. If we by nature wanted only that which satisfies our appetites, there would have been no art, no philosophy, and no religion. Our being is such that side by side with the tendencies that take us to the satisfaction of our appetites or to sense-gratifications, there are others which in an unaccountable manner lift us higher. The senses when properly exercised give us sense pleasures; the mind,through its activities of logical thinking, affords the corresponding joys and the satisfaction of truth-seeking; and the spirit longs to associate itself with some higher ideal, with a greater and superior being, or with a transcendent unspeakable something of which it has at first only an indistinct vision.

Reason moves within a circle and cannot get beyond it. When the ultimate reason of reasoning is to be sought, we have to rest in a tendency, temperament or feeling. Ask a philosopher why he engages in philosophical speculation. He may say that he seeks to know the truth of some particular or some universal problem. But ask him again why he so seeks and he will probably say that he does it because he finds therein a special satisfaction. The satisfaction, though not measureable in physical terms, is yet enough for him. He possesses intellectual curiosity and it must be gratified. Ask a scientist and you will probably receive the same answer. One can never explain our endeavors in any of the higher planes of life, philosophy, art or religion, by reference to any of the ordinary needs and objects of life. These higher activities are apparently without any reason, but still they justify themselves and they are our very existence. That bread alone should not satisfy man is part of his very nature and there is no getting away therefrom. It is an absolute fact with man. The case of religion is very similar. There is a spiritual longing in the heart of man, indistinct and undefined, but steady like a flame tapering upwards to some divine goal. The mystics of the Bhagavata Purana of whom I am now speaking called it the love of God. They felt that there is nothing higher than the culture of this love. The seed of it they regarded as latent within the individual. Hearing and singing the praises of God stimulates its growth—sprinkles it with water, as it were—until it ascends higher and higher and eventually reaches God. Like an expert gardener the individual has always to see that no beast of a sin, tramples this tender creeper, and that no offshoots, no branches of worldly desires, obstruct its upward growth. Whenever he is tempted by worldly desires or to pray to God for worldly good, he is allowing offshoots to grow on the body of the tender creeper of God's love and to interfere with its upward growth. He must cut them off and make the creeper of love grow freely in one direction, until it connects him with God and he thus comes to enjoy its sweet fruits.

The type of bhakti which is preached in the Bhagavata Purana is well illustrated in the life of Chaitanya, who was born in Navadvip, in Bengal, in 1486 and died in 1534. In his life we find an exemplification of how love of God may be cultivated for its own sake, without any kind of ulterior motive whether of liberation or of happiness. In the accounts which his biographers have given of his mysticism, a distinction is drawn between the experience of God's love as self-surrender to Him, or taking refuge in Him through attachment to Him, and a driving passion of love for God, i.e., between what they call rati and preman. A distinction is also drawn between a course of attachment and love of God adopted out of a sense of duty or of reverence for the scriptures and a passion of love which springs spontaneously and overflows unrestrainedly. A distinction is further made between love of God with an overwhelming sense of His greatness and superiority, awe and reverence, and love of God as an easy flow of affection to one who is nearest and dearest to us. Real intimacy with God is only possible in the case of the latter alternative, when a free flow of passionate love springing spontaneously from within associates us with God as the most intimate friend and beloved without whom we cannot live. Chaitanya acknowledges, of course, the peaceful calm and tender love for God called shanta, and the submission of the heart to God in obligation and service to Him, called the service attitude, dasya; but to look upon God as one's own most intimate friend, sakhya, is regarded by him as higher than either of the first two attitudes. To look upon God as one's dearest beloved or lover, or to love Him with a feminine love as that with which a woman loves her beloved, he considers the deepest, sweetest and most perfect love, madhura.

According to the legend, Lord Krishna was born of Devaki and Vasudeva in a prison-house where the King Kansa, who was afraid of the birth of the infant who was foretold to be his future destroyer, had confined his mother Devaki. Later Krishna was carried to the house of a cowherd chief, Nanda. There he grew up, having as his associates cowherd boys with whom he was very friendly. He came to be regarded as God incarnate, as the result of a number of miracles which he performed. The wives of most of the cowherd people, who were, in reality but the female incarnations of God's energy, became attached to him and loved him dearly. They were sorely pained over the separation when he later on left for Mathura, a city at some distance from Brindaban, the scene of his early activities. Krishna's early life illustrates the love for him of his fostermother Yashoda, wife of the cowherd chief Nanda, the love for him of his cowherd friends, and the love of the cowherd girls for him as their lover. Inasmuch as Krishna was considered to be God, these three kinds of love for Krishna as described in the tenth chapter of the Bhagavata Purana, together with the other two time-honored modes of loving God, viz., the peaceful quiet love of God and the love of God as God's servant, came to be considered as the five fundamental modes of loving God. The attention of the later Vaishnavas was so much drawn to the excellence of the three kinds of love described in the Bhagavata, and particularly of the love of God as one's lover, that no less than four-teen commentaries have been published dealing with this portion of the Bhagavata Purana. Love of Krishna was the most absorbing passion of Chaitanya's life and, though he came to taste all the different ways of loving God, it was the sweet love of Krishna as the lover, husband and Lord that was the most important feature of his life.

Chaitanya's elder brother had turned a recluse. So his mother Sachi Devi would not at first send Chaitanya to school, since she believed that it is through knowledge that one learns the transitoriness of all things, and she thought it better that her son should grow untutored than that he become learned and renounce the world. So Chaitanya, or Nimai as he was called in his early life, grew wild. But he gradually grew so wild that he could no longer be tolerated, and so he was sent to school. He mastered Sanskrit grammar and logic very

thoroughly and at twenty started a school himself. Numerous anecdotes are told
by his biographers of his great scholarship and of occasions when he defeated
reputed scholars in open debates. At this period he scoffed at all religions and
was considered by many to be absolutely godless. In the meanwhile he had
settled down in life. His first wife having died, he married again. But at this
time Chaitanya's deeper nature began to reveal itself and he wanted to visit the
temple of the God Krishna at Gaya, several hundred miles distant from his
village. On his way thither he met a great Vaishnava saint and at his sight his
higher spiritual life was stirred into life. When he reached the temple of Gaya
he experienced a rapturous fervor of love for Krishna, and he became an
entirely different man. "Where is my God Krishna," became his chief cry. In
thinking of Krishna, in seeking Him, in relating his vision of Him, he would be
so overpowered as often to become unconscious. It was in this condition that he
was brought home from Gaya by his friends. He spent his days and nights in
reciting and singing the name of God. He, his intimate friend Nityananda, and
his other friends used thus to sing the name of God and to dance about with a
particular type of music produced by special musical instruments. This music
touched the inner, spiritual chords of life and brought on a great religious
intoxication in all the hearers, and particularly in Chaitanya and his followers.
Chaitanya lived continually in this state of religious intoxication. He had no
respect for caste or creeds but was a friend of all. He could not continue this sort
of life midst the worldly conditions of his native village. Hence he renounced the
world to preach the love of God all over India. In this work he spent the rest of
his years, going about from place to place, thousands of miles, on foot. The
vision of God was always before him in the form of Lord Krishna. His whole life
was a passionate flow of love for this deity, and this emotion was generally so
intense that as he sang and danced like a mad man he often became
unconscious. He had so thoroughly identified himself as a partner in the
episodes of the life of Krishna as described in the Bhagavata that the slightest
incidents deriving either from personal conversations and relations or from the
scenes of nature sufficed to suggest to him similar adventures or events in the
life of Krishna.

Chaitanya described God's love in its most exalted form as being like the
love of a woman in deep attachment to a man, where the attachment is so deep
that all sex considerations have ceased a love so intense that only an insatiable
desire of union in love remains and all the earthly relations of man and woman
have ceased. God, he taught, is himself a great controller of us all, and in His
eternal love is always attracting us, drawing us up toward greater and greater
perfection. Love is His very nature. So it is only through a passionate love of
Him that we can enjoy His deep love for us. The older ideals of liberation, of
heavenly happiness, of the destruction of the mind and the like were
considered by Chaitanya to be absolutely insignificant for a person whose mind
has been fired by a great passion that flows in torrents to God, the great ocean

of love, who washes away all his sins and defects. In the end, Chaitanya, in an outbreak of divine passion which he was unable to restrain, jumped into the deep blue ocean on the South and was lost forever to human eyes. So passed away one drop of God's love in human shape into that eternal and limitless Ocean of divine love from which it had descended upon the earth.

LECTURE VI: POPULAR DEVOTIONAL MYSTICISM

THE chief features of the passionate devotion for God described in the last lecture are its spontaneity and its transference of human relations and emotions to God through the medium of the Krishna legend described in the Bhagavata Purana. It presupposes the theory of the incarnation of God as man, which makes it possible to think of God in human relations and in human ways. The idea of God as father is indeed as old as the Vedas. It is expressed also in several passages of the Gita (9.17, 11.43, 11.44, 14.4) and in the Puranas, in the Nyaya-bhashya of Vatsyayana, as well as elsewhere. Nevertheless it did not, during this period, seem to gain much strength in the way of fostering an intimate relation with God or of affecting worship. Wherever it appears it seems to be but one of the many passing phases in which God's relation to man is viewed when God is praised and extolled in His greatness as Lord and Master. But in the new school of bhakti the conception of God as creator, supporter, father, lord and master, or as the ultimate philosophical principle, is subordinated to the conception of god as the nearest and dearest. The most important feature is His nearness to and His intimacy with us—not His great powers, which create a distance between Him and us. That He is the greatest of the great and the Highest of the high, that there is nothing greater and higher than Him is admitted by all. His greatness, however, does not reveal the secret of why He should be so dear to us. He may be the greatest, highest, loftiest and the most transcendent, but yet He has made His home in our hearts and has come down to our level to give us His affection and love. Indeed He is conceived as so near to us that we can look upon Him and love Him with the love of a very dear friend, or with the devotion and the intensity of love of a spouse. Love is a great leveller; the best way of realizing God is by making Him an equal partner in life by the force of intense love.

The legend of Krishna supplies a human touch to God's dealings with men. With the help of this legend the bhaktas of the new school, by a peculiar mystical turn of mind, could conceive of God as at once a great being with transcendent powers and also as an intimate friend or a dear lover maintaining human relations with his bhaktas. The episodes of Krishna's life in Brindaban are spiritualized. They are often conceived to happen on a non-physical plane where both Krishna and his partners are thought to play their parts of love and friendship in non-physical bodies. Thus they are not regarded as particular events that took place at specific points of time in the life of a particular man, Krishna. They are interpreted as the eternal, timeless and spaceless play of God with His own associates and His energies, with whom He eternally realizes Himself in love and friendship. The part that his bhaktas had to play was to identify themselves, by a great stretch of sympathy, as partners in or spectators of God's love-play, and find their fullest satisfaction in the satisfaction of God. For a true bhakta, it is not necessary, therefore, that his sense-inclinations should be destroyed. What is necessary is merely that these should be turned towards God and not towards himself, i.e., that he use his senses not for his own worldly satisfaction but to find enjoyment and satisfaction in the great love-drama of God by identifying himself with one of the spiritual partners of God in his love-play. Hence it is not essential that all desires and sense-functions, as the Gita says, be destroyed, or that the individual behave as if he had desires while yet being absolutely desireless. It was required that the bhakta have the fullest satisfaction of his sense and inclinations by participating in the joys of Krishna in his divine love-play. For such participation and vicarious enjoyment was regarded as true love (preman), while the satisfaction of one's own senses or of one's own worldly purposes was viewed as a vicious passion. Thus here we have a new scheme of life. The ideal of desirelessness and absolute self-control is replaced by that of participation in a drama of divine joy, and the desires are given full play in the direction of God. Desires are not to be distinguished; only their directions are to be changed.

Though this form of bhakti has in various circles at times been debased and encroached upon by diverse kinds of eroticism or erotic mysticism, it cannot be denied that many of the immediate and later followers of Chaitanya achieved great spiritual success in this form of bhakti-worship. In the Narayaniya chapter of the fifth canto of the Mahabharata God is spoken of as a father, mother and teacher; and in the Yoga Sutra of Patanjali and elsewhere the idea is often expressed that God originally taught the Vedas to the sages and that He is therefore the original teacher. In all these writings, however, the love of God supercedes deep reverence. The true bhakta looked upon God as the divine dispenser; he considered all that he had—kingdoms, riches, wife and all that he could call his own—to be God's. Love of God as the mother of the world plays an important part in the religious attitude of many bhakti worshippers. This is particularly true in the case of Ramprasad and others, notably the sage Ramakrishna of recent times. And in this attribution of motherliness to God both Ramprasad and Ramakrishna view Him as a tender mother who is always helping her child, condoning his sins and transgressions, partial to his weaknesses and concerned to better him. Nevertheless He cannot be attained by mere formal worship but only through a whole-hearted worship, with a proper control of the sense-inclinations.

The theory of bhakti seems to have its original source in the Pancaratra school of Vaishnavism. However, the doctrine of supreme self-surrender to Narayana, Hari or Krishna as the one and only God in disregard of all other mythical gods, represents a teaching of the Gita, the chief work of the Ekanti school of Vaishnavas; and this doctrine forms the universal basis of all kinds of bhakti worship, though among the Shaktas or Shaivas the supreme deity went by the name of Shakti or Shiva. The Gita plainly teaches, as we have already pointed out in our previous lecture, that there is no other God but Narayana or Krishna, that He alone is great and that we should lay aside all other modes of religious worship and take refuge in Him. In Chaitanya this devotion to God developed into a life-absorbing passion; yet in all advanced forms of bhakti the chief emphasis is on supreme attachment to God. The sort of bhakti which Prahlada asked as a boon from Hari was such an attachment for Him as worldly persons have for the objects of their senses. Such a bhakti, as described in the Bhagavata or the Shandilya sutra, is not worship out of a sense of duty or mere meditation on God or mere singing of His name, but it is deep affection (anurakti). It is therefore neither knowledge nor any kind of activity, but is a feeling. And the taking of refuge (prapatti) in God is also not motivated by knowledge but by a deep affection which impels the individual to take his first and last stay in Him. But though a feeling, this bhakti does not bind anyone to the world. For the world is but a manifestation of God's maya, and God so arranges for those who love Him that His maya cannot bind His bhakta to the world.

But how is such a bhakti possible? For this also we have ultimately to depend on God. There is a passage in the Upanishads (Katha II. 23) which states that He can be attained by him whom He (God) chooses. This text has often been cited to indicate that it is only the chosen man of God who has the privilege of possessing a special affection for God. Vallabha declares this special favor (pushti) of God indispensable for the rise of such an affection for God. He further holds that according to the different degrees of the favor of God one may have different degrees of affection for Him, though by avoiding the commission of sinful actions, by cleansing the mind of the impurities of worldly passions, and by inclining the mind towards God, one may go a great way in deserving His special favor. It is only by the highest special favor of God that one's affection or attachment for Him can become an all-consuming and all-engulfing passion (vyasana—see the Prameyaratnarnava). True devotion to God, affection or love for Him, must always be an end in itself and never a means to any other end, not even salvation or liberation, so much praised in the classical systems of philosophy. This all-absorbing passion for God is the bhakta's eternal stay in God, and dearer to him than liberation or any other goal of religious realization.

It is not out of place here to mention that among various Hindu sects it was held that an engrossing passion of any kind may so possess the whole mind that all other mental functions may temporarily be suspended, and that gradually, through the repeated occurrence of such a passion, the other mental functions may be altogether annihilated. Thus, absorption in a single supreme passion may make the mind so one-pointed that all other attachments are transcended and the individual attains Brahmahood (see the Spandapradipika). In the Upanishads (Brihadaranyaka IV. 3.21) we find that the bliss of Brahman is compared with the loving embrace of a beloved woman. To love one's husband and to serve him as a god was regarded from very early times as the only spiritualizing duty for a woman. Hence the idea that ordinary man-and-woman love may be so perfected as to become a spiritual force easily won acceptance in certain circles. This man-and-woman love developed an absorbing and dominant passion, completely independent and unaided by other considerations of marital and parental duties. In its non-marital forms, it was considered to be capable of becoming so deep as to become by itself a spiritualizing force. Moreover, it was thought that the transition from human love to divine love was so easy that a man who had specialized in the experience of deep man-and-woman love of a non-marital type could easily change the direction of his love from woman to God, and thus indulge in a passionate love for God. The story is told that in his early career the saint Bilvamangala became so deeply attached to a courtesan named Cintamani that one night he swam across a river supported by a floating corpse, then scaled a high wall by holding on to the tail of a serpent, and finally well-nigh broke his limbs in jumping down from the wall into the yard of Cintamani. The woman, however, rebuked him, saying that if he entertained toward God a little of the love that he had for her he would be a saint. This produced such a wonderful change in Bilvamangala that he forthwith became a God-intoxicated man. Later, in his saintly life, when he once again felt attracted by a woman, he plucked out his eyes so that external forms and colors might not further tempt him. This blind saint became one of the best-reputed among all the saints, devoting his life to the love of God.

Thus there grew up a school of mystics, including the great poet Candidas and others, who devoted themselves to the cultivation of the spirituality of love and the deification of human love, and who thought that more could be learned through such efforts than through any other mode of worship. "There is no god or goddess in Heaven who can teach spiritual truths more than the person whom one loves with the whole heart." The goddess Basuli whom Candidas worshipped is said to have admonished him to adhere to his love for the washerwoman Rami, saying that Rami would be able to teach him truths that no one else could, and to lead him to such bliss as not even the creator himself might do. A somewhat similar idea of the purificatory power of intense human love is found in the Vishnupurana. In describing the illicit love of a cowherd-girl for Krishna, the Vishnupurana says that at her separation from him she underwent so much suffering that all her sins were expiated, and that in thinking of him in her separation from him she had so much delight as would be equal to the collective culmination of all the happiness that she could enjoy as a reward of her virtuous actions. By the combination of the suffering and the bliss, she exhausted all the fruits of her bad and good deeds, and thus by her thoughts of Krishna she attained her liberation. Somewhat allied with the idea of human worship, though not of the man-and-women type just mentioned, is a certain attitude sometimes adopted toward man as a religious teacher. The latter was considered in many circles as the representative of God on earth, and self-surrender, love and devotion to him was considered to lead one to God. This sort of worship was prevalent among the Hindus and the Buddhists from pretty early times. One fact should be noted. It was associated with reverence and a sense of the religious teacher's superiority, whereas the other type of worship (through romantic love) raised the man and woman by their constancy and sufferings for each other and the happiness that each enjoys in the company and thought of the other. In this latter case, love is religion, and all pain endured for the beloved, joy. With the exception of the phase of love-mysticism just mentioned, I have thus far confined myself to a description of different forms of mysticism as portrayed in Sanskrit writings. I shall now turn to the mysticism of divine love that found expression in the vernaculars of North India and of the South. But this is a vast subject and I can say only a few words.

Let me advert first to the Alvar saints of the South, the earliest of whom belonged to the second and the latest to the tenth century, A. D. They all wrote psalms or songs in Tamil, a Dravidian tongue of South India. They were inspired by the teachings of Vaishnavism when it travelled from the North to the South. Their doctrines were more or less similar to those touched upon in the preceding lecture in connection with the bhakti mysticism of the Bhagavata Purana and the Gita. They are embodied in psalms and not in any connected philosophical treatise. Describing his insatiable love of God, Nam Alvar says:

"As I dote on the Lord of Katkarai (God)
Whose streets with scarlet lily are perfumed
My heart for his wonderful graces melts
How then can I, my restless love suppress?"

With reference to Nam Alvar, Govindacarya has said: "Briefly, Saint Nam Alvar declares that when one is overcome by bhakti exaltation, trembling in every cell of his being, he must freely and passively allow this influence to penetrate his being, and carry him beyond all known states of consciousness; never from fear or shame that bystanders may take him for a madman, ought the exhibition of this bhakti-rapture that deluges his being, to be suppressed. The very madness is the means of distinguishing him from the ordinary mortals to whom such beatific vision is necessarily denied. The very madness is the bhakta's pride. In that very madness, the saint exhorts, "run, jump, cry, laugh and sing, and let every man witness it."

Let us now pass on to other saints of the South, Namdev and Tukaram. The bhakti school referred to in the last lecture, and most of the other branches of this school, developed under purely Brahminic traditions and in the shadow of Brahminic scriptures,the Puranas and the like. And though in the Bhagavata we find that even the foreign and aboriginal races of the Kiratas, Hunas, Andhras, Pulindas, Pukkasas, Abhiras, Suhmas, Yavanas, Khasas, etc., become pure if they are attached to God, yet the Brahminic civilization had such a hold over the country that the cult of bhakti grew up around the traditional cult of Rama, or Krishna, Shiva or Shakti. Representation of God in images and their worship by the bhaktas, faith in the legends of Krishna and other inferior deities as told in the Puranas, preferential treatment of the Brahmin caste, respect to the Vedas, etc., became very intimately associated with the doctrine of bhakti preached in the Puranas and other Sanskrit scriptures. We know, of course, that the bhakti cult spread also among foreigners. Thus, in the second century B. C., the Greek king Heliodorus, son of Dios, dedicated to Vasudeva a flagstaff bearing an image of the bird Garuda, on which the God Vasudeva or Krishna was said to ride. Now, though the sons of some demons are also known to have been great bhaktas, as described in the Puranas, yet the latter all accepted the traditional God Vasudeva and they regarded the legends associated with Krishna or Vasudeva as real episodes of his life. In the thirteenth century A. D., we find that Visoba Khecar, the teacher of the bhakta Namdev, denounced the worship of images as a substitute for the God Krishna or for any other god. He is said to have instructed Namdev to abandon image-worship, saying: "A stone god never speaks. What possibility then of his removing the disease of mundane existence? A stone image is regarded as God, but the true God is wholly different. If a stone god fulfills desires, how is it he breaks when struck? Those who adore a god made of stone, lose everything through their folly. Those who say and hear that a god of stone speaks to his devotees are both of them fools. Whether a holy place is small or large there is no god but stone or water. There is no place which is devoid of God. That God has shown Nama in his heart and thus Khecar conferred a blessing on him." Namdev was a tailor by caste and he worshipped the idol at Pandharpur in the Maratha country in South India. However, he had a full knowledge of the true nature of God, as had other bhaktas of Sanskritic traditions. Thus he says: "The Veda has to speak by Thy might and the Sun has to move round; such is the might of Thee, the Lord of the Universe. Knowing this essential truth I have surrendered myself to Thee. By Thy might it is that the clouds have to pour down rain, mountains to rest firm and the wind to blow." Again: "Vows, fasts and austerities are not at all necessary; nor is it necessary for you to go on a pilgrimage. Be you watchful in your hearts and always sing the name of Hari. It is not necessary to give up eating food or drinking water; fix your mind on the foot of Hari. Neither is it necessary for you to contemplate the one without attributes. Hold fast to the love of the name of Hari." "Recognize him alone to be a righteous man, who sees Vasudeva in all objects,eradicating all pride or egoism. The rest are entangled in the shackles of delusion. To him all wealth is like earth, and the nine gems are mere stones. The two, desire and anger, he has thrown out, and he cherishes in his heart quietude and forgiveness." Again he says: "Firmly grasp the truth which is Narayana. Purity of conduct should not be abandoned; one should not be afraid of the censure of people and thus accomplish one's own purpose. Surrender yourself to your loving friend (God) giving up all ostentation and pride. The censure of people should be regarded as praise and their praise not heeded. One should entertain no longing for being respected and honored, but should nourish in oneself a liking for devotion. This should be rendered firm in the mind and the name of God should not be neglected even for a moment."

The essence of the teachings of Namdev, as of almost all the other bhaktas of whom I shall now be speaking, is purity of mind, speech, and deed, utter disregard of castes, creeds and other social distinctions, a tendency to leave all for God, and in love and joy to live in God always, utterly ignoring all social, communal and religious prejudices, narrowness, dogmas and bigotry. It is held that God is omnipotent and omnipresent and that He cannot be identified with any particular deity or his character properly narrated by any particular legendary or mythical ways of thinking. At the same time it is contended that we may call him by any name we like, for He is always the same in all.

Another great Maratha saint was Tukaram of the seventeenth century. Tukaram was a low class Hindu. His father was a petty trader. When his father, in his old age, wanted to give over his business to his eldest son Savji, the latter refused the task since he did not wish a worldly life. So the business was entrusted to Tukaram when he was at the age of thirteen. Four years later his father died. Then Tukaram was imposed upon by crafty persons and his business was wrecked. His wife, however, procured a loan; the business was restored and then he began to prosper. Once, however, while he was returning home, Tukaram met a man who was on the point of being dragged to prison for his debts. Tukaram at once gave all that he had to this debtor in order to achieve his release. From that time on Tukaram renounced all worldly vocations and devoted his life to singing the glories of God and the dearness of our relations to Him. He employed a particular kind of verse which he often composed extempore and in which he frequently spoke. Thus Tukaram says: "God is ours, certainly ours, and is the soul of all souls. God is near to us, certainly near, outside and inside. God is benignant, certainly benignant, and fulfills every longing even of a longing nature." Again he says: "This thy nature is beyond the grasp of the mind or of words, and therefore I have made devoted love a measure. I measure the endless by the measure of love. He is not to be truly measured by any other means. Thou art not to be found by processes of concentration, sacrificial rites, practice of austerities, or any bodily exertions, or by knowledge. Oh Kesava, accept the service which we render to thee in the simplicity of our hearts." Still again: "The Endless is beyond, and between him and me there are lofty mountains of desire and anger. I am not able to ascend them, nor do I find any pass. Insurmountable is the ascent of my enemies. What possibility is there of my attaining my friend Narayana (God)?" He expresses his heart full of longing for God in the following words:

"As on the bank the poor fish lies
And gasps and writhes in pain,
Or, as a man with anxious eyes
Seeks hidden gold in vain,—
So is my heart distressed and cries
To come to thee again.
Thou knowest, Lord, the agony
Of the lost infant's wail
Yearning his mother's face to see.
(How oft I tell this tale.)
O, at thy feet the mystery
Of the dark world unveil.
The fire of this harassing thought
Upon my bosom prays.
Why is it I am thus forgot?
(O, who can know thy ways?)
Nay, Lord, thou seest my hapless lot;
Have mercy, Tuka says."

Desolate and disconsolate for the love of God he prays at His door:

"A beggar at thy door,
Pleading I stand;
Give me an alms, O God,
Love from thy loving hand.
Spare me the barren task,
To come, and to come for nought.
A gift poor Tuka craves,
Unmerited, unbought."

Again:

"O save me, save me, Mightiest,
Save me and set me free.
O let the love that fills my breast
Cling to thee lovingly.
Grant me to taste how sweet thou art;

Grant me but this, I pray,
And never shall my love depart
Or turn from thee away.
Then I thy name shall magnify
And tell thy praise abroad,
For very love and gladness I
Shall dance before my God.
Grant to me, Vitthal, that I rest
Thy blessed feet beside;
Ah, give me this, the dearest, best,
And I am satisfied."

Leaving this bhakti movement of the South, which dates from the thirteenth to the seventeenth century, from Jnanesvar and Namdev to Tukaram, we pass to the bhakti movement of North India, represented by Kabir, Nanak and others. It followed the line traced by the Gita and the Bhagavata. Having been developed in the vernacular, however, it appealed directly to the masses. It largely dissociated itself from the complex entanglements of Hindu mythology which had enmeshed the devotional creed of spiritual loyalty to God in the legend of Krishna and his associates.

Kabir (1440-1518) was an abandoned child, probably because of the illegitimacy of his birth. He was brought up by a weaver, Niru, and his wife, Nina. Throughout his life he lived in Benares, probably himself following the profession of a weaver. He is said to have been a disciple of Ramananda, a disciple of Ramanuja, the great Vaishnava teacher of the South. But he likewise came into touch with some Mohammedan Pirs and was also probably acquainted with certain forms of Sufism. His was a religion which derived its life from what was best among both the Hindus and the Mohammedans. However, he disliked the bigotry and superstitions of all formal religions and was consequently persecuted by both the Hindus and the Mohammedans. With him and his followers, such as Ruidas and Dadu, we find a religion which shook off all the traditional limitations of formal religions, with their belief in revealed books and their acceptance of mythological stories, and of dogmas and creeds that often obscure the purity of the religious light and contact with God. Kabir considered the practice of yoga, alms, and fasting, and the feeding of Brahmins, not only useless but improper without the repetition of God's name and love for Him. He discarded the Hindu ideas regarding purity, external ablutions and contact with so-called impure things with as much force as he rejected the Mohammedan belief in circumcision or the requirement that a Brahmin should wear a holy thread, or any other marks of caste. When Kabir's parents found that they could not subdue his Hindu tendencies they wanted to circumcise him, and at this he said:

"Whence have come the Hindus and Mussulmans? Who hath put them in

their different ways,
Having thought and reflected in thy heart, answer this—who shall obtain
Heaven and who Hell."

Now we know that the doctrine of bhakti had a great levelling influence.
Even according to the Gita and the Bhagavata Purana, bhakti removed all
inequalities of caste and social status. We know that Haridas (his
Mohammedan name is not known) was converted from Mohammedanism to
Vaishnavism by Chaitanya and Nityananda. In lauding him Chaitanya once
said: "Your holy thoughts are as the streams of the Ganges in which your soul
bathes every hour. Your pious acts earn for you that virtue which the people
seek in sacrificial rites prescribed in the scriptures. You are constantly in touch
with the loftiest of ideals which give you the same merit as the study of the
Vedas. What sadhu or Brahmin is there who is good and great as you are?" In
the Brihat Naradiya Purana we find that even a candala (the lowest caste
among the Hindus) becomes the greatest of all Brahmins if he loves God. So the
new religious ideal of bhakti, in all its enthusiastic circles, dispensed with the
considerations of caste, creed, and social status.

There was, therefore, nothing particularly novel in Kabir's insistence that
the time-honored distinctions of caste, creed and social status are absolutely
valueless or in his emphasis upon the need of bhakti for all, as that which alone
exalts a man. But in Kabir we find a reformatory zeal. He never tires of
reiterating the worthlessness of all these superstitions of caste, creed, social
status, external purity and impurity, penances, asceticism, and all sorts of
formalities which passed by the name of religion though in fact having nothing
to do with it. Thus Kabir says:

"If union with God be obtained by going about naked,
All the deer of the forest shall be saved.
What mattereth it whether man goeth naked or weareth a deerskin,
If he recognize not God in his heart?
If perfection be obtained by shaving the head,
Why should not sheep obtain salvation?
If, O brethren, the continent man is saved,
Why should not a eunuch obtain the supreme reward?
Saith Kabir, hear, O my brethren,
Who hath obtained salvation without God's name?"

Again he says:

"They who battle in the evening and the morning
Are like frogs in the water.
When men have no love for God's name,
They shall all go to the god of death.

They who love their persons and deck themselves out in various guises,
Feel not mercy even in their dreams.
Many leading religious men call them quadrupeds,
And say that only holy men shall obtain happiness in this ocean of trouble.
Saith Kabir, why perform so many ceremonies?
Forsaking all other essences quaff the great essence of God's name."

These allusions to bathing and other activities refer to religious practices followed by many Hindus but vigorously denounced by Kabir.

To a Yogin who said to Kabir that one could not attain deliverance without chastening his heart by the performance of yoga Kabir said:

"Without devotion the qualities of the heart cling to the heart,
Who secured perfection by merely chastening his heart?
What holy man has succeeded in chastening his heart?
Say who bath saved any one by merely chastening his heart.
Every one thinketh in his heart that he is going to chasten it,
But the heart is not chastened without devotion.
Saith Kabir, let him who knoweth this secret
Worship in his heart God, the lord of the three worlds."

Kabir in speaking of the search after God says:

"When I turned my thoughts toward God, I restrained my mind
and my senses, and my attention became lovingly fixed on Him.
O Bairagi, search for Him who neither cometh nor goeth, who neither dieth nor is.
My soul turning away from sin, is absorbed in the universal soul."

Describing the view that God is not confined to any mosque, church or temple, Kabir says:

"If God dwell only in the mosque, to whom belongeth the rest of the country?
They who are called Hindus say that God dwelleth in an idol:
I see not the truth in either sect.
O God, whether Allah or Ram, I live by Thy name,
O Lord, show kindness unto me.
Hari dwelleth in the south, Allah hath his place in the west.
Search in thy heart, search in thy heart of hearts; there is his place and abode.
The Brahmins yearly perform twenty-four fastings . . . the Mussulmans fast in the month of Ramzan.
. . . Kabir is a child of Ram and Allah and accepteth all gurus and Pirs."

Describing his great love and intoxication for God, Kabir says:

"I am not skilled in book knowledge, nor do I understand controversy:

I have grown mad reciting and hearing God's praises.
O father, I am mad; the whole world is sane; I am mad;
I am ruined; let not others be ruined likewise;
I have not grown mad out of my own will; God hath made me mad—
The true guru hath dispelled my doubts—
I am ruined, and have lost my intellect;
Let nobody be led astray in doubts like mine.
He who knoweth not himself is mad;
When one knoweth himself he knoweth the one God.
He who is not intoxicated with divine love in this human birth shall never be
so.
Saith Kabir, I am dyed with the dye of God."

Thus, on the one hand, Kabir waged war against the prevailing superstitions, rituals and litanies of all religions and religious sects; and, on the other hand, he dived deep in the depth of God's love and he beheld nothing but God on all sides, becoming as it were one with Him in spiritual union. Thus, he says:

"With both mine eyes I look,
But I behold nothing save God;
Mine eyes gaze affectionately on Him."

The motto of his life was, as he often said, "Remember God, Remember God, Remember God, my brethren;" and in his own life he felt that he was absorbed in the Infinite.

Rui Das (also called Ravi Das), a shoe-maker by caste, was another great disciple of Ramananda. His songs and hymns are full of humility and devotion. However, he evidences none of the reformatory zeal that animated Kabir. I shall quote the translation of only one hymn which seems to me typical of Rui Das's attitude of love towards God. He says:

"There is none so poor as I, none so compassionate as Thou;
For this what further test is now necessary?
May my heart obey thy words, fill thy servant therewith.
I am a sacrifice to thee, O God;
Why art thou silent?
For many births have I been separated from Thee, O God;
This birth is on thine own account.
Saith Rui Das, putting my hopes in Thee, I live; it is long since I have seen thee."

Still another great saint of love was Mira Bai, a princess of Rajputana, who from her childhood (born about 1504 A. D.) was devoted to an image of Lord Krishna called Girdharlal. Her marriage proved unhappy. At the time of going to her husband's place she became very disconsolate. She wept until she became unconscious at the idea of leaving the image of Girdharlal behind. So her parents gave her the image as a part of her marriage dowry. It proved that Mira could not get on well with the family of her father-in-law, for she was always given to the adoration and worship of her little image, representing to her Lord Krishna, and it was this image that she considered as her husband. Her father-in-law made attempts to kill her, but she was miraculously saved. Ultimately she left his abode and went to Brindaban, the place of Lord Krishna's activities, to have her passion for Krishna realized. Here again, in the case of this princess saint who left her all for Krishna, we find the potency of the Krishna legend.

I shall quote here the translation of one of Mira Bai's hymns which show her great attachment for Krishna, in an image of whom, at Dvaraka, she was, as the tradition says, ultimately lost. Her soul was so full of deep longing for Lord Krishna, or Girdhar as she called him, that she proclaims:

"I have the god Girdhar and no other;
He is my spouse on whose head is a crown of peacock feathers,
Who carrieth a shell, discus, mace and lotus, and who weareth a necklace;
I have forfeited the respect of the world by ever sitting near holy men.
The matter is now public; everybody knoweth it.
Having felt supreme devotion I die as I behold the world.
I have no father, son, or relation with me.
I laugh when I behold my beloved; people think I weep.
I have planted the vine of love and irrigated it again
and again with the water of tears,
I have cast away my fear of the world, what can anyone do to me
Mira's love for her god is fixed, come what may."

India is a land of saints. There are hundreds of them of whom one could say much. But my time is limited and I have well-nigh exhausted your patience. Yet I cannot conclude without referring briefly to Tulsidas, the greatest Hindu poet of India and a great saint.

Tulsidas lived in the seventeenth century. He did not inaugurate any new faith, but accepted the Hindu mythology and the theory of the incarnation of God, the appearance of the attributeless God as a God of infinite attributes. In his view Rama was the incarnation of God, the savior and father of mankind. An all-surrendering devotion to him, he believed, is our only duty and the sole legitimate passion of life. God is great not only in His greatness, but also in his mercy. He knows the sins and the frailties of men, and is always prepared to help them repel their temptations. To run counter to the will of God is sin, and it is only by acknowledging our sins and taking an all-surrendering refuge in Him, in love and faith, that we can be saved. Connected herewith was the doctrine of the brotherhood of man and of our duty toward our neighbors.

Tulsidas is said to have been very much attached to his wife in his early life. On one occasion he followed her to her father's place, much to her annoyance, and she said that if he had as much love for God Rama as he had for her he would be saved. This struck Tulsidas to the heart and he renounced the world. By his great strength of character, his remark-able poetic gifts which he applied to religious subjects, and by his strong faith, Tulsidas soon endeared himself to his countrymen. No one has exercised a greater influence than he over the Hindi-speaking people of North India.

I have now described, though but briefly, some of the main types of Indian mysticism in their mutual relations; others could not be so much as touched upon owing to the limitations of time. I am fully alive to the imperfections of my treatment. Great as they are, they must have appeared to you even greater on account of the difficulty that you must have experienced in placing yourselves on the mental plane of these mystics. The subtle metaphysical and philosophical background of these different types of mysticism I have here been compelled to disregard. But I have elsewhere undertaken an historical survey of all the different systems of Indian Philosophy. Through oral instruction, tradition, and the example of great men who renounced the world in pursuance of the high ideals of philosophy, the essence of these different systems, with their spiritual longings and their yearnings after salvation and the cessation of rebirth, have gradually been filtering down into the minds of the masses of the population. The tiller of the soil and the grocer in the shop may be uneducated and often wholly illiterate, but even they, while tilling the ground, driving a bullock cart or resting after the work of the day, will be singing songs full of mystical meaning, and for the moment transporting themselves to regions beyond the touch of material gains and comforts:

"The sky and the earth are born of mine own eyes.
The hardness and softness, the cold and the heat are the products of my own body;
The sweet smell and the bad are of my own nose."

Or,

"Nobody can tell whence the bird unknown
Comes into the cage and goes out.
I would feign put round its feet the fetter of my mind
Could I but capture it."

A traveller in the village of Bengal or on board the steamers plying the rivers of the interior of rural Bengal, may often hear a middle-aged or old Mohammedan or a Hindu singing mystical, philosophical or mythical songs of the love of Krishna and Radha, or of the renunciation of the world by

Chaitanya, while a large crowd of men is assembled around the singer listening to him with great reverence and feeling. The singer is probably describing the world as a mirage or a mere phantom show of maya, or is expressing the futility of his worldly life on account of his having lost his friendship with his own self.

"My hope of the world is all false,
What shall be my fate, O kind, good lord?
I am not in love with him (self) with whom
I have come to live in this house (body)
O kind, good lord."

So the sublime teachings of philosophy and the other-worldly aspirations of mysticism, with their soothing, plaintive and meditative tendencies, have watered the hearts of Bengal right into the thatched cottages of this land. Wealth and comfort they all appreciate as do people everywhere, but they all know that money is not everything, and that peace of mind and the ultimate good of man cannot be secured through it or any other worldly thing. They are immersed in the world; but still the wisdom of the ages and the teachings of the saints have not been in vain, and at times they are drawn away from the world—their souls unknowingly long for deliverance and find a mystic delight in it. It is only the educated or Anglicized Hindu who, dazzled by the gay colors of the West, sometimes turns a deaf ear to the old tune of his country—the flute of Krishna calling from afar through the rustling leaves of bamboos and the cocoanut groves of the village homes—and, in the name of patriotism and progress, installs a foreign god of money and luxury in the ancestral throne of the god of the Indian heart—the god of deliverance. The thoughts and aspirations of the ages, our myths, our religions, our philosophies, our songs and poetry, have all interpenetrated and formed a whole which cannot be expressed through a portrayal of its elements. They represent a unique experience which I feel with my countrymen, but which is incommunicable to any one who is unable imaginatively to bring himself into tune with that spirit. The British in India have understood as much of the country as is necessary for policing it, but no foreigner has ever adequately understood our land. Those of you who see India through newspapers and the strange tales and stories of tourists who "do" India in a month, can hardly hope to go right to the place where the heart of India lies.

But, you may perhaps ask, what may I gain by knowing India as it really is at its heart? Well, that is a different matter. Perhaps you may derive gain, perhaps not. You may further ask what is it that one gains through such spiritual longing, realization, or mystical rapture. And I shall frankly confess that one certainly gains nothing that will show itself in one's bank account. But with all my appreciation and admiration of the great achievements of the West in science, politics and wealth, the Upanishad spirit in me may whisper from within: What have you gained if you have not gained yourself, the immortal, the infinite? What have you gained if you have never tasted in your life the deep longing for deliverance and supreme emancipation? And the spirit of the saints of ages whispers in my ears: What have you gained if you have not tasted the joys of self-surrender, if your heart has not longed to make of you a flute in the hands of Krishna, that master musician of the universe, and if you have not been able to sweeten all your miseries with a touch of God?

The Great Learning
by Confucius
translated by James Legge

WHAT THE GREAT LEARNING teaches, is to illustrate illustrious virtue; to renovate the people; and to rest in the highest excellence.

The point where to rest being known, the object of pursuit is then determined; and, that being determined, a calm unperturbedness may be attained to. To that calmness there will succeed a tranquil repose. In that repose there may be careful deliberation, and that deliberation will be followed by the attainment of the desired end.

Things have their root and their branches. Affairs have their end and their beginning. To know what is first and what is last will lead near to what is taught in the Great Learning.

The ancients who wished to illustrate illustrious virtue throughout the kingdom, first ordered well their own states. Wishing to order well their states, they first regulated their families. Wishing to regulate their families, they first cultivated their persons. Wishing to cultivate their persons, they first rectified their hearts. Wishing to rectify their hearts, they first sought to be sincere in their thoughts. Wishing to be sincere in their thoughts, they first extended to the utmost their knowledge. Such extension of knowledge lay in the investigation of things.

Things being investigated, knowledge became complete. Their knowledge being complete, their thoughts were sincere. Their thoughts being sincere, their hearts were then rectified. Their hearts being rectified, their persons were cultivated. Their persons being cultivated, their families were regulated. Their families being regulated, their states were rightly governed. Their states being rightly governed, the whole kingdom was made tranquil and happy.

From the Son of Heaven down to the mass of the people, all must consider the cultivation of the person the root of everything besides.

It cannot be, when the root is neglected, that what should spring from it will be well ordered. It never has been the case that what was of great importance has been slightly cared for, and, at the same time, that what was of slight importance has been greatly cared for.

COMMENTARY OF THE PHILOSOPHER TSANG

In the Announcement to K'ang, it is said, "He was able to make his virtue illustrious."

In the Tai Chia, it is said, "He contemplated and studied the illustrious decrees of Heaven."

In the Canon of the emperor (Yao), it is said, "He was able to make illustrious his lofty virtue."

These passages all show how those sovereigns made themselves illustrious.

On the bathing tub of T'ang, the following words were engraved: "If you can one day renovate yourself, do so from day to day. Yea, let there be daily renovation."

In the Announcement to K'ang, it is said, "To stir up the new people."

In the Book of Poetry, it is said, "Although Chau was an ancient state the ordinance which lighted on it was new."

Therefore, the superior man in everything uses his utmost endeavors.

In the Book of Poetry, it is said, "The royal domain of a thousand li is where the people rest."

In the Book of Poetry, it is said, "The twittering yellow bird rests on a corner of the mound." The Master said, "When it rests, it knows where to rest. Is it possible that a man should not be equal to this bird?"

In the Book of Poetry, it is said, "Profound was King Wan. With how bright and unceasing a feeling of reverence did he regard his resting places!" As a sovereign, he rested in benevolence. As a minister, he rested in reverence. As a son, he rested in filial piety. As a father, he rested in kindness. In communication with his subjects, he rested in good faith.

In the Book of Poetry, it is said, "Look at that winding course of the Ch'i, with the green bamboos so luxuriant! Here is our elegant and accomplished prince! As we cut and then file; as we chisel and then grind: so has he cultivated himself. How grave is he and dignified! How majestic and distinguished! Our elegant and accomplished prince never can be forgotten." That expression-"As we cut and then file," the work of learning. "As we chisel and then grind," indicates that of self-culture. "How grave is he and dignified!" indicates the feeling of cautious reverence. "How commanding and distinguished! indicates an awe-inspiring deportment. "Our elegant and accomplished prince never can be forgotten," indicates how, when virtue is complete and excellence extreme, the people cannot forget them.

In the Book of Poetry, it is said, "Ah! the former kings are not forgotten." Future princes deem worthy what they deemed worthy, and love what they loved. The common people delight in what delighted them, and are benefited by their beneficial arrangements. It is on this account that the former kings, after they have quitted the world, are not forgotten.

The Master said, "In hearing litigations, I am like any other body. What is necessary is to cause the people to have no litigations." So, those who are devoid of principle find it impossible to carry out their speeches, and a great awe would be struck into men's minds;-this is called knowing the root.

This is called knowing the root. This is called the perfecting of knowledge.

What is meant by "making the thoughts sincere." is the allowing no self-deception, as when we hate a bad smell, and as when we love what is beautiful. This is called self-enjoyment. Therefore, the superior man must be watchful over himself when he is alone.

There is no evil to which the mean man, dwelling retired, will not proceed, but when he sees a superior man, he instantly tries to disguise himself, concealing his evil, and displaying what is good. The other beholds him, as if he saw his heart and reins;-of what use is his disguise? This is an instance of the saying -"What truly is within will be manifested without." Therefore, the superior man must be watchful over himself when he is alone.

The disciple Tsang said, "What ten eyes behold, what ten hands point to, is to be regarded with reverence!"

Riches adorn a house, and virtue adorns the person. The mind is expanded, and the body is at ease. Therefore, the superior man must make his thoughts sincere.

What is meant by, "The cultivation of the person depends on rectifying the mind may be thus illustrated:-If a man be under the influence of passion he will be incorrect in his conduct. He will be the same, if he is under the influence of terror, or under the influence of fond regard, or under that of sorrow and distress.

When the mind is not present, we look and do not see; we hear and do not understand; we eat and do not know the taste of what we eat.

This is what is meant by saying that the cultivation of the person depends on the rectifying of the mind.

What is meant by "The regulation of one's family depends on the cultivation of his person is this:-men are partial where they feel affection and love; partial where they despise and dislike; partial where they stand in awe and reverence; partial where they feel sorrow and compassion; partial where they are arrogant and rude. Thus it is that there are few men in the world who love and at the same time know the bad qualities of the object of their love, or who hate and yet know the excellences of the object of their hatred.

Hence it is said, in the common adage,"A man does not know the wickedness of his son; he does not know the richness of his growing corn."

This is what is meant by saying that if the person be not cultivated, a man cannot regulate his family.

What is meant by "In order rightly to govern the state, it is necessary first to regulate the family," is this:-It is not possible for one to teach others, while he cannot teach his own family. Therefore, the ruler, without going beyond his family, completes the lessons for the state. There is filial piety:-therewith the. sovereign should be served. There is fraternal submission:-therewith elders and superiors should be served. There is kindness:-therewith the multitude should be treated.

In the Announcement to K'ang, it is said, "Act as if you were watching over an infant." If a mother is really anxious about it, though she may not hit exactly the wants of her infant, she will not be far from doing so. There never has been a girl who learned to bring up a child, that she might afterwards marry.

From the loving example of one family a whole state becomes loving, and from its courtesies the whole state becomes courteous while, from the ambition and perverseness of the One man, the whole state may be led to rebellious disorder;-such is the nature of the influence. This verifies the saying, "Affairs may be ruined by a single sentence; a kingdom may be settled by its One man."

Yao and Shun led on the kingdom with benevolence and the people followed them. Chieh and Chau led on the kingdom with violence, and people followed them. The orders which these issued were contrary to the practices which they loved, and so the people did not follow them. On this account, the ruler must himself be possessed of the good qualities, and then he may require them in the people. He must not have the bad qualities in himself, and then he may require that they shall not be in the people. Never has there been a man, who, not having reference to his own character and wishes in dealing with others, was able effectually to instruct them.

Thus we see how the government of the state depends on the regulation of the family.

In the Book of Poetry, it is said, "That peach tree, so delicate and elegant! IIow luxuriant is its foliage! This girl is going to her husband's house. She will rightly order her household." Let the household be rightly ordered, and then the people of the state may be taught.

In the Book of Poetry, it is said, "They can discharge their duties to their elder brothers. They can discharge their duties to their younger brothers." Let the ruler discharge his duties to his elder and younger brothers, and then he may teach the people of the state.

In the Book of Poetry, it is said, "In his deportment there is nothing wrong; he rectifies all the people of the state." Yes; when the ruler, as a father, a son, and a brother, is a model, then the people imitate him.

This is what is meant by saying, "The government of his kingdom depends on his regulation of the family."

What is meant by "The making the whole kingdom peaceful and happy depends on the government of his state," this:-When the sovereign behaves to his aged, as the aged should be behaved to, the people become final; when the sovereign behaves to his elders, as the elders should be behaved to, the people learn brotherly submission; when the sovereign treats compassionately the young and helpless, the people do the same. Thus the ruler has a principle with which, as with a measuring square, he may regulate his conduct.

What a man dislikes in his superiors, let him not display in the treatment of his inferiors; what he dislikes in inferiors, let him not display in the service of his superiors; what he hates in those who are before him, let him not therewith precede those who are behind him; what he hates in those who are behind him, let him not bestow on the left; what he hates to receive on the left, let him not bestow on the right:-this is what is called "The principle with which, as with a measuring square, to regulate one's conduct."

In the Book of Poetry, it is said, "How much to be rejoiced in are these princes, the parents of the people!" When a prince loves what the people love, and hates what the people hate, then is he what is called the parent of the people.

In the Book of Poetry, it is said, "Lofty is that southern hill, with its rugged masses of rocks! Greatly distinguished are you, O grand-teacher Yin, the people all look up to you. "Rulers of states may not neglect to be careful. If they deviate to a mean selfishness, they will be a disgrace in the kingdom.

In the Book of Poetry, it is said, "Before the sovereigns of the Yin dynasty had lost the hearts of the people, they could appear before God. Take warning from the house of Yin. The great decree is not easily preserved." This shows that, by gaining the people, the kingdom is gained, and, by losing the people, the kingdom is lost.

On this account, the ruler will first take pains about his own virtue. Possessing virtue will give him the people. Possessing the people will give the territory. Possessing the territory will give him its wealth. Possessing the wealth, he will have resources for expenditure.

Virtue is the root; wealth is the result.

If he make the root his secondary object, and the result his primary, he will only wrangle with his people, and teach them rapine.

Hence, the accumulation of wealth is the way to scatter the people; and the letting it be scattered among them is the way to collect the people.

And hence, the ruler's words going forth contrary to right, will come back to him in the same way, and wealth, gotten by improper ways, will take its departure by the same.

In the Announcement to K'ang, it is said, "The decree indeed may not always rest on us"; that is, goodness obtains the decree, and the want of goodness loses it.

In the Book of Ch'u, it is said, "The kingdom of Ch'u does not consider that to be valuable. It values, instead, its good men."

Duke Wan's uncle, Fan, said, "Our fugitive does not account that to be precious. What he considers precious is the affection due to his parent."

In the Declaration of the Duke of Ch'in, it is said, "Let me have but one minister, plain and sincere, not pretending to other abilities, but with a simple, upright, mind; and possessed of generosity, regarding the talents of others as though he himself possessed them, and, where he finds accomplished and perspicacious men, loving them in his heart more than his mouth expresses, and really showing himself able to bear them and employ them:-such a minister will be able to preserve my sons and grandsons and black-haired people, and benefits likewise to the kingdom may well be looked for from him. But if it be his character, when he finds men of ability, to be jealous and hate them; and, when he finds accomplished and perspicacious men, to oppose them and not allow their advancement, showing himself really not able to bear them: such a minister will not be able to protect my sons and grandsons and people; and may he not also be pronounced dangerous to the state?"

It is only the truly virtuous man who can send away such a man and banish him, driving him out among the barbarous tribes around, determined not to dwell along with him in the Auddle Kingdom. This is in accordance with the saying, "It is only the truly virtuous man who can love or who can hate others."

To see men of worth and not be able to raise them to office; to raise them to office, but not to do so quickly:-this is disrespectful. To see bad men and not be able to remove them; to remove them, but not to do so to a distance:-this is weakness.

To love those whom men hate, and to hate those whom men love;-this is to outrage the natural feeling of men. Calamities cannot fail to come down on him who does so.

Thus we see that the sovereign has a great course to pursue. He must show entire self-devotion and sincerity to attain it, and by pride and extravagance he will fail of it.

There is a great course also for the production of wealth. Let the producers be many and the consumers few. Let there be activity in the production, and economy in the expenditure. Then the wealth will always be sufficient.

The virtuous ruler, by means of his wealth, makes himself more distinguished. The vicious ruler accumulates wealth, at the expense of his life.

Never has there been a case of the sovereign loving benevolence, and the people not loving righteousness. Never has there been a case where the people have loved righteousness, and the affairs of the sovereign have not been carried to completion. And never has there been a case where the wealth in such a state, collected in the treasuries and arsenals, did not continue in the sovereign's possession.

The officer Mang Hsien said, "He who keeps horses and a carriage does not look after fowls and pigs. The family which keeps its stores of ice does not rear cattle or sheep. So, the house which possesses a hundred chariots should not keep a minister to look out for imposts that he may lay them on the people. Than to have such a minister, it were better for that house to have one who should rob it of its revenues." This is in accordance with the saying:-"In a state, pecuniary gain is not to be considered to be prosperity, but its prosperity will be found in righteousness."

When he who presides over a state or a family makes his revenues his chief business, he must be under the influence of some small, mean man. He may consider this man to be good; but when such a person is employed in the administration of a state or family, calamities from Heaven, and injuries from men, will befall it together, and, though a good man may take his place, he will not be able to remedy the evil. This illustrates again the saying, "In a state, gain is not to be considered prosperity, but its prosperity will be found in righteousness."

The Yengishiki

THE HARVEST RITUAL

I declare in the presence of the sovereign gods of the Harvest, If the sovereign gods will bestow, in many-bundled spikes and in luxuriant spikes, the late-ripening harvest which they will bestow, the late-ripening harvest which will be produced by the dripping of foam from the arms, and by drawing the mud together between the opposing thighs, then I will fulfil their praises by presenting the first-fruits in a thousand ears, and in many hundred ears; raising high the beer-jars, filling and ranging in rows the bellies of the beer-jars, I will present them in juice and in grain. As to things which grow in the great field plain - sweet herbs and bitter herbs; as to things which dwell in the blue sea plain things wide of fin, and things narrow of fin, down to the weeds of the offing, and weeds of the shore; and as to Clothes, with bright cloth, glittering cloth, soft cloth, and coarse cloth will I fulfil their praises. And having furnished a white horse, a white boar, and a white cock, and the various kinds of things in the presence of the sovereign gods of the Harvest, I fulfil their praises by presenting the great Offerings of the sovereign Grand-child's augustness.

THE RITUAL FOR THE WIND-GODS

I declare in the presence of the sovereign gods, whose praises are fulfilled at Tatsuta.

Because they had not allowed, firstly the five sorts of grain which the Sovereign Grand-child's augustness, who ruled the great country of many islands at Shikishima, took with ruddy countenance as his long and lasting food, and the things produced by the people, down to the least leaf of the herbs, to ripen, and had spoilt them not for one year, or for two years, but for continuous years, he deigned to command: "As to the Heart of the god which shall come forth in the divinings of all the men who are learned in things, declare what god it is."

Whereupon the men learned in things divined with their divinings, but they declared that no Heart of a god appears.

When he had heard this, the Sovereign Grand-child's augustness deigned to conjure them, saying: "I sought to fulfil their praises as heavenly temples and country temples, without forgetting or omitting, and have so acted, but let the god, whatever god he be, that has prevented the things produced by the people of the region under Heaven from ripening, and has spoilt them, make known his Heart."

Hereupon they made the Sovereign Grand-child's augustness to know in a great dream, and made him to know their names, saying:

"Our names, who have prevented the things made by the people of the region under Heaven from ripening and have spoilt them, by visiting them with bad winds and rough waters, are Heaven's Pillars augustness and Country's Pillars augustness." And they made him to know, saying: "If for the Offerings which shall be set up in our presence there be furnished various sorts of

Offerings, as to Clothes, bright cloth, glittering cloth, soft cloth, and coarse cloth, and the five kinds of things, a shield, a spear, and a horse furnished with a saddle; if our house be fixed at Wonu, in Tachinu, at Tatsuta, in a place where the morning sun is opposite, and the evening sun is hidden, and praises be fulfilled in our presence, we will bless and ripen the things produced by the people of the region under Heaven, firstly the five sorts of grain, down to the least leaf of the herbs."

Therefore hear, all ye wardens and vergers, by declaring in the presence of the sovereign gods that, having fixed the House-pillars in the place which the sovereign gods had taught by words and made known, in order to fulfil praises in the presence of the sovereign gods, the Sovereign Grandchild's augustness has caused his great Offerings to be lifted up and brought, and has fulfilled their praises, sending the princes and counselors as his messengers.

THE FIRE RITUAL

I declare with the great ritual, the Heavenly ritual, which was bestowed on him at the time when, by the Word of the Sovereign's dear progenitor and progenitrix, who divinely remain in the plain of high Heaven, they bestowed on him the region under Heaven, saying: "Let the Sovereign Grandchild's augustness tranquilly rule over the country of fresh spikes which flourishes in the midst of the reed-moor, as a peaceful region."

When the two pillars, the divine Izanagi and Izanami's augustness, younger sister and elder brother, had intercourse, and she had deigned to bear the many tens of countries of the countries, and the many tens of islands of the islands, and had deigned to bear the many hundred myriads of gods, she also deigned to bear her dear youngest child of all, the Fire-producer god, and her hidden parts being burnt, she bid in the rocks, and said: "My dear elder brother's augustness, deign not to look upon me for seven nights of nights and seven days of sunshine"; but when, before the seven days were fulfilled, he looked, thinking her remaining hidden to be strange, she deigned to say: "My hidden parts were burnt when I bore fire." At such a time I said, "My dear elder brother's augustness, deign not to look upon me, but you violently looked upon me "; and after saying, "My dear elder brother's augustness shall rule the upper country; I will rule the lower country," she deigned to hide in the rocks, and having come to the flat hill of darkness, she thought and said: "I have come hither, having born and left a bad-hearted child in the upper country, ruled over by my illustrious elder brother's augustness," and going back she bore other children. Having born the Water-goddess, the gourd, the river-weed, and the clay-hill maiden, four sorts of things, she taught them with words, and made them to know, saying: "If the heart of this bad-hearted child becomes violent, let the Water-goddess take the gourd, and the clay-hill maiden take the river-weed, and pacify him."

In consequence of this I fulfil his praises, and say that for the things set up, so that he may deign not to be awfully quick of heart in their great place of the Sovereign Grandchild's augustness, there are provided bright cloth, glittering cloth, soft cloth, and coarse cloth, and the five kinds of things; as to things which dwell in the blue sea plain, there are things wide of fin and things narrow of fin, down to the weeds of the offing and weeds of the shore; as to liquor, raising high the beer-jars, filling and ranging in rows the bellies of the beer-jars, piling the offerings up, even to rice in grain and rice in ear, like a range of hills, I fulfil his praises with the great ritual, the heavenly ritual.

THE RITUAL FOR EVIL SPIRITS

I (the diviner), declare: When by the word of the progenitor and progenitrix, who divinely remaining in the plain of high Heaven, deigned to make the beginning of things, they divinely deigned to assemble the many hundred myriads of gods in the high city of Heaven, and deigned divinely to take counsel in council, saying: "When we cause our Sovereign Grandchild's augustness, to leave Heaven's eternal seat, to cleave a path with might through Heaven's manifold clouds, and to descend from Heaven, with orders tranquilly to rule the country of fresh spikes, which flourishes in the midst of the reed-moor as a peaceful country, what god shall we send first to divinely sweep away, sweep away and subdue the gods who are turbulent in the country of fresh spikes "; all the gods pondered and declared: "You shall send Amenohohi's augustness, and subdue them," declared they. Wherefore they sent him down from Heaven, but he did not declare an answer; and having next sent Takemikuma's augustness, he also, obeying his father's words, did not declare an answer. Ame-no-waka-hiko also, whom they sent, did not declare an answer, but immediately perished by the calamity of a bird on high. Wherefore they pondered afresh by the word of the Heavenly gods, and having deigned to send down from Heaven the two pillars of gods, Futsunushi and Takemika-dzuchi's augustness, who having deigned divinely to sweep away, and sweep away, and deigned divinely to soften, and soften the gods who were turbulent, and silenced the rocks, trees, and the least leaf of herbs likewise that bad spoken, they caused the Sovereign Grandchild's augustness to descend from Heaven.

I fulfil your praises, saying: As to the Offerings set up, so that the sovereign gods who come into the heavenly house of the Sovereign Grandchild's augustness, which, after he had fixed upon as a peaceful country - the country of great Yamato where the sun is high, as the center of the countries of the four quarters bestowed upon him when he was thus sent down from Heaven - stoutly planting the house-pillars on the bottom-most rocks, and exalting the cross-beams to the plain of high Heaven, the builders had made for his shade from the Heavens and shade from the sun, and wherein he will tranquilly rule the country as a peaceful country may, without deigning to be turbulent, deigning to be fierce, and deigning to hurt, knowing, by virtue of their divinity, the things which were begun in the plain of high Heaven, deigning to correct with Divine-correcting and Great-correcting, remove hence out to the clean places of the mountain streams which look far away over the four quarters, and rule them as their own place. Let the sovereign gods tranquilly take with clear hearts, as peaceful offerings and sufficient offerings the great offerings which

I set up, piling them upon the tables like a range of hills, providing bright cloth, glittering cloth, soft cloth, and coarse cloth, as a thing to see plain in - a mirror: as things to play with-beads: as things to shoot off with - a bow and arrows: as things to strike and cut with - a sword: as a thing which gallops out - a horse; as to liquor - raising high the beer-jars, filling and ranging in rows the bellies of the beer-jars, with grains of rice and ears; as to the things which dwell in the hills things soft of hair, and things rough of hair; as to the things which grow in the great field plain - sweet herbs and bitter herbs; as to the things which dwell in the blue sea plain things broad of fin and things narrow of fin, down to weeds of the offing and weeds of the short, and without deigning to be turbulent, deigning to be fierce, and deigning to hurt, remove out to the wide and clean places of the mountain streams, and by virtue of their divinity be tranquil.

THE ROAD-GODS' RITUAL

He (the priest) says: "I declare in the presence of the sovereign gods, who like innumerable piles of rocks, sit closing up the way in the multitudinous road-forkings... fulfil your praises by declaring your names, Youth and Maiden of the Many Road-forkings and Come-no-further Gate, and say: for the offerings set up so that you may prevent the servants of the monarch from being poisoned by and agreeing with the things which shall come roughly acting and hating from the Root-country, the Bottom-country, that you may guard the bottom of the gate when they come from the bottom, guard the top when they come from the top, guarding with nightly guard and with daily guard, and, may praise them peacefully take the great offerings which are set up by piling them up like a range of hills - that is to say, providing bright cloth, etc., and sitting closing-up the way like innumerable piles of rock in the multitudinous road-forkings, deign to praise the Sovereign Grandchild's augustness eternally and unchangingly, and to bless his age as a luxuriant age."

RITUALS TO THE SUN-GODDESS

He (the priest envoy) says: "Hear all of you, ministers of the gods and sanctifiers of offerings, the great ritual, the Heavenly ritual, declared in the great presence of the From-Heaven-shining-great deity, whose praises are fulfilled by setting up the stout pillars of the great house, and exalting the cross-beam to the plain of high Heaven at the sources of the Isuzu river at Udji in Watarahi."

He says: "It is the Sovereign's great Word. Hear all of you, ministers of the gods and sanctifiers of offerings, the fulfilling of praises on this seventeenth day of the sixth moon of this year, as the morning sun goes up in glory, of the Oho-Nakatomi, who-having abundantly piled up like a range of hills the tribute thread and sanctified liquor and food presented as of usage by the people of the deity's houses attributed to her in the three departments and in various countries and places, so that she design to bless his (the Mikado's) life as a long life and his age as a luxuriant age eternally and unchangingly as multitudinous piles of rock; may deign to bless the children who are born to him, and deigning to cause to flourish the five kinds of grain which the men of - a hundred functions and the peasants of the countries in the four quarters of the region under Heaven long and peacefully cultivate and eat, and guarding and benefiting them deign to bless them - is hidden by the great offering-wands."

1 declare in the great presence of the From-Heaven-shining-great deity who sits in Ise. Because the Sovereign great goddess bestows on him the countries of the four quarters over which her glance extends, as far as the limit where Heaven stands up like a wall, as far as the bounds where the country stands up distant, as far as the limit where the blue clouds spread flat, as far as the bounds where the white clouds lie away fallen-the blue sea plain as far as the limit whither come the prows of the ships without drying poles or paddles, the ships which continuously crowd on the great sea plain, and the roads which men travel by land, as far as the limit whither come the horses' hoofs, with the baggage-cords tied tightly, treading the uneven rocks and tree-roots and standing up continuously in a long path without a break - making the narrow countries wide and the hilly countries plain, and as it were drawing together the distant countries by throwing many tens of ropes over them - he will pile up the first-fruits like a range of hills in the great presence of the Sovereign great goddess, and will peacefully enjoy the remainder.

THE PURIFICATION RITUAL

[The ritual opens by calling upon the assembled princes of the Mikado's family, the ministers of State, and all other officials, to listen, in words which are a modern addition after the establishment of a form of administration modeled on that of the Chinese. To this succeeds a second enumeration of the Sovereign's servants, according to the old division, into scarf-wearing companies (women attendants), sash-wearing companies (cooks), quiver-bearing and sword-bearing companies (guards), with which begins the genuine ancient text. The nature of the Mikado's title to rule over the land is then stated, as in the ritual of the gods of pestilence, already quoted, after which we have a list of the offenses of which the nation is to be purged.]

Amongst the various sorts of offenses which may be committed in ignorance or out of negligence by Heaven's increasing people, who shall come into being in the country, which the Sovereign Grandchild's augustness, hiding in the fresh residence, built by stoutly planting the house-pillars on the bottom-most rocks, and exalting the cross-beams to the plain of high Heaven, as his shade from the Heavens and shade from the sun, shall tranquilly rule as a peaceful country, namely, the country of great Yamato, where the sun is seen on high, which be fixed upon as a peaceful country, as the center of the countries of the four quarters thus bestowed upon him - breaking the ridges, filling up watercourses, opening sluices, doubly sowing, planting stakes, flaying alive, flaying backward, and dunging; many of such offenses are distinguished as Heavenly offenses, and as earthly offenses; cutting living flesh, cutting dead flesh, leprosy, proud flesh, the offense committed with one's own mother, the

offense committed with one's own child, the offense committed with mother and
child, the offense committed with child and mother, the offense committed with
beasts, calamities of crawling worms, calamities of a god on high, calamities of
birds on high, the offenses of killing beasts and using incantations; many of
such offenses may be disclosed.

[The high priest then arranges the sacrifices, and, turning round to the
assembled company, waves before them a sort of broom made of grass, to
symbolize the sweeping away of their offenses. At this point occurs in the
original a direction to the priest to repeat " the great ritual, the Heavenly
ritual." Several versions of what seems to be the missing document have been
discovered, and it turns out to have been a short address to all the gods, calling
upon them to bear the remaining part of the principal ritual, after which the
original proceeds:]

When he has thus repeated it, the Heavenly gods will push open Heaven's
eternal gates, and cleaving a path with might through the manifold clouds of
Heaven, will hear; and the country gods, ascending to the tops of the high
mountains, and to the tops of the low hills, and tearing asunder the mists of the
high mountains, and the mists of the low hills, will bear.

And when they have thus heard, the Maiden-of-Descent-into-the-Current,
who dwells in the current of the swift stream which boils down the ravines from
the tops of the high mountains, and the tops of the low hills, shall carry out to
the great sea plain the offenses which are cleared away and purified, so that
there be no remaining offense; like as Sbinato's wind blows apart the manifold
clouds of Heaven, as the morning wind and the evening wind blow away the
morning mist and the evening mist, as the great ships which lie on the shore of
the great port loosen their prows, and loosen their sterns to push out into the
great sea plain; as the trunks of the forest trees, far and near, are cleared away
by the sharp sickle, the sickle forged with fire; so that there cease to be any
offense called an offense in the court of the Sovereign Grandchild's augustness
to begin with, and in the countries of the four quarters of the region under
Heaven.

And when she thus carries them out and away, the deity called the
Maiden-of-the-Swift-cleansing, who dwells in the multitudinous meetings of the
sea-waters, the multitudinous currents of rough sea-waters shall gulp them
down.

And when she has thus gulped them down, the lord of the
Breath-blowing-place, who dwells in the Breath-blowing-place, shall utterly
blow them away with his breath to the Root-country, the Bottom-country.

And when he has thus blown them away, the deity called the
Maiden-of-Swift-Banishment, who dwells in the Root-country, the
Bottom-country, shall completely banish them, and get rid of them.

And when they have thus been got rid of, there shall from this day onward
be no offense which is called offense, with regard to the men of the offices who
serve in the court of the Sovereign, nor in the four quarters of the region under
Heaven.

[Then the high priest says:]

Hear all of you how he leads forth the horse as a thing that erects its ears toward the plain of high Heaven, and deigns to sweep away and purify with the general purification, as the evening sun goes down on the last day of the watery moon of this year.

O diviners of the four countries, take the sacrifices away out of the river highway, and sweep them away.

www.ingramcontent.com/pod-product-compliance
Lightning Source LLC
Chambersburg PA
CBHW030921090426
42737CB00007B/270